At the field's end, in the corner missed by the mower,
Where the turf drops off into a grass-hidden culvert,
Haunt of the cat-bird, nesting-place of the field-mouse,
. . . .
One learned of the eternal. . . .

From *The Far Field*
by Theodore Roethke

AT THE
FIELD'S END

*Interviews with Twenty
Pacific Northwest Writers*

NICHOLAS O'CONNELL

MADRONA PUBLISHERS • Seattle

First Edition
10 9 8 7 6 5 4 3 2 1

Published by
Madrona Publishers
PO Box 22667
Seattle, Washington 98122

Library of Congress Cataloging-in-Publication Data

O'Connell, Nicholas.
At the field's end.

1. Authors, American--Northwest, Pacific--Interviews.
2. Authors, American--20th century--Interviews.
3. American literature--Northwest, Pacific--History
and criticism.   4. American literature--20th century--
History and criticism.   5. Northwest, Pacific, in
literature.   6. Northwest, Pacific--Intellectual life.
7. Authorship. I. Title.
PS282.026   1987   810'.9'9795   87-7053
ISBN 0-88089-025-8
ISBN 0-88089-026-6 (pbk.)

Thanks to the following for their photographs of the authors: Warren Morgan (Barry Lopez); J. Phil Samuell (Ursula K. Le Guin); Robin Seyfried (David Wagoner); Nicholas O'Connell (James Welch, Norman Maclean); Jerry Bauer (Raymond Carver); John Wood-bridge (Carolyn Kizer); Fran Martiny (James Mitsui); James P. Bell (A.B. Guthrie); Lisa Stone (Richard Hoyt); Jim Heynen (Tess Gallagher); Tom Victor (Jean M. Auel); Laurie Foley (Marilynne Robinson); Kit Stafford (William Stafford); Wayne Sourbeer (Charles Johnson); Eric Edwards (Tom Robbins); Mary Randlett (Murray Morgan); Jim Bates (Ivan Doig); Hank Meals (Gary Snyder).

Design by William James

FOR MY PARENTS

Contents

Preface

*F*OR most of its cultural history, the Pacific Northwest—Washington, Oregon, Idaho, and the western half of Montana—has been a region without a distinct literary identity. It is still a late American frontier, a new West, and its literature, until well into this century, has been dominated by the chronicles of early explorers and settlers, romances that could have been set in any fantastic land, and the tailings of westering adventures which placed it at the end of the Oregon Trail.

From a land inhabited largely by recent immigrants with roots and traditions from a variety of other places, the Pacific Northwest is now assuming its own sense of place with its own regional character. It is now recognized as a region of immense natural wealth and beauty not yet irreversibly destroyed by industrialization or development, still allowing easy access to wilderness and the pleasures of the outdoors, and still aware of the presence of its earliest Native American inhabitants.

The people of the region are seen as healthy, independent, innovative—measuring achievement as much in terms of climbing mountains as in climbing corporate ladders. Surrounded by the power and majesty of the natural world, familiar with the woods, waterways, and the high country, we are finding our identity within nature as well as within human history.

Writers with a strong connection to the region, like the poet Theodore Roethke, have been translating this identification with the natural world into literature. In their way they are continuing in the tradition of Emerson, Thoreau, Twain, and Melville, but with the advantages of new materials to work with. They have had access to the resources of modern biological investigation and the understanding of Oriental and Native American cultures with which to present a vision of people integrated within the natural world, not above or outside it.

This view of people's relation to nature is less alienated than much of what is seen in contemporary literature. When the division between the human and the natural world is obliterated, men and women are not seen simply as souls imprisoned in flesh but as whole and integrated, healed of some of the old dichotomies of body and spirit. Pacific Northwest writers are not alone, of course, in proclaiming the close connection between people and place, but they have the advantage of a vast natural laboratory within which to carry out their investigations.

At the Field's End is an exploration and celebration of Pacific Northwest literature. In their own words, twenty of the region's finest writers discuss the practice of their craft and the influence the region has had on their work.

Only writers who live or have lived in the Pacific Northwest for much of their lives were considered for inclusion. Some of the most prominent representatives of particular genres or traditions were interviewed, with the hope that they would sketch in the full body of regional literature.

All of the interviews were conducted in person except for Jean Auel's, which took place over the phone. Most of them ran two to four hours, although Ernest Gann's lasted only an hour and Barry Lopez took the better part of two days. Each interview was tape-recorded, and the tapes were then transcribed and edited. The transcriptions were sent to the authors for their corrections or changes.

This book began as a quest for what the Pacific Northwest stood for and what its literature was about, and it was with the enthusiasm of an explorer that I began to piece together some of its patterns. I hope that this collection conveys some of the excitement I felt as I began to discover that this was a literature firmly rooted within American letters, but which contributed something new, going beyond the farthest field of human culture and back into the mysterious wild heart of the world itself.

My exploration has depended upon the support of a number of people. I particularly want to thank Professor Lois Hudson of the University of Washington for first getting me interested in Pacific Northwest literature, Professor Charles Johnson of the University of Washington for his wise advice and continued encouragement, Dan Levant of Madrona Publishers for his early commitment to the book, my agent John Pickering for his valuable counsel, Sean Bentley at Madrona for his care in editing the manuscript, my parents for their understanding and material assistance, Roland Stephan and Vence Malernee at Outdoor Empire Publishing for allowing me a flexible work schedule, and all the friends and acquaintances who helped me work out and refine what the book should be about. Finally, I want to express my deepest gratitude to the writers themselves, who gave so generously of their time and attention during the interviews and throughout the process of reading, editing, and completing *At the Field's End*.

Nicholas O'Connell

Seattle, 1987

AT THE FIELD'S END

Interviews with Twenty
Pacific Northwest Writers

Barry Lopez

BARRY *Lopez's work illuminates and celebrates the intimate connection between people and place. In the nonfiction books* Arctic Dreams *(1986) and* Of Wolves and Men *(1978), he employs many different perspectives and methodologies to clarify this connection. The short stories in* Winter Count *(1981),* Desert Notes *(1976) and* River Notes *(1979) turn on humans' relationship with the environment in which they are living. Many of the images of peace or coherence in these stories come from people touching the land. Lopez's work helps us appreciate the power of landscape and its importance in our lives.*

Born January 6, 1945 in Port Chester, New York, Lopez received an A.B. (cum laude) from the University of Notre Dame in 1966 and an M.A.T. in 1968. He did graduate work in 1969 and 1970 at the University of Oregon before becoming a full-time writer in 1970. He has received numerous awards, including the American Book Award for Arctic Dreams *and the John Burroughs Medal for* Of Wolves and Men. *He was honored with a Distinguished Recognition Award from Friends of American Writers for* Winter Count, *and received an Award in Literature from the American Academy and Institute of Arts and Letters in 1986. His other works include* Giving Birth to Thunder, Sleeping with His Daughter: Coyote Builds North America *(Native American trickster stories, 1978),* Desert Reservation *(chapbook, 1980) and numerous works of nonfiction published in magazines such as* Harper's, North American Review *and* National Geographic.

The interview took place May 6th and 7th, 1985 in Spokane, Washington. Lopez lives with his wife, Sandra, on the banks of the McKenzie River in Oregon, but was staying in Spokane while teaching at Eastern Washington University. His apartment was simple, clean and full of light; no unnecessary furniture or decoration cluttered it.

Lopez is a sturdy, thick-chested man with dark brown hair and a well-trimmed beard. He wore jeans, a pressed dress shirt and cowboy boots and looked as if he'd be as much at home following a wolf biologist around the Brooks Range in Alaska as doing research in the Pierpont Morgan Library in New York. At times during the interview, especially when asked abstract questions, he would cease talking and whistle back at the birds singing outside the apartment window.

How did you first become interested in writing about the wilderness?

I don't know. I've always been deeply interested in animals, in what they were doing and where they lived. They are for me parallel cultures. I think about them a lot and spend a certain amount of time with them. Natural history is the metaphor I feel most comfortable with as a writer—a kind of natural history that includes geography.

What do you mean about natural history as a metaphor?

Well, a writer has a certain handful of questions. Mine seem to be questions of tolerance and dignity, for example. You can't sit down and write directly about these things, but if they are on your mind, they're going to come out in one form or another. The form that I feel most comfortable with, where I do a lot of reading and aimless thinking, is in natural history—in the biology and ecology of animals or the differences between desert and arctic ecosystems, for example. This has been an area of concentrated reading for me since leaving the university. That and anthropology. Those are the two areas where I have a certain amount of material at hand that I can work with; and then inevitably I end up talking about these other things I'm concerned about.

Has our culture as a whole lost touch with the natural world?
Oh, sure.

And when this occurs, what happens to the culture?
The culture becomes solipsistic. It produces too much self-referential material and loses a sense of itself in the world because it creates too much of the world in which it lives. The reason you go into unmanaged landscapes is in part to get out of a world in which all the references are to human scale or somehow devised from a sense of human values.

So by going into these landscapes, you have a chance to learn about something that's nonhuman?
It encourages you to think in a pattern that's nonhuman. The proportion, line, color, and activity in wild landscapes are not arranged according to human schedules or systems of aesthetics. It's important to expose yourself to this. Otherwise you have no check on your philosophy except what you make up.

It allows you to check your philosophy?
Yes. Opening yourself up to an unmanaged landscape is the same as opening yourself up to another culture. Other cultures force you to consider that the way you approach reality is not the one and only way. If you aren't familiar with the metaphors of other cultures, then you can have no real depth perception. The issue is not which is the best way to think or what's the best moral framework, the issue is that there are other, valid frameworks.

And so human culture needs landscape as a reference point?
Yes. Landscape is the culture that contains all human cultures.

And when that reference point is destroyed. . . .

You have nothing to verify anything against. You have created an environment in which totalitarianism thrives.

When you go to the wilderness, what kind of order do you find there?

The order I bring with me, until I start listening. Then I find many different orders. When you come to a wild place, you unconsciously impose your taxonomies on it. Part of what should come to you there, however, is that your taxonomies are an imposition. You can't bring the orders with you and apply them.

How does story help us come to terms with the land?

There is an unmanipulated order in unmanaged landscapes. Story grows out of this order in the land; it heals you in much the same way the land itself does. The mind tends toward chaos and longs to move toward order. Story makes you feel healed and healthy because it restores that order within you.

Why is the story a particularly human need? Why don't animals need something similar?

Animals have not broken out of their environment to the extent that we have. The Inuit people have an interesting observation here. A word they have for us translates "the people who change nature." It has two meanings: we are people who manipulate landscape, and we also have managed something that baffles them—making nature an object. They look at themselves as part of what's going on out there. They understand the complete absorption of the grizzly bear in the land, and they look at the white person as someone who has managed this quite extraordinary thing of completely removing himself from the land.

So the native peoples, or at least some of them, are still closely tied to the natural world. Is that why you've spent time studying their cultures?

When I first began reading the serious thinking of Native American people, I realized another culture had put into formal terms a way of thinking I'd felt inclined toward since I was a child. I just never knew that there were other people thinking along these lines outside my own culture. All cultures, of course, are flawed; the serious question for me became, "How do we bring together the best of what each culture has to offer?"

I'm disturbed sometimes by the amount of hatred directed

against my own culture, as if it consisted of nothing but industrial imperialism, greed, duplicity, and Vietnam. Our culture is older than those things and it has had a great deal to offer: cathedral architecture, the thinking of Darwin, Mendel, Copernicus, Leibnitz, Carl Jung, the library at Alexandria, the ideas that came out of the Renaissance and the Enlightenment.

Obviously we're in difficult straits at the moment. We have chilling issues before us—the manufacture and deployment of nuclear weapons, heavy metals pollution, habitat destruction all over the world. We're not doing very well with these problems. Other cultures dissimilar to our own have insights that are worth paying close attention to, thought processes that would be useful. Because if we don't solve these problems we're not going to be around very long.

One of the things we're trying to do today is understand what we've thrown away in the Holocene, those 10,000 years since we emerged in northern Mesopotamia as a people with inclinations toward agriculture and urban living. During this 10,000-year period we threw these things away in the belief that we were improving ourselves. And now it seems that maybe we shouldn't have thrown some of them away, for practical reasons and for reasons of the heart, mind and spirit.

Writers, anthropologists, philosophers, thinkers and scholars are trying to go back and look at Native American cultures and ask, "What of the original wisdom remains with these people, and how might it serve us who are beginning to doubt seriously the tack we have taken?" But it is important, of course, to be careful about the extraction of that original wisdom, not to choose only the things we like, for example. And among all the people in a specific tradition, maybe there will be one or two articulate about ways of behaving. In our culture, we produce people like Thomas Merton. When we go among the Inuit, we should be interested in finding the Thomas Merton kind of mind. There's a word for that person, *isumataq*, a person who can create the atmosphere in which wisdom reveals itself. This person is not necessarily a political leader but a human being the world has invested, in some strange way, with this ability. Occasionally, in our culture, writers do this.

Would this be deliberate on the writer's part?

Well, it's like everything else in writing. I don't think you set out to do certain things with a story. I think story is so subtle that sometimes more is going on than you can consciously grasp. If you're paying close attention to what you're doing, you can create an atmosphere in which truth can reveal itself, and reinforce in a community a sense of what is good behavior and what are worthy ideals. Part of the function of literature is to make the quality of aspiration in a culture real, to make it clear that this is a real part of life.

As a human being you have concerns about the world in which you live, as a writer you tell a story. It may be that the story seems to have no direct connection with the issues that concern you as a human being, but there is a connection. And that's where the moral dimension comes in. Everyone has things that disturb them about literature; one thing that disturbs me is that so much writing today has no moral framework.

Is it true that you trained to become a monk?

That was something that I considered very seriously when I was in college. It still occurs to me occasionally. I went to Gethsemani in Kentucky, where Thomas Merton was, in 1966. That's the point at which I made the decision that I wasn't going to go into a monastery. The work I wanted to do with my life—I didn't have anything specific in mind—I was going to do outside. The monastic life is very attractive to me, probably more as an abstraction than as a reality.

Did you enter the noviate?

No. I just made a visit. I stayed there for a while, thought about it and decided no. That was the last time I seriously addressed the question.

I grew up in a Roman Catholic tradition, and was deeply affected by it. The part that affected me was the tradition of the Desert Fathers, the Jesuits, and the monastic tradition—not the things one normally hears about Catholicism.

Catholicism comes out for me especially in the memory of the Church Latin *te Deus laudamus*, we praise you God. In the middle of an arduous trip, I sometimes think, *peccata mundi*, the sins of the world.

Another image I have from childhood is of a group of men and women praying somewhere in the desert, and the reason chronically myopic and selfish people have not destroyed us with nuclear weapons is that, in a rarified and metaphorical way, there have been these enclaves of monastics praying. What keeps these things from exploding, perhaps, is that each of us in his own way is saying his prayers.

How does this part of your background make a difference in your writing?

At Notre Dame it was a requirement for undergraduates to take four years of philosophy and two years of theology. You were exposed to the thinking of Hegel, Descartes, Kant, Kierkegaard. The courses that were of lasting importance were these in philosophy and theology, not because you believed one way or the other, but because you realized from them that you had to be responsible in your life for what you did. You had to be responsible as a human being, responsible as a writer.

Would you say that your first orientation as a writer is toward the spiritual?

No. I don't think in terms of dividing the material from the spiritual. My response is to a phenomenon that has many dimensions, some of which can be addressed in a story. When I was working on the wolf book, I was attracted to the animal itself. When I began that book I realized that part of what I wanted to do was to look at the animal from the point of view of different people, because the notion that one kind of thinking could make the animal clear seemed completely ridiculous to me. Every animal is a mysterious entity. There is a certain amount of information that you can gather, but there is a great deal that you never will know.

In your book Of Wolves and Men, *why was the wolf singled out for annihilation?*

Why did it become the focus of blame?

Yes. Why not the grizzly bear, or some other animal?

The level of interference wasn't as high with any other animal. Wolves to some extent occupy a niche that human beings occupy, so there was going to be some conflict. Part of what I wanted to do in *Of Wolves and Men* was to show that the different threads of connotation, including the sense of its being a warrior or a wanton murderer, had nothing to do with the wolf. I can't imagine another animal that would fit the bill, so to speak, as far as projection is concerned. There was no coyote or jackal in Europe, that's part of the explanation. Another part was that the wolf was a social animal and appeared in a formidable pack, rather than all alone like a bear. It looked like a dog but wasn't a dog. It was also of a size to do some damage. Many things come into play.

How did you first become interested in writing?

I don't remember. I was writing stories when I was in high school. I continued to write stories through college and after I graduated. I published a few book reviews, but I had no clear idea that I was going to be a writer. I guess it was just what I was, and after a while I was aware of that. I had no schemes, no plans about it.

Did you admire the work of other writers?

Oh, yes. Going back I can see that writing was a principal interest. I was strongly influenced by Hemingway and Faulkner. I admired Hemingway's ability to get rid of what was not working, and to make things very tight. And with Faulkner I admired that wonderful vision of people moving around and doing things in a place, and the thicker texture of the work.

I think I read *Moby Dick* five or six times before I was eighteen. I read almost all of John Steinbeck when I was young. Later I tried to read him again but he didn't hold up as well. I also think of Gerard Manley Hopkins as an influence. But I was never interested in imitating anybody. My sense of imitation had to do with admiring how well somebody did their work, and wanting to do my work as well.

Nowadays, do you do a lot of traveling in the process of researching and writing your books?

Yes.

Does that hold for pieces like those in Winter Count?

Oh, no. I don't intentionally go anywhere for pieces like that. I'm talking about nonfiction, magazine pieces, for *Outside* and *National Geographic* and *Harper's*.

But you continue to write both fiction and nonfiction?

Oh, yes. I work in one area and then the other, back and forth. It would never occur to me not to work in one or the other.

The kind of nonfiction I like to do comes out of going to a place. Traveling is very much a part of what I write about. There's a certain amount of travel in the wolf book and a great deal of travel in *Arctic Dreams*. It's very pleasant for me to go someplace and do a story. I like that. I like seeing a different part of the landscape and traveling around with different kinds of people and seeing what's on their minds and talking to them and seeing the world from their point of view.

When you come back, is there another part of the process?

You sit and think about it, or split wood and think about it, or drive to town and think about it. Just keep turning it over until a light bursts through. After thinking about it for a long time, parts of it will just fall away and I'll be left with what I was after all along.

That's the problem when you try to go out with the story all figured out. So much is going to happen that you're not going to see. For this reason, I rarely work on assignment. I don't want to work with someone's preconceived notions of what's out there. What if you find something different? What if you find something you never dreamed was going to be there?

It's important for me to be able to go to a place for a while and think about it and read a lot about it and talk to people who are there. And then fiction is a completely different thing. Fiction is completely out of your imagination.

That's interesting, because some reviewers have thought that many of your short stories were nonfiction.

They're all fiction. There's no character as far as I know that corresponds to a character in the real world. The places are real—Nebraska, North Dakota, Madrid—but the rest of it is completely fictional.

How do your fictional pieces start?

A line or an image around which the story begins somehow. I don't think I've ever known how a story was going to end. I might have some feeling for events toward the end of the story, but not in how they are going to come into play.

How does the story take shape?

I don't think about that. I just try to be attentive at those moments when the story is getting outside me onto a piece of paper. I don't think about these things much at all.

How do you know when the story's finished?

There's never a question. The order or organic quality of the story is such that it's whole: more would be too much, less would not be enough. It's just whole.

Is this an intuition that you've developed?

I guess it's an intuition. I don't quite know what's going on there and I'm not interested in finding out.

Do you rewrite much?

I rewrite a great deal. The language is very important to me and it takes a long time to get the language right. Rewriting a piece is a matter of getting rid of some things, making things sharper, just making them tighter. I always think of that image of making the pieces fit together more tightly. It's not the kind of rewriting where I write a different end or a different beginning—I never do that. I'll probably do it now that I've said I never do it.

Is there something you learn in the process of writing?

Sure. You're bringing order out of chaos. You know a lot more about it when you're finished.

Is that why you write?

I don't know, could be. An image just occurred to me that I hope is not too peculiar. I don't know if it's right or not. But there is this thing called prayer. Prayer is a way to formalize in a conventional sense with language the relationship between yourself and a spiritual entity or entities. But I think of prayer as larger than that; in the monastic traditions your work is your prayer. So you don't create this dichotomy that Monday through Saturday you're doing one thing, and Sunday you're doing another. In the monastic traditions there are times for prayer, meditation or reading the breviary, but there is an understanding that your work is your prayer. And there must be a similar idea in Buddhism, that your life is your prayer. There must be moments in your life when you are saying your prayers better, and that's what writing is for me. In writing a story, you're trying to make something intelligent and beautiful and worthy, the same thing you're trying to do as a dancer on a stage or the same thing a painter is trying to do. I had never thought about it, but I think this idea about prayerful activity is probably very close to something for me and the way I think about things.

How is your writing developing?

You mean where is it going?

Yes.

I don't know. I've been so buried in this arctic book that that's about all I've been thinking about.

What about the earlier books? Do you see a progress in them?

I don't ever think of progress. I think of being a different person a little bit. I just continue to try to write well about what interests me. I don't have any sense of improvement. You would hope that over a period of time you would learn to be a better writer, but so much comes into play when you have the subject and the language. You have a certain amount of control over the language, so you can bring good language to a bad subject. And then every once in a while you bring good language to a good subject and there's something quite memorable in the piece. Most writers do a few things of great value and some other things that are good but in some ways not as successful. It's idiotic to think that as you grow older you inevitably grow better or wiser, where it's really a matter of what frame of mind you are in when you encounter a certain subject. So the good books can come early or late or scattered through your career.

It's important to consciously break patterns a little bit, not to do everything one way. I'm interested now in writing for *National Geographic*. This is a new one for me. I keep trying different kinds of things. I don't want to fall into the habit of trying to imitate myself. The arctic book has certain things in common with the wolf book, but it's different.

Why did you move to the West Coast?

I grew up in Southern California and I've always felt more comfortable on this side of the continent. When I was a child I was in the Mojave Desert and the Grand Canyon and places like that. That's where I got the feelings about landscape that have remained with me the longest. My family moved to New York City when I was eleven. I loved living in New York; I've always considered it a privilege to have lived there and I like going back, but I'm just more comfortable out here. More people out here are thinking about the relationship between human beings and the landscape. It's a topic of conversation that you can strike up more easily with

people here than you can back East. I'm very interested in talking
with students at eastern universities about these issues, however.
They are thinking about some of these things, but they're not
thinking about them in ways I'm used to. So I want to talk to them,
to find out how they're doing it, because I want to understand it. I
know something about the relationship between human beings
and landscape out here, but I want to know a lot more about it
from people back East because I want to understand it as a national
issue rather than a regional issue.

So the landscape is a big part of your writing?

Certainly. The issue at the heart of *Arctic Dreams* is the relationship between landscape and imagination—how do we describe
the land and how do we explore it? Certainly I would say that
landscape is a central issue for me. Overall it probably has more to
do with my work than any strict consideration of dignity and
tolerance. The relationship between human beings and that part of
the landscape called *Canis lupus* is what the wolf book is about.
And many of the stories in *Desert Notes* and *River Notes* turn on
people's relationship with an environment in which they are
living. Many of the images of peace in those stories come from
people touching the land.

So you don't consider landscape as part of the background?

God no. Anything but. It's an integral part of what's going on.
Eventually what American literature is going to offer among the
world's literatures, I think, is an illumination of this issue of man
and landscape, particularly modern man trying to come to grips
with a reorientation toward landscape. In some ways I think of
Moby Dick as a landscape novel, or Stephen Crane's *The Open
Boat*. I think of the role that landscape plays in Faulkner, the role
of landscape in South American literature, some of which derives
from Faulkner. So I tend to think what has distinguished and what
will distinguish American literature from European literature is an
elucidation of this issue.

Is language an outgrowth of a particular landscape?

I think so. The indigenous quality of language is probably
most clear in the poetic, more clearly rhythmic forms of the language, or in songs or music. With some words, some rhythms, you

might be able to say, "Yes, the relationship is clear." Instances turn up constantly in native languages. One I just ran across for Baird's sandpiper, an Inuktitut word, is *tuituek* [two-EE-two-ek]. Isn't that wonderful? Saying the word is just what Baird's sandpipers sound like. So when you tell a story about *tuituek*, right away you've sewn yourself into something that is familiar aurally to the listener or reader. I said in the essay about landscape and narrative ["Story at Anaktuvuk Pass," *Harper's*, December, 1984], that the writer has a responsibility to establish intimacy with the landscape and intimacy with the reader. A critical quality to me in story is intimacy. When you say, "I want to tell a story about *tuituek*," the intimacy is already starting to work.

In the terms you used in that essay, how does the "exterior landscape" of the Northwest become part of people's "interior landscape"?

They begin to think in terms of the topology that is there. They think, if they're living on the west side of the mountains, less about the sun and its circuits, less than somebody living, say, in Nebraska. In a completely indigenous literature, one that grows out of the country west of the Cascades and north of Mount Shasta or Trinity Alps, the emotional shadings of the story will in some ineffable way be part of, will have reference to, that landscape. I don't think it will be one to one, but a mind shaped in the Pacific Northwest is not like a mind shaped in the Sonoran Desert, or the Piedmont Country in the Carolinas. I think that people out here have a way of putting things together a little bit differently.

Is it possible that someone from another place who reads a story set out here might not find the story comprehensible?

Could be that it wouldn't be completely comprehensible to them. That's very true.

Is it difficult to make a story set in a particular landscape meaningful to someone not familiar with the landscape?

Good work is always difficult. I try to create a place where the reader can walk around on a solid floor, where a reader can get the feeling that the writer has built a solid foundation; that it's not just off the top of his head. Having built a solid floor on which to stand, I then try to address things that I think will be understood for what they are, but are also rich enough as incidents to be understood in a larger context, so that the metaphorical part of the human mind comes into play.

One of the things that happens for me in rewriting a piece is that I'll get up to my ears in scientific jargon. I don't worry about it in the beginning, but I worry about it when I rewrite because I want to get rid of that. It puts off the reader, not only because the reader wonders what the hell the word means, but because you can seem to be affecting a pose—that you're a biologist when you're not, you're a writer.

So your job as a writer is to do all that research to build a floor on which a reader can wander around, and then create an environment in which thinking and reaction and wonder and awe and speculation can take place, and not try to do it in a dogmatic way, or to be adamant that one thing or another has to be understood in precisely this way or otherwise it's no good. A book should be rich with suggestion. I mean, obviously, you want to bring the reader to the point of view that you have, but you must do it in a respectful way. I told the students the other day, "What you are doing when you write nonfiction, the frame of mind that you should have, is to make a bow of respect toward the material and make a bow of respect toward the reader—that's what the piece is." The bow of respect toward the material means try to understand what's coming from it, not what you are trying to impose on it. Listen. Pay attention. Do your research. Try to learn. Don't presume. And always imagine that there's more there than you could possibly understand or sense. The bow to the reader is to say, "I have assembled this material. I have tried to bring order to these disparate elements. I have tried to use the language elegantly. Everywhere I could I have sought illumination, clarity. I have tried to organize things with a proper sense of the drama of human life. I have tried to think hard about these things. I have tried to get rid of all that is unnecessary."

So it's just to show some regard for the reader. You're asking the reader for time and a certain amount of attention. Somebody said that what you want from a reader is someone who reads as attentively as you write. One way to get that is to cultivate a sense of respect for the reader.

Your stories grow out of a particular place, but if you do these things you just mentioned, can they be widely understood?

Yes, I think so, at least understood within your own country. I had an experience recently talking with some Japanese. A Japanese man said through the translator, "What have you learned from wolves?" I said, "Tolerance." The translator turned to me and said, "This might not work. What you mean is a pretty foreign, esoteric notion to the Japanese. They are not a tolerant people. What you're saying is going to sound pretty strange to them." So I got through it, but I found that some of the things I'm trying to talk about as a writer are not things of interest to other cultures. If you can make sense of things for your own culture, that's quite enough.

Is this what you were trying to do in Arctic Dreams?

Yes. The Arctic was a place where I could examine some of these large issues. One of the critical things in the book for me is coming to an understanding of what North America has to offer us. When Frobisher sailed into Frobisher Bay in 1576, he thought the land to the north was Asia, and what lay to the south was North America. He thought he had discovered a passage down which he could sail to the Spice Islands and China. When he came back to England and made his presentation to Queen Elizabeth, he offered her the opportunity to name the southern land. She called it *meta incognita*, the unknown land.

North America is the meta incognita of our Judeo-Christian, Western European civilization. We are still in the process of discovering North America. We are still looking for the Northwest Passage, trying to find a passage through our projected understanding of North America to a real understanding of it.

Animals and the landscape have more protection here than any place in the world. There is legal and social pressure here to preserve the heritage of a relationship between a native people and a native landscape, which can be plumbed for some of its original wisdom. But we've been here for 450 years and we continue to destroy instead of stopping to look at what lies before us.

One of the questions that *Arctic Dreams* addresses is, "What does it mean to be rich?" Is it to possess the material, tangible wealth of North America—the gold and the silver, the timber, the fish and the furs? Or is real wealth, lasting wealth, something else?

Most of us, I think, believe that it is something else. We have taken the most obvious kind of wealth from this continent and overlooked the more lasting, the more valuable and sustaining experience of intimacy with it, the spiritual dimension of a responsible involvement with this place.

Ursula K. Le Guin

URSULA K. *Le Guin has created a rich, imaginative literature out of the popular genres of science fiction and fantasy, as well as many other traditions. Her work ranges from the realistic to the fantastical, and synthesizes many different literary genres and styles. In her hands, science fiction becomes "an infinitely variable metaphor...a way of talking about the world right now, right here." Her works of fantasy start in a "very irrational place deep inside you, probably from feelings you don't understand. There is something out of your control and you're trying to control it as you write." Though she is best known for her work in science fiction and fantasy, Le Guin continues to experiment with other genres, inventing new literary styles and forms, new ways of interpreting the world, new ways of approaching her subjects.*

She has garnered numerous awards for her work. Among these are: Boston Globe/Hornbook Award, A Wizard of Earthsea *(1968);* Nebula and Hugo awards for The Left Hand of Darkness *(1969);* Newbery Honor Medal, The Tombs of Atuan *(1972);* Hugo Award, The Word for World is Forest *(1972);* National Book Award, The Farthest Shore *(1972);* Hugo Award, The Ones Who Walk Away from Omelas *(1973); Nebula and Hugo awards,* The Dispossessed *(1974); Nebula Award,* The Day before the Revolution *(1975); Gandalf Award for fantasy (1979); American Book Award runner-up, Kafka Award,* Always Coming Home *(1985).*

As of 1986, she had published fifteen novels, some sixty short stories (many reprinted in three collections), two books of poems, a chapbook, two children's books, a collection of criticism and a screenplay.

The daughter of writer Theodora Kroeber and anthropologist Alfred L. Kroeber, Le Guin was born in Berkeley, California in 1929. She received a B.A. in French from Radcliffe College in 1951 and an M.A. in Romance Languages from Columbia University in 1952. In 1953 she married historian Charles A. Le Guin. They have three children.

The interview took place in the spring of 1986 at the Le Guins' home in Portland, Oregon. Though she writes about other worlds, Le Guin seemed perfectly at home on the planet Earth, and talked and gestured with great vibrancy and enthusiasm about everything from her own approach to science fiction to the current research on dreams.

When you were growing up did you think you'd end up writing as many books as you have?

I didn't think in those terms. I thought of myself as a writer, as a person who was going to write. I didn't have a specific ambition of writing a lot of books, or of being famous. I just wanted to get the writing done. And I wanted to get published. You have to publish if you're a writer—sooner or later—it's part of being a writer.

When did you first get published?

I published poetry early, in my twenties. But I didn't get any prose published until I'd been sending it out to editors for seven or eight years. That's a long time. I was writing novels and short stories both and not getting any of them published.

What kept you going?

Obstinacy. And the fact that, although it's very hard work, I like writing. It is where I feel I function best. It's what I do best. I knew I had a long way to go. This is what I wanted to do.

Did you have any formal training in writing?

No. I took one course in creative writing in school and hated it. I felt really out of place. It was about marketing, all that stuff that has nothing to do with writing. What I did in college was to train myself to earn a living as a French teacher, so that I could eat while I was writing.

Did your parents encourage you to write?

Sure. They encouraged all of their kids in anything we wanted to do seriously. And they made no difference between the boys and the girl. But it was my father who encouraged me also to get this other skill, a saleable skill, being able to teach French, so that I wouldn't have to depend on the writing. He said, "It will leave you free of the editors; you won't have to do what they say." And that was good advice. I give that advice to young writers now. If you want to be totally free as a writer, if you want to write what *you* want to write, marry rich, have a rich aunt—anything—so you don't have to live every penny off your writing. I couldn't have done it. For fifteen years I would have starved.

But no advice fits everybody. I have friends whose entire income is from their writing. I admire them, because it's a very hard and often pretty bare life, but they have a certain freedom too; at least all their time is free for writing.

Was it helpful to have someone in your family who was a published author?

That was my father when I was a kid. My mother didn't start writing until her fifties. Our careers went along about the same pace. She started getting published just a little before I did. But when I was a kid I saw my dad spend several hours a day writing. So I had a model: this is something that grownups do, and it's respectable, and he enjoys it. He loved his time at work. That was a good model.

My mother didn't write at all until she was in her fifties, and then she never stopped until she died at eighty-three. So that's impressive to watch too. And of course she was quite successful. Her book *Ishi* was a bestseller. It surprised us all—"Hey, ma wrote a bestseller." It surprised her too—pleasantly!

Why did you start writing science fiction?

I had published poetry, and one short story in a literary magazine. My first sale—the first money I ever got paid for writing—was from *Amazing Stories*, a pulp science-fiction magazine. They paid me thirty whole dollars. That was a pretty good rate those days. The magazine had a woman editor, Cele Lalli, a very sharp editor. She started a lot of us with her magazine. Most of us that are now in my generation of science-fiction writers were publishing with her: Harlan Ellison and the rest. She had pretty good literary taste, and she had an eye for a young writer that was going somewhere. So I thought, "Okay, if they see what I'm doing and they like it, I will write whatever this stuff is." Actually, my first story wasn't science fiction at all. It was called "April in Paris" and it's a time fantasy. There's no science in it. But I did write some science fiction, and of course my first four or five books, novels, were definitely science fiction. I liked it. I enjoyed it very much.

Did it give you a lot of latitude?

It's called a genre or a field of literature, but actually you can do an immense variety of different things in science fiction. Other genres, westerns or mysteries, are narrower. You can only do certain things with them. But science fiction covers this incredible range of things all the way from absolutely bang-bang pulp stuff to completely serious, complex fiction. And of course it blends into fantasy too, another kind of writing. So I thought, "This is a great place. All the doors are open and there are a lot of good people." Because as I say, my generation came in saying, "We're going to make science fiction into something really good." And we did. Took it out of the old pulp gutter. It's harder to sneer at science fiction than it used to be.

Because science fiction is sort of a world to itself and fans and writers meet together, I made some writer friends. It's good for a young writer to meet some other writers. Writing is a lonesome job.

Did you have a lot of fans early?

In science fiction, you get response to your books. People write back and say, "Hey, I really liked that, but why did you do such and such?" Kids always do that. If you write young-adult fiction, you get great letters from kids and teenagers. And science-fiction fans aren't shy toward the writers, so you get response, and that's neat. Because, boy, you can publish a serious novel and it's like dropping something into a black hole. Because if it doesn't get widely reviewed, you don't get any response at all. Your friends say, "Hey, it was great." But that's it. That's hard. That's hard on a writer. After all, artists are performers—they want a response. They want applause, or even boos and jeers.

They want attention.

You want to know that people heard you. So that's one reason why science fiction is a nice place for a young writer who has that gift to start. They'll know who's reading them.

Did you feel that there was room there?

Lots of room. Particularly for a woman. There were hardly any women writing it then. I just barged in, said, "Hey, move over fellas."

Was it traditionally a male field?

It had been very much a men's field. Mostly read by young men, and written by men. The generation before me the women were using mostly initials—C.L. Moore, or Andre Norton who took a name that could be either a man or woman. And of course the young men who would be scared off by a woman writer assumed that they were men.

Were a lot of those books adventure stories?

The science fiction of the generation before me—the '30s, '40s, '50s—a lot of that was engineering stories, adventure stories, *Star Wars* stuff—just like Spielberg's movies—pretty mindless. Some of it wasn't mindless, but it was emotionless. It had all the wiring diagrams, it told you how the space ship worked, but nobody had any feelings. Cardboard characters being moved through the adventure. So there was a lot to be done when we started writing science fiction. And people liked it when we started doing it. People responded, said, "Hey, wow, this is great."

And then there were some writers whom I really admired and used as models, like Philip K. Dick, who actually was my age, but who had been publishing much longer than me. And Cordwainer Smith, and other writers, showed me what you could do with this material, making real literature, really exciting stuff.

It seems like a lot of women are writing in science fiction now.
Oh, they are.

Vonda McIntyre, for instance.
A very fine writer. Vonda's ten years younger than me; she's part of the next wave. With her generation a good many women came in. We women almost dominated the field for a while. And influenced it permanently. I can tell you one reason women started writing it when they did. We're talking mid-'60s, just about the time when the women's movement was getting restarted. And this imaginative, speculative fiction gave us a place where we could do thought experiments, where we could say, "Well, what if it isn't the way it is now? What if men and women had a different relationship?" *The Left Hand of Darkness* is a thought experiment. Science fiction gave us freedom; we could get away from the way things were and talk about how things might be. It was exciting, and I know that's one reason so many women went into it. They thought, "Hey, I can do my thinking through fiction, as a feminist." That has continued to be true. You get people like Marge Piercy who is not "a science fiction writer," or Doris Lessing, or Margaret Atwood now, using the medium for the same purposes: thinking, thinking something through. "What if this happened, what if that happened, what would it be like?" It's a beautiful medium for that.

It always reminds me of taking a trip somewhere. There's always a quality of strangeness about it.
There should be strangeness. If there isn't strangeness, then it isn't quite successful. That's what makes fantasy or science fiction. It isn't quite like this world right now. People love strange things.

Why is science fiction appealing for a reader?
Some people hate it. Some people don't like imaginative fiction at all. They want realism. They want to read stories that tell you what brand name of something people are using: Anne Beattie stories. Some people are allergic to imaginative fiction. If you do like it, you read it for pleasure. That's what it's for, for pleasure. Like all art.

Do you know why science fiction is popular now?
Just now there's a lot of escapist science fiction being written —the stuff I call sci-fi. Lucas's and Spielberg's movies have had a

big influence on the literature. There's a lot of low-grade escapism. I suppose the reason why that's so popular is that people are really quite scared. This is a very frightening time we're living in. People are rushing around bombing each other; we'd all like to get away. So readers turn to escapist, simplistic stories and films. But that to me is not the real heart of science fiction; that is schlock stuff. The stuff that I like to read and like to write is not escaping from the world. It's just the opposite. It's a way of talking about the world. It's a metaphor for us, right now, right here. It's an infinitely variable metaphor. I write about us. I'm not trying to get away. . . . In my books, the future is a metaphor. I'm not predicting. People are always asking me, "What's going to happen in thirty years?" I don't know! You know as much as I do.

Is good science fiction finally getting some respect?

Sure. It's being taught in schools and colleges. It's being taken seriously by reviewers, critics. High time, too.

So there's an intelligent audience out there?

Yes. There's an audience of serious readers, as well as an audience of escapist readers.

Is it much different from fantasy?

There's a spectrum. On one end you get pure fantasy like Tolkien's *The Lord of the Rings*, which has no science or anything like science in it, although it's not irrational; it's a very intelligent book. And then way over on the other end you get what I call wiring-diagram science fiction, which is all about the innards of the machinery—they're always explaining things to each other—which I think goes a little too far; but some people love that too. In between is most of the rest of it. But science fiction either is genuinely exploring some scientifically plausible idea, or it's using science as a metaphor. There is science in science fiction, no matter how well buried. As there is technology in the most "primitive" camping week in the Cascades. . . . Of course some people say, "*You* don't write science fiction because you don't have physics, astronomy in there." And I say, "Well, isn't anthropology a science? Isn't psychology a science? Sociology? Don't they rate?" Then they say, "Oh, that's social science fiction." All right, call it what you like. All genre names are just labels, essentially publishers' and booksellers' labels—or labels used by conservative, conventional academics to keep "popular" books out of the sanctum of literature. They are highly artificial categories, which describe only the most conventional books. They are seldom really useful on any but a superficial, cataloguing level.

In the Earthsea *trilogy, did you have less latitude because you were using mythological characters, rather than creating a whole new race as you might in a science-fiction novel?*

I was working in a tradition, a Western European tradition of wizardry and magic. That's an enormously old tradition and it goes very deep in people. I could get down to that ground and do what I pleased, invent my own kind of magic. The magic in the *Earthsea* books has to do with naming, right? That is a metaphor for science, and it's a metaphor for art. So right there, you see, things get confused again. Because obviously I don't believe in magic. I don't think that you can say the true name of the sofa and the sofa will turn into a rhinoceros. Magic doesn't work, but magic is a wonderful metaphor for things that do work, like science, like art.

None of this was clear in my head when I wrote the books. This is what I see afterwards. When I write the book, I have the story to tell, and I do not know what the story means. I don't have a message; I just have a story. Then I look back and see that the story said something. Or, hopefully, said a few hundred different things, some of which might contradict each other.

Some writers seem to be getting away from telling a story. But that doesn't seem to be true of your work.

In my last book, *Always Coming Home*, I have taken the story apart quite radically. There is a narrative running through it, and it's full of short stories, and there's a piece of a novel in it, but I'm also doing a whole lot of stuff that isn't narrative, or is part of the narrative in a way that we're not quite used to. A lot of us novelists are playing with storytelling and narrative. Artists have to keep making things new; you can't stick to the old way. You have to make things difficult for yourself. The easy way is the wrong way, in art, alas!

What prompted you to write the Earthsea *trilogy?*

I was invited. It was the first time I was asked to write a book by a publisher. There was a small West Coast press, Parnassus, that did children's books. He [the publisher] wanted to start doing what is called "young-adult" fiction for people eleven or twelve up. He said, "Would you like to write me a book?" I said, "I don't know how to write for kids." And he said, "Well, give it a try. Maybe you can write a fantasy or something." And it just clicked. The story began to come to me very quickly. So I sat down and wrote it. And it was very interesting for me because I had never thought of writing for young people before.

Did you read those kinds of books when you were little?

There weren't so many to get ahold of. Tolkien's books weren't out yet. Now it's so easy, but even fifteen years ago, fantasy was really rare; most of the books were out of print. You'd look for them in second-hand bookstores. As a child, I read a lot of folk and fairy tales—that's related. And a writer such as Lord Dunsany—I read him when I was a kid. But the bookstores weren't crawling with unicorns, back then.

Did you do a lot of research?

No. Fantasy has to come out of your own deep feelings to carry any real power. You can't spin it out of your head.

But things like the sorcerer's school. How did you make that up?

I wondered what a "wizard" was before he was an old man with a grey beard. . . . It was fun figuring that out. I'm not saying that you don't use your head, but that's not where it starts. Fantasy starts in a very irrational place deep inside you. It's got to start, probably, from feelings that you don't understand, so that there is something that is out of your control, and you're constantly trying to control it as you write. This is something that is true of all art. It's like riding a horse. You want the horse to have his own will, because you're doing something together. If the horse is too docile then you won't go far. Any real art that isn't just hack work, grinding things out of the bologna machine, is going to come from places inside the writer that the writer didn't know about until she or he started writing. The writing is a means of exploring. It's like going into a country I didn't know was there. And therefore the strangeness you talked about. It is strange country. It has to be strange country. If I've been there before I don't want to go back. That's why my books may be getting less conventional, and stranger: I want to take more risks.

When you were writing the Earthsea *trilogy, was it hard to model the characters so that they didn't become too stereotypical?*

I didn't think about that. That's not how one's mind works while writing. These characters appeared; there they were, and I described them as best I could. The characters started pushing the author around. The character Ged, the wizard, was always doing that, doing something I didn't expect him to do, or saying something I didn't understand and had to figure out. "Why is this happening? Why is the book taking this turn? Why is Ged doing that?" This is a very common phenomenon with novelists. I've compared notes with lots of them; they agree that if the character doesn't have a will of its own, the character may be dead. Stillborn.

Why does the book end if the character keeps changing and things keep happening?

Well—*Earthsea*: it's a trilogy, but I didn't intend it to be. At that time trilogies weren't a dime a dozen like they are now. There was Tolkien's, and that was about it. I wrote this book, *A Wizard of Earthsea*. A year or so later, I realized that at the end of the book there are a lot of hints that something else is going to happen. And then the second book arrived. Then the third book came fairly promptly. At the end of the third book my wizard left. He didn't tell me where he was going and he's never come back. I couldn't write about him. He's gone. So that's one way a book ends. When your character decides, "That's all I'm going to tell you."

I missed him sometimes terribly. Sure, you miss a novel when you are done with it. You've been living this life for years maybe. I miss the people and place, just like I was homesick.

It works for readers too. I felt that way when I first read Tolkien, in my twenties. I read the three books in four days. I was living in Middle Earth. I love writers who make you a world, whether it's a fantasy world or a real world. Dickens does the same thing. Any true novelist does—"fantasist" or "realist."

If you were creating a world like the Northwest, how would the form of it change as you turned it into science fiction?

Well, if you set it on other planets, you have to make it exotic, unworldly. But the fact is, people tell me that my other worlds are very easy to get into, not all that unearthly; they're just a little different. This last book, *Always Coming Home*, is about the Napa

Valley, where I have been to every year of my life. I love that place very deeply, and try, in the book, to describe it just as it is. Only the people I put there are different. The place is as it is. "Real gardens—imaginary toads. . . ."

Do the people fit with the place?

It's a long, long time in the future. And they've lived there a long time, so they fit the place. Have you traveled abroad? Have you ever been to Italy?

Yes.

You know how the little towns there look like they grow up out of the hills? That's so beautiful. We've only lived in California 150 years, and the Spanish another 150 years or so; we don't know how to use California. We mostly just ruin it. We exploit, exhaust, misuse that beautiful place—we rape it. Endlessly. So I tried to put some people there who use it right, who live with it. Who fit in. And that was a lot of fun, figuring out how to fit in. How to not do the harm we've done, but also not just sit on your hands and do nothing.

So the society wasn't static?

To us it seems very static, but we have such crazy ideas about the necessity for immediate, continuous progress. I was kind of standing all that progress stuff on its head in the book. I was trying to take a deliberately subversive attitude toward Western civilization. It was a pleasure. It was hard, too. It's hard to think yourself out of your own culture. And of course you can't really do it; but you can try.

Do you have much hope for the progress of Western civilization?

Let's not call it progress, because I'm anti-progress. I think we've "progressed" quite far enough. Hope, yes. You have to have hope or you'd jump off the cliff. I must say sometimes it's an act of will to believe that we won't irrevocably and disastrously damage ourselves and the whole earth—worse than we have done already.

Is that why you wrote The Word for World Is Forest?

That was written out of a specific anger. Anger generally comes from some kind of despair. I was feeling desperate. It looked like we were never going to get out of Vietnam. We would just go deeper and deeper. That book was a direct response to that rage that a lot of us felt. A lot of us are feeling it again, now that we have a government that seems determined to go and bomb people wherever it can get away with it. That anger is building up, whatever our administration may think.

When you get mad at something like the Vietnam War, why is it that you write a science-fiction novel?

Well, that's what I did then, who knows what I'd do now? I might not have written that novel that way if I'd been home that year. I was in London. As a foreigner, an American in a foreign country, I did not feel that I could be active politically; it was almost like being a traitor. I don't know if that was a dumb way to feel, but it seemed to me that if I was demonstrating against the United States in England, that was really different from going down here to Pioneer Courthouse Square and demonstrating against the government in America as an American. I'd been very active politically, and my hands were tied. I had nothing to do but write. That's why that book is quite different from any of my other books. There was this urgency. Usually I would blow off steam in some kind of activism politically. But I do try to keep them separate. And that time they came together.

What kind of perspective does The Word For World Is Forest *have on the Vietnam War that a more reportorial book wouldn't have?*

I don't know that it would have a different value. I would hope that it might generalize the subject a bit more. Every good book does that. No matter what it's about. It can be about something very small and specific and momentary, but in that you can read its relevance to other things. Homer wrote about a stupid nasty little war a couple of thousand years ago, but we still are enlarged in mind and soul by Homer, because he's a great writer. The more serious, large-minded the writer, the more permanent the relevance. Jane Austen's stories seem like nothing, a few people in a drawing room, but they give us permanent strength and understanding because they're talking about us, on a deep level. So there's that aspect to any book about a specific place or incident. If you can hit the deep chords, they keep vibrating.

It's hard to do that though.

It's not the same as preaching or polemics. The more you are preaching directly, saying, "You should stop this, you should do this," that's not art. It's going to hurt the work. *The Word for World Is Forest* is a bit soap-boxy. That's its fault as a novel. It gets preachy. Fortunately there are other aspects to it which I like and which aren't preachy, which counteract that. The whole dream thing picks it up and changes it. At any rate, Vietnam's over, but people still seem to be reading the book.

When you write stories like that, do you try to get down to a level that is archetypical?

It isn't like getting down to it, it's like trying to start from there. You're calling on something that is deep and obscure probably, that's so far in that...see, if you could describe it rationally, if you could intellectualize it, you wouldn't have to write a book about it.

Do you believe in the idea of the collective unconscious?

It's a nice image. I don't know how far you can take it in actuality. I came to Jung very late. I read him after I'd written the *Earthsea* books. People kept saying, "That's Jungian, isn't it, that shadow?" They finally shamed me into reading him. I liked Jung a lot. He was very helpful to me, as an artist, and in a troubled part of my life. I'm grateful to Jung. But some of his ideas seem to work better for me as metaphors than as literal truths. I like the way he talks about art. He knows much better than Freud what art is. Freud didn't have any idea what art was—had it all assbackwards.

Do you think that there's some commonality in people that allows them to respond in much the same way to a given story?

Absolutely. Whatever Jung meant by the archetypes, there are certain kinds of images, or events, or stories, that we all respond to. There seems to be no doubt about that. It's part of our common humanity.

Are you getting better at discovering what these are?

I don't know. I might be getting worse. But the shadow in the first *Earthsea* book, I hit something there. It was amazing when I came to read Jung. It *was* the same thing. We had approached the same idea from totally different directions. That was kind of uncanny. I thought either Jung or I must be right, probably both of us; we were saying the same thing so differently.

Do you see a big difference between what you wrote when you were first starting out and what you write now?

There's a difference. I'm more skillful. I'm surer on my feet. But no, I don't see a great difference. I hope I've gotten a little larger and more skillful, but I still like my early stuff, most of it. I couldn't write it now. That's not a difference in artistic level, that's a difference in age. I'm a different person now. I'm a grandmother, for God's sake.

When you make up these other worlds, is it important that the people you create fit within the world?

Very important. The word ecology or ecosystem was hardly invented when I started writing science fiction, but it is the relevant word here. It means that everything does fit together. We now have this perception scientifically; I think novelists always had it. Everything in the world that you're making has to be part of everything else, or else it all falls apart.

Is this something that you realized early, or did you develop it?

I just felt my way into it. It was the way I worked. I didn't think about it rationally. Making a novel isn't that different from making a pottery pot in some ways. Your mind is at work all the time, shaping and controlling, but you are doing it with your feelings. I've never been able to explain this satisfactorily. This is about the hundredth time I've tried to say it.

Do you draw a map of the world you plan to create?

If there's any travelling around in it, I always have a map. You have to know how long it's going to take to get from here to there, even if it's just a city. I think a lot of novelists do that. You want to *know*, you don't want to be fudging and faking and making stupid mistakes.

What are the rules that you have to follow in making up these other worlds?

It all has to hang together. If you say anything about it, it has to fit with everything else about it. This is one of the things that comes up when I'm doing workshops in writing speculative fiction. If I have inexperienced writers, they try to throw in an orange sun and eight blue moons and you have to say, "Okay, that's beautiful but what does that mean about, for instance, the tides? What kinds of shadows are you going to have if you have eight moons?" This is part of the fun, making it all fit.

Things have to go together.

They have to go together. And if they don't go together, you have a shaky, weak story. You've got a story that isn't founded solidly and it's going to fall apart. And some reader sure enough is going to think, "I don't know what's wrong, but there's something wrong." Because readers are very smart. Readers, after all, are making the world with you. You give them the materials, but it's the readers who build that world in their own minds. I am very aware of writing as a collaborative act. You've got to play fair with the person you're working with.

Do you do a lot of research for your books?

For some of them, but some of it's research in fields you wouldn't really think about. In *Left Hand of Darkness* the two things I really had to read about were sexual physiology so I could figure out how they worked, being androgynous, and how people live in very cold climates. So I read a bunch of books about Finland and Tierra del Fuego and things like that.

So you had the idea in advance that you were going to create a winter environment?

I had the idea for the book and then I had to find out how things worked.

Do you enjoy creating languages and naming your characters?

That's part of the game.

How do you go about doing that?

I listen till it sounds right. It's very strange. I have no explanation for it. But if the name isn't right, I can't write about the character. In *Lathe of Heaven*, I couldn't start the book till I knew his name was George Orr. Once I knew it was George, George Orr, I was off. Some psychologist probably could explain it, but I can't.

Do your stories ever start out of dreams?

A couple of stories use bits of dreams. When I'm writing I don't dream very much; it's like the dreaming gets used in the writing. If you're asking when the unconscious comes up and gets into the work, it's if I can wake up slowly, early in the morning, and just be undisturbed for ten, fifteen minutes; that's often when

I solve the problem, I see how to go on with the next chapter. Between sleep and waking you're between the two worlds, and that's a really good time for me. It's not the dreaming. It's coming up between. You're still in touch with your unconscious.

Do you think your writing is a way of dreaming?

No. I would say perhaps it fulfills some of the same psychological functions of dreaming for me the writer, but probably not for the reader. Sometimes obviously it's therapy too. If it can work for you, maybe it'll work for them.

Do you think it's therapy for you?

Sometimes, not always. I don't think I'm that sick.

Do you need to keep writing?

Yeah.

Could you stop?

I think I'd die. It's more than therapy. It's the way I live. It is life to me. Where I live my life most intensely is in my writing.

And your output of books shows no sign of dropping off?

Oh, I wouldn't want to say that. Because I just finished a big book, and I haven't written anything much since. And writers are always afraid [wrings hands], "That was the last book. I'm through." You can have a year or two of feeling perfectly miserable. Usually what it means is that the well is filling back up and you can't get any water for a year or two. I'm getting older, I'm fifty-six. Writers vary a lot in old age. I'm very curious to see if I can go on. I hope so. I'll be bored to tears if I can't.

Some people do their best work when they get older.

I used to think that poets were people who died at thirty, like Keats and so on. In this century it seems like a lot of our poets only get really good as they get older, like Yeats. He just got better and better and better as he got older. That's one way we can use older people.

Yes, they could offer the value of experience.

Which we don't use in our society. We shove old people under the carpet. But the older artists often can go on, in writing, painting, photography, and we continue to respect them; we don't just shove them under the carpet.

Did you have trouble reconciling your other responsibilities with writing?

Sure. If you're working—even a part-time job—that takes up a lot of energy. If you're bringing up three kids, that takes not only energy, it means that you are totally responsible while they are awake and home. You can't give yourself entirely to anything else, and to do any art you must give yourself to it totally—without any reserve. And so that means that when I was responsible for the kids and they were awake, I couldn't write. I wrote at night, while the kids were little. I would get impatient. It seems like forever. But it isn't forever. It's actually only a few years of your life. Then they go off to school one by one. And you begin to have time. You use the time you get. Most mother writers learn to be incredibly efficient in their use of time. You just have to. Grab it when you get it. I think artists in general don't dilly-dally around. They pretend to, but actually they're pretty hard-working people with pretty regular hours.

Do you keep pretty regular hours?

Yeah. Don't all the writers you've talked to?

Most of them do, some incredibly strict.

I know very few that don't. Some of them are really rigid about it. Seven o'clock to noon is my writing time. When I'm home that's where I am. I don't answer the phone. And even if I'm not writing, I'm there ready to go. You learn to use your time intensely if you only have a couple of hours. You can wear yourself out in a couple of hours. That may be all you *can* work that day; then you've had it.

With other responsibilities such as interviews and public appearances, do you have to make an effort to get time to write?

I have to fight pretty hard.

Is that a cost of being successful?

It is. We are very hard on our artists in America. We demand an enormous lot of public giving from them. I'm not saying that it's wrong, but I think that people might sometimes realize that in order to do their art, artists do need five or six hours a day, and privacy. Look what we do to popular artists. I don't know how those kids survive, except that they're young and have lots of vitality.

And anybody that goes on the road—musician, poet, anything—oh, that's hard. I did some weeks of that this year and I'll never do it again.

Is your personality such that you just don't like public speaking?

No. I love to read my work. And doing gigs you meet all these neat people. It's great. But you do it over and over. . . . I tell you what's the hardest thing for me: book signing. I did it once for five hours straight in Los Angeles. That means a new person every minute or two. And they want contact and you want to give contact. I find that really hard.

We've sort of built that into being a successful writer. It's a little off base. I'm not saying it's wrong, but saying that I can't handle it too well.

Are you in any way religious?

Not formally. The springs of religion are completely familiar to me. I've been there. It's just that I was brought up completely outside all sects. My father was an anthropologist, a man trained and by nature relativistic about religions, disbelieving that there is one true one. So I don't have this feeling I "need" religion. Some people think they must have some "belief." I don't. But I do know that, whether it's a great work like the Bach B-minor Mass, or just a gospel song, I know where it comes from; I understand that. I know what that feeling is. So I would never say I was anti-religious; that would be an incredibly cheap, stupid thing to say.

So you recognize the source?

I think so. And I think all religions rise from the same needs and feelings. I dislike religions when they become opinions and start pushing other people around, saying, "You must believe this. You must do that." I don't like that. I don't like being pushed around, seeing other people being pushed around.

Did the feminist movement change your perception of things?

It has changed me and is changing me. I'm deeply grateful to feminism, because I feel it has liberated me in many ways. It's liberated me from ways of thinking and being that I didn't even know I was caught in. But I was caught. And now I'm free of certain rigidities—for instance, the fact that all my early books are about men, and women are very secondary. In the first and the third *Earthsea* books there really aren't any women to speak of. That's very strange. I'm a woman. Why was I writing that way? Well, I was in a certain box. It was partly a literary box. In literature, it has conventionally been the men who did things. And it was a social box: in our culture it's been the men who do things, the women who stay home and wait for them. I had to become conscious of that to work through it. And now I'm getting free of it. And it makes me happy.

I'm sure I have thereby gotten on top of certain fears and hatreds that were suppressed. They're gone. I don't need them anymore. And now I have my tradition as a woman, as a woman writer. I was afraid of it, apparently, I wasn't strong enough to use it.

What tradition?

The tradition of women writing. Very few women are accepted as great writers—the Brontës, George Eliot, Jane Austen, and maybe Virginia Woolf and that's about it. Well, there's a lot more women than that. Part of the fun I'm having now is reading novels by women you've never even heard of. Feminist theory and criticism of literature I have found incredibly exciting and interesting. This is the first school of criticism that's ever made any sense to me.

Has this commitment to feminism changed your language?

Well, take pronouns: I don't say *he*, meaning *he and/or she* anymore. And I never will again, except by old bad habit. I realize that *he* doesn't mean *he-and-she*. We're told that it does, but it doesn't. People don't take it as such. They understand it as meaning *he*. And it does reduce the world to the male. It's a big problem: what do you use instead? I use *them* and *they* wherever I can. That was the original English usage; the grammarians arbitrarily decided it was "wrong," because it wasn't like Latin. There are places you can't use *they* and keep clear, so we've got a problem. But I'll do anything rather than reduce the human world to the masculine. And I don't talk about *man* meaning human beings anymore. . . . Beyond that, I don't think it's changed my language all that much in detail. Women are just learning how to take back the language, make it their own property.

How about your characters?

There I would say, look at the new book and tell me what you think. I get some queer reactions. Some reviewers, because it's not a patriarchy, assume that it's a matriarchy. They think that there's no other choice: somebody "has to be" top dog. That is hierarchic thinking refusing to question itself.

Does reading anthropology help to figure these things out?

Sure. It makes us realize how much our thinking is caught in our own culture. And that's why some people are afraid of it, while others find it very exciting.

Are the differences between cultures becoming less distinct?

Western industrial civilization has taken over everything all over the world, and all the other cultures are dominated by it. I hate that. My father spent his life working with cultures that were dying because of us, talking to Indians who were the last few people of what had been a whole culture. Now we're all industrialized; we all want the same things. I think that is dangerous and sad. That may be one reason why I keep inventing cultures. We've got to have variety somewhere; do it imaginatively if you can't do it any other way.

David Wagoner

*I*N HIS *essay "Walking," Henry David Thoreau called for the kind of poet who could "...impress the rivers and streams into his service, to speak for him; who nailed words to their primitive senses,...transplanted them onto the page with earth adhering to their roots...." David Wagoner has answered that call. In his thirteen books of poetry to date, Wagoner has wrought poems from the plants, the trees, the rocks, the animals and the people of the Pacific Northwest. He packs his poems with vividly rendered details of the lives of gulls, owls, ospreys, crabs, salmon, geese, grebes, goldeneyes. He has recreated the landscape of the Northwest on the page, and in the process has made clear the sometimes mysterious connections between humans and landscape.*

His books of poetry include: First Light *(1983),* Landfall *(1981),* In Broken Country *(1979),* Who Shall Be the Sun? *(1978) and* Collected Poems *(1976). Nearly as prolific a novelist as he is a poet, he has ten novels to his credit. Among them:* The Hanging

Garden *(1980),* Whole Hog *(1976),* Tracker *(1975),* Where Is My Wandering Boy Tonight? *(1970) and* The Escape Artist *(1965). The Escape Artist was filmed by Francis Ford Coppola and released in 1982. Wagoner is the editor of* Straw for the Fire: From the Notebooks of Theodore Roethke, 1943-63 *(1972), and has received numerous awards: Pushcart Prize in poetry, 1983; nomination for American Book Award in poetry, 1980; Pacific Northwest Booksellers Award for Excellence in Writing, 1979; nomination for National Book Award in poetry, 1977; Guggenheim Fellowship in Fiction, 1956.*

Born in Massillon, Ohio, in 1926, he grew up in Whiting, Indiana. He received a B.A. in English from Penn State in 1947 and an M.A. in English from Indiana University in 1949. He has taught English at the University of Washington since 1954, and has edited Poetry Northwest *since 1966.*

The interview took place in the spring of 1985 at Wagoner's home in Mill Creek, outside Seattle. He is a soft-spoken man whose voice takes on an incantational quality when talking of the rivers, forests and wild creatures of the Pacific Northwest.

Most of your poems are rooted in the climate, the geography, the flora and fauna of the Pacific Northwest. Why is this?

The impulse to write the kind of dramatic lyric that you're talking about, based on real live organisms and real places, may be a result of my upbringing in a place where things didn't grow easily, where everything had a great deal of difficulty making it to adulthood. This was the area between between Gary, Indiana, and Chicago, where the soil is very sandy, where the weather is very harsh, where growing things have about the same kinds of lives as the people do.

It was an enormous surprise to me to come to the Northwest in my late twenties, and to see a place where almost anything would grow, where growing things had a kind of furious life about them, a kind of lavishness that I admired a lot.

I think I had associated myself with what didn't grow very much, where I was brought up. So I responded very strongly to a completely different kind of environment. It has a lot of complicated aspects, and I don't pretend to understand them all, but when I came over the Cascades and down into the coastal rain-forest for the first time in the fall of 1954, it was a big event for me, it was a real crossing of a threshhold, a real change of conscious-ness. Nothing was ever the same again.

How did this change your poetry?

Well, it took a while. I remained a city boy for some time after that. I was a little frightened by the wilderness, as I should have been. I didn't get out into the woods and out to the seashore and up into the mountains for a year and a half or so. Until I had oriented myself that way it had no effect on my poetry at all. I kept writing more or less the same way that I had. But the change had something to do with a reassurance that I belonged in the world. That's partly it. I recognize a lot of my own work as an attempt to discover what my place is in the natural order of things. Where I grew up there was no natural place, everything was unnatural and/or dying or already dead. So I had to come to terms with other growing things for the first time—nonhuman growing things.

Did the subjects of your poetry change?

I think so. I think that my poetry before then was a great deal more literary, more bookish, more cerebral than it became there-after. My teacher had been Theodore Roethke, who reveled in this growth in the Northwest. A change came in his work after he got here. So I had a foreshadowing of what was apt to happen to me.

I had already begun, before coming out here, to think about the whole biological world differently, because I'd had Roethke as a teacher. He made a sort of revolution among the roots for us all.

Did this change of subject imply a change of style?

Yes. I think it's quite obvious looking at the poems that I worked much more conversationally, in a middle level of diction thereafter. I had been a lot more artificial before that. It was partly the result of that exposure to a natural world in which I could feel some kinship that made me want to write in a way that Thoreau talked about in one of his essays called "Walking." He foresaw the coming of a kind of poetry in which the language still had the dirt clinging to its roots, which had an air of being part of the living earth. I saw some of that in Roethke and that was the direction that I wanted to go.

That's what I have tried to do. Whether I have done it or not is an entirely different matter. This has been my aim: to find the poetry of common, American speech. Instead of pushing out the boundaries of poetic diction, I have turned inward to its middle.

Most of my poems have a clear surface; they're not difficult for even a semiliterate adult to make something of. I don't explore—as a rule—the kind of world that John Ashbery is looking at now. I'd rather have my poems sound like talk, though I don't go to the extremes that some have in this respect. I don't see this as a cause, in the manner of William Carlos Williams or at times William Stafford.

Is your poetry a way of coming to terms with the Northwest, a way of discovering it?

I don't think of it as a region at all. For me, the Northwest stands for the whole world now, to a large extent anyway.

As you began to incorporate the Northwest landscape into your poetry, did the poetry change?

Yes, but the change in my poetry also had something to do with the discovery of the ability to love. For me it spread out of that into the natural world. I suddenly realized I had been a lost stranger everywhere I had been because I had closed myself off. When I was able to open myself, it was like being in Eden. It was like naming day in Eden. Is it in the Apocrypha where God asks Adam to name the creatures? It was a feeling very much like that when I realized I was in a place like the Olympic rainforest and I didn't know the names of anything. I didn't know these other living entities, even by name, let alone in any other way.

How did your writing develop from the time you moved out here to now?

I changed my working habits. I began working more freely. I spent more time in revision, and more time than ever before in the evolving of the raw material for a poem. I discovered ways to get at my unconscious mind in ways I had never been able to before.

In writing a poem I had tried simultaneously to be the dreamer, the explorer, the poet and the critic—all at once. As soon as I divided those into three stages, everything changed. I allowed myself to be crazy and very free in working, and then tried to make a poem out of the raw materials, and then criticized the poem after that.

Roethke set me an example there. I don't know if I would have done it so soon if he hadn't done what he did.

So Roethke had a powerful influence on you?

Oh, a great influence, especially in terms of the rudiments of how to think about writing and revising a poem.

Stylistically do you think that there's a resemblance between your work and his?

I doubt it, and nobody has told me so for a long time. I think we went quite different ways. He was interested in a more ecstatic kind of elevation of the language than I had ever been interested in.

How did you go about developing your own style?

I began writing poems when I was very young, when I was in grade school, and I have not stopped. I don't know why I did it. I didn't have any living examples; I didn't know any poets. The first living, practicing adult poet I met after I came into the thinking part of my life was Theodore Roethke. I met him when I was a senior in college.

He was a role model, somebody who was completely devoted to poetry, who was teaching it, who was writing it, who was reading it aloud. I simply accepted that model. I said, "That's what I want to be."

He told me whom to read. He told me what was wrong with my poems. He showed me how I could think further about them, how I could try harder, where I could apply mechanical effort if I couldn't think of any other kind of effort, or if I didn't have sufficient imagination yet.

I have worked hard. I really have, and I have read a great deal, and continue to do so. As an editor and teacher I read an enormous amount of poetry. I also judge a number of contests. So I have a fair idea of what's going on in American poetry. I read a great deal of bad poetry, and it isn't necessarily healthful to do so, but I haven't killed myself or silenced myself so far.

You have to want to be a poet. The world doesn't seem to want poetry. You have to want to write it and impose it on a rather indifferent market. If it were a matter of vote whether or not there would be any poets in the United States, I suspect that we would not get very many votes. Or perhaps society in general would decide that a half a dozen would be quite enough, thank you, and that we'd do with them. You have to be stubborn.

When did you start writing novels?

It depends on what you call a novel. In college I wrote long fiction of a very strange, sloppy sort. I read with enormous astonishment the early novels of Graham Greene, and emulated him. I wrote a spy novel without ever having been in Germany or Denmark, which was the setting. I did crazy things, in other words.

I was an English instructor and about twenty-three when I made my first serious try at a novel, one I have discarded. The second one I really tried on, finished, and it eventually sold. I had to change a good deal of it, though. It's called *The Man in the Middle*. It was rejected by fifteen publishers before it was taken by Harcourt Brace.

I had an agent by then, and he helped me a lot. Malcolm Cowley encouraged me early, bless him, and got me my agent. He liked that novel and tried to get it published at Viking, but it was voted down, so he then sent it to an agent.

Why is there such a disparity between the voice you employ in your novels, which is often humorous, and the voice that appears in your poetry, which is usually serious? Why is there no overlap?

They do overlap, but frequently it's the novels that didn't get published that are the most overlapping with the poems. I have written, for instance, several novels that didn't get published, and should not have been published, and which I'm grateful were not published, which I then went back to and made into poems.

I remember one out of which I extracted nine poems. In each case they were events, the kernel of which had happened to me, much disguised in the novel form. I then turned them into poems which I can read without being ill.

I have tried to write fiction of the sort that I have used in poems. It hasn't worked. I don't know why. I guess because I didn't work hard enough. I tried to write the novels too easily. I became too impatient. I didn't follow my working methods in poetry. I was less careful and gave up instead of revising extensively. I didn't put the same degree of effort into writing fiction as I did into writing poetry.

Sometimes I'd be lucky with novels, and those are the ones that got published. But my novels are almost all about events that never happened. My poems are frequently the truth. I steer away from the truth in fiction.

To what extent are your poems fictional?

I write a great deal out of personal experience, and I remain, as far as I can and as close as I can, true to that experience. I also write about fantastic things at times—I write about dreams. I deal with my own experience the majority of the time in my writing. It may be a limitation; I wonder about it at times. It's not that I don't feel free to lie, but I can't lie about important matters.

Why is naming things so important to your poetry?

I was just talking about this. I had a letter from Bill Matthews, who's writing an introduction to the personal memoirs of Richard Hugo, and he asked if I knew any anecdotes about Dick in the early years that he might use, especially the 1950s about which he didn't write very much.

I knew him then when he was a technical writer at Boeing. It was Dick Hugo that helped get me out of town in Seattle. I went fishing with him and I learned about a number of the places that I have come to love through being with Dick Hugo.

He knew a great deal about fish and the habits of fish and the names of fish, but he knew almost nothing about flowers, shrubs, trees, birds. He knew thousands of place names and could remember the place and was very sensitive to the landscape. But he didn't know the names of the things that were around him when he was out in the woods going from stream to stream, even the things that were biting him on the back of the neck.

I had a phone call from Dick Hugo one time that began, "What's a one syllable seabird besides gull?"

"Grebe," I said.

"Grebe," he said. "That's good." He hung up.

It showed up in a poem of his called "Port Townsend." I noticed that birds show up in Hugo's poetry again and again and again, frequently toward the end and often as a crowning image. But they make their appearance either as gulls or most of the time just as birds.

Now that's not good enough for me. Birds have many different habits and feelings and appearances. They stand for a great many different things. I am an ardent birdwatcher. I am as particular about birds, I suppose, as the Eskimos are supposed to be about snow and ice—they have a huge vocabulary related to snow and ice because they have to deal with it daily.

Those who don't need to know the names of birds and animals and can simply say, "That's a bird," have a different attitude from me. I can't believe that birds are that important to them.

"Tree" is a favorite word, and what would you do without "tree" as a poet? But trees again have vastly different looks and characteristics and habits and seasonally are quite different.

I share the interest that I understand Hardy had in the landscape. His notebooks are full of minute descriptions of growing things in different seasons: the way dead leaves lie in icy puddles. I have that love, too, for the minutiae of growing things. Hopkins's notebooks are full of detailed observation of twigs and the leaves of bushes. I love that, too. Thoreau had a lot of these same feelings. I think Thoreau knew a great deal more about growing things than he knew about people, and maybe I'm the same, though I write novels that have lots of people in them.

Is there something within these things which you discover when you start writing about them, as Hopkins discovered signs of God in the natural world?

Right, the inscape. Everything expresses its own nature and its own growth, in its manner of existence and its changes.

Do you find this true for you too?

Yes, I do. I absolutely do. I used to think I knew what Hopkins was talking about when I was an undergraduate and a graduate student. I don't think I did. I think I'm coming a little closer to understanding what he meant.

Is there any way that you can get at the larger things without first getting at the minute details?

I don't think so. And the recent discoveries in biology such as DNA and the inherent characteristics of living matter have confirmed that Hopkins was quite right. The whole notion of the in-scape as emblematic of the soul is a biological commonplace right now.

What kind of pictorial dimension do you try to get at in your poetry?

I work out of scene frequently. Many of my poems have a narrative quality, many occur in real places and remain there throughout the poem. This is what I mean by the dramatic lyric. So I set the scene often before something happens in it. That's thinking dramatically, like a dramatist.

In your poetry, do you work out the oral and pictorial dimensions separately or together?

I don't think of them as separate. The sound and rhythm come first; everything else is secondary. If they're not right, nothing's right. Much of my early revision on a poem will be an attempt to discover the right way for the poem to move. Sound you can tend to fix later, but the right movement and the right level of diction are very important very early. If they're not right, nothing will come of it.

So your poetry starts with the aural dimension?

Yes. I know this was the case with Dick Hugo and Jim Wright, who were also students of Theodore Roethke, because this was what Roethke emphasized in his teaching. We all came to believe that the sound had to be right, that a poem is not ideas, fundamentally, that a poem is not its paraphrasable meaning. If you hadn't entered that uncanny world of the right sound, the right movement, you were not being a poet.

In what ways are your poems emblematic, such as your poem about Hemingway, where you described the cicada found near his grave?

The cidada, yes. Well, I saw that there. I wouldn't have put that there if it hadn't been there; that would have been cheating. But it was there at the Hemingway memorial, and it suddenly occurred to me that that shucking off of an old life was maybe what he had done. A cicada looks very threatening. It has a kind of ugly, hunched boxerlike quality, built like Hemingway. It was empty. It had moved on. So it occurred to me as a natural image for an elegy.

Do you keep the metaphorical, allegorical levels in mind when you're writing poetry?

You hope for them. It happens that a whole bunch of layers come together, implode. You suddenly know that a poem is happening to you. You know you're going to have to wait, sometimes maybe for years, before that will be a poem, but you recognize the connections. You know there's a metaphor, even a group of metaphors, waiting for you.

Stanley Kunitz told me he had one miraculous summer when he wrote thirty poems, all of which were in his *Selected Poems* which won the Pulitzer Prize. He said that all but a few came from old notes. He had written down the central metaphors of an experience, had sketched out a few lines and then just left them, unable to write the poems. And suddenly he was free to write them.

This has happened to me too. This is the thrill of recognitition that I associate with making a poem, when in Housman's phrase, the hair stands up on the back of your neck.

How do you decide on a structure for your poems?

This is a decision I try to leave till late. I try never to impose that on a poem; I let the poem seek its own form. If you ask just in the abstract, "What's the difference between a poem in quatrains and a poem in a single verse paragraph?" you can make observations such as the one in quatrains is more songlike, is more suggestive of a cyclic shape, is more likely to be narrative, whereas the other is more likely to be monologue and reflective, meditative.

But there are certain types of structures that seem to lend themselves more readily to a more songlike poem, to the repetition of verses, in the old sense, turns, the suggestion that there had been a refrain there, even if there was not one in the final draft.

Whether it should be a long line or short, or a combination of long lines and short is a matter of feeling your way. This has to do in my case with the relative density of the connotative level. If the poet is in a sense saying, "All right, you must listen and look at every word of this because it is more than it seems on the surface," that poem tends to be in a shorter line. You're asking the eye to linger longer over the sounds of words, their reverberations, that jelly of the language, that memory that we all carry with us which is the product of everything we've ever read and heard.

In the longer line, the voice tends to be louder and nearer the surface: the angry voice, the extremely agitated voice, the more openly passionate voice, any of the stronger emotions of that kind, less the singing voice.

Poems with a combination of long lines and short are like a sine curve, a wavelike motion, a giving and a taking back, an expansion and contraction, a swaying and rocking. The rhythm of the heart is in that, the rhythm of the breath. The true breath unit for me is not the William Carlos Williams three-line stanza, but the long, middle and short line, alternating; long, middle, short; long, middle, short. That for me is the rhythm of the breathing creature, including the breathing earth. Poems about water, about flowing or waving, tend to do that.

When you make a decision about something in a poem, can you always point to why you're doing it, or does it just come down to ear?

It often comes down to ear. If asked, or if I'm curious about how the hell I'm ever going to be able to do anything like that again, I may go back and look and question myself, "Why did I decide that?" I can look at some of my old poems now and be angry with myself for having forced them into shapes that they should not have been in. They feel all wrong. I didn't do my job right. All I can hope is that I'll be wiser next time. It's easy to be wise after the fact. It doesn't make me any readier to be free of error tomorrow, but it's easier to be objective about your own work when you're looking way back.

How did you develop your ear?

I hope I have it. I think I do, because I certainly pay attention to it. I use it to criticize the poems of others, especially students. I feel it in the poets I most admire. It's a characteristic of the poems I like best. I think I hear them in this way, in ways that I would like to emulate.

I hear that kind of ear at work in the poems of Roethke, James Wright, Wallace Stevens, Hopkins, and much of the time in the poems of John Donne, and Keats.

I don't know whether you can develop one or not. You can conceal the lack of one. There are ways to hide the evidence.

There are a number of widely published poets who have very weak ears, and who have managed to conceal that fact through very adroit handling of the line in a mechanical way, the breaking of the line in a particular manner, or by their very strong gifts of invention, metaphor or some other characteristic that makes up for a flawed ear, an overly mechanical one which has discovered a neutral territory that it can occupy but can never sing in.

Was it from people such as Roethke and Hopkins that you developed this ear?

Roethke sent us to the ones with the best ears for our models. He sent us to Hopkins and to Yeats. Yeats was at the top of the list; he had a magnificent ear for musical speech. James Joyce, too. The Irish seem to value their speakers and singers, and the spoken and written word, far more than most ethnic groups and maybe as much as any. It may have something to do with their political powerlessness. It's often true of subject groups. The power of the spoken word in Harlem is notorious. The people whose weapons have been taken away from them develop the power of language. Once you've been cursed by a gifted Irishman or a gifted black, you know you've had it.

Could you describe the process of composition of your poetry?

Every morning I sit down at the writing desk touch-typing, writing free-associatively. This may be a rehashing of my recent reading or what happened to me yesterday or some memory, speculation, idea—I don't care. Get black on white is the old advice, and I try to do that.

If I feel especially verbal, I may get into a lengthy session of free-associative writing. If I'm doubly fortunate I may come across something that seems like an idea. It may have been an idea that I've had before. I have many notebooks that are the product of this kind of writing, and I may browse through some of those to get myself started. I have lists of titles of unwritten poems by the thousands, and I may see one that I suddenly know how to write and the notes may be there.

If I get on to something, I then write down everything I can imagine on the subject. I let myself go; I let myself run off at the mouth as freely as possible without self-criticism. I do this until

I'm tired; then I quit. I don't reread; I look at it the next day or the next time I'm fresh.

If I think I've had a rich time, if I think I've been productive, I may approach it with the attitude of a poet, and look for the poem in this. In the middle of it I may find something very like the first line of a poem. And then I begin to use all the means that I've accumulated over the years, that are a product of my reading and my other writing; the carpenter's tools that I've learned how to handle.

So if I have good hunting I might come out of that second session with a rough draft of a poem. Depending on the length of the poem, degree of difficulty, my mental and emotional poise that day, I may have to have a second session of either free association or another complete rough draft, if I've imposed the wrong form or if I don't have the rhythm right or if my ear hasn't been working right.

The third session as a rule will be as critic. I come back then as poetic policeman, as the one who's looking for trouble and trying to find out what is wrong. "Is there anything here that doesn't belong here? Is there anything missing that's crucial? Is it in the right order? Is it the right shape? Is it the right voice? Is it the right rhythm? Is it the right sound?" And so on.

I permit myself to be as critical as I can be. I attempt to be as objective as possible, pretending that I didn't write it. "How can this damned thing be made better?" is my key question. Those are roughly the three stages. Any one of them may be prolonged.

What prompted you to write Who Shall Be The Sun?

I had become interested in Indian lore through meeting Northwest Indians, and through being in a number of places that they had called theirs. I realized for the first time, though it had also been true of the Midwest, that I was living on Indian land. The more I read about Indians and the old ways, the more I recognized some of the ways I was feeling about the woods, and the earth and plants and animals. The more I read about animism, the more I recognized a kind of natural religion that I have come to believe in.

So I went to their lore in earnest, and reread a lot of the verbatim prose translations of Indians' stories and myths that Franz Boas and his students had collected in the Bureau of American Ethnology Bulletins in the 1880s and 1890s. I realized that some of their stories were marvelous, and had never been retold in any form that anybody could use. Some were very poetic. A lot of these were transliterations, that is, the Indian language was directly translated into English in the same order as the Indian. The Indian was given phonetically. So I could get the voice and the movement of the sentences and see some of the ways they thought. I heard a voice that I could use. So I started retelling some of these. And then after I had found as many as I could, I quit. I felt a little worried about being white and manipulating Indian material like that. Because I had to choose among different versions of the stories, I had to omit things, and to tamper with the originals to a fair extent sometimes.

What did the Indians think of your efforts?

I read them aloud to a large group at an all-tribes party in the University District, and got nothing but praise. They had representatives from almost all the tribes along the coast and some interior tribes, too, the Blackfeet, for instance.

I had read them at a Blackfeet powwow in a tent with twenty Blackfeet, including a seventy-five-year-old shaman, and got away with it, with nothing but praise. I don't think I'll do any more of that, but it was a very curious experience. The poems came out rather quickly, maybe too quickly, but I'm not ashamed of them. I can reread them without difficulty.

The Indians that evolved these myths and tales were far more sophisticated psychologically than they've been given credit for, and that was another aspect that urged me on. I thought that they had been underestimated and that this would be a way to prove it. The Indian moved in the world in the way I felt I wanted to, as if among equals. In the old way, they did not try to dominate the earth, they saw themselves not as superior to trees or even to rocks, but as members as a kind of community of mysteries. I had had that feeling repeatedly and had been very moved by it. To find it there in their lives gave me a weird kind of reassurance. It seemed to me far better and far more useful than the Scotch Presbyterianism I had been raised on.

How did you change the myths in retelling them?

I had to shorten them. A lot of them were told to Boas, his students and early anthropologists—people who weren't very good storytellers. They even would get things garbled or backwards. In some cases, I found nineteen different versions of one of those stories. What is the right one? I had to pick and choose. That, generally speaking, is the type of alteration. I'd have a choice of ten different endings to the story of Star Woman. Each Indian storyteller would have told his own way.

How did you choose the diction, form and structure of the stories?

I stuck as closely as I could to the stories. They made metaphors infrequently. They imitated animal noises, they acted out stories often, especially the ones for children. A lot of what seems unlikely in them is true. The sentences tended to be short. They loved abrupt surprises, they loved the repetitions of sound, and were amused by them, apparently.

The stories were in prose, but it is not like ordinary speech. If you look at a translation of a description of how they cooked vegetables, or how they prepared fish—and there are lots of those—it isn't the same at all as the prose of a story. That is more intense, it is more gnarled. Everything is condensed. So it seemed more poemlike to me.

Were they the first ecologists of this region?

They performed a lot of rituals that would seem to be ecological in spirit, not just motivated by fear. The killing of a bear, for instance, involved all kinds of ritual behavior thereafter. You had to ask forgiveness, had to honor the spirit of the dead bear, had to prepare the skin in a particular way. In another instance, you had to return all of the bones of the first salmon of the season to the river of its origin—all of them—or the ghost of the salmon would come back imperfect. There are a number of kinds of behavior like this.

There were all kinds of holy places. They moved with respect in the natural world, partly because it was peopled by what they called "the first people." When they [the first people] learned that Indians were coming, they were transformed from their original shapes into rocks, stones, trees. You didn't know which of these

were the first people. The rock you picked up might be a holy rock
and you didn't know what powers it might have.

They moved very cautiously in a land they didn't feel they
owned. The idea of the ownership of land was nonsensical. There
were traditional hunting places and fishing places, but that's different. You didn't own them. They assumed the right to fish there,
but that's not the same thing as buying and selling it.

*Is is possible to integrate the Indian's view of the world with
that of the white man's?*

It's not too late for individuals like me to do it privately.
There's nothing that prevents me except the people who cut down
whole forests or ruin streams. It's not too late to suggest to school
children that they can gain more by thinking and feeling this way,
can gain a greater insight into their own lives and into the whole
shape of the existence of living things.

I don't believe man is Nature's last word, or that he was
brought here to be the lord of creation. I feel that he's been a very,
very poor proprietor of this country, in particular. He came damn
close to ruining the earth where I grew up. I have been back there
in recent years. It's not completely dead, but the nearest thing to
it. Pollution there, throughout my growing up, was an accepted
commonplace. There was nothing that you could do about it because these industries were so powerful—Standard Oil of Indiana,
Bethlehem Steel, Inland Steel, Union-Carbide—they were everywhere in my home town. Standard Oil of Indiana was larger,
richer, more powerful than my home town.

So that's wrecked for me. I don't know what a school child
would think about Lake Michigan, which you can't even put your
foot into without having something bad happen to it, without having it break out with ringworm, infections or worse. Lake
Michigan was closed to swimming but we swam there anyway and
got sick.

But that hasn't happened here. It's not too late here in the
Northwest. And that's another reason I honor it. We can still drive
for an hour, walk for a little ways, and be in a place where there is
absolutely no trace of man, where what the earth was like before
us has been preserved, where you get some notion, some humbling notion about your rank in the universe. The woods pay very

little attention to the wishes of man—individually. If he comes with a wrecking machine that's something else.

Do you think that people are more ecologically aware out here?

Yes, because the process had too far advanced, at least where I was. You would have had to drive a long ways there before you found a place that had no trace of man. A long ways. Northern Michigan or northern Wisconsin.

So are there a lot of people who have seen what's happened back East and who want to protect the landscape out here?

Of course. Many like me. Many of us have been transplanted from places that have gone the way that the Northwest can go but hasn't yet.

And because they've seen what can happen, do they value what's here even more?

I believe so. To give one example, I had never slept outdoors until I was almost thirty. This was because nobody did where I came from; it was too hazardous. There were no places where you could get away from the mosquitoes, and everything was polluted and oily. It was not a natural part of growing up where I came from. So when I did finally do that, it was a very strange experience. It was strange to me in a way that it would never be to a Northwesterner who would tend to do this at an early age and take it for granted. I didn't take it for granted. It was remarkable.

Where was it?

In the foothills of the Cascades. And I got lost too, for the first time. Not for very long, only a half hour. But I wasn't a Midwesterner anymore after that.

Why is poetry an appropriate means of expressing such experiences? Is it a more primitive means of expression than prose? Does it hit a deeper level?

I hope so. I believe it does. And primitive in all senses of the word, with major emphasis on prehistory and preliteracy. I have no doubt at all that the song predates the prose narrative, that the chanted hunting story, the boast or the charm predated every explanation that tends to be prose.

Is that why you chose to express yourself in poetry?

I don't know that I chose it, and I write a great deal of prose. I've published ten novels and I've written twenty-three, so it's not that I have something against prose as such; I have something against my own prose; I wish it were better. No, it's a very flexible and marvelous medium and many novelists and writers of non-fiction have proved that. I don't underestimate the value or power of prose. My God, it's glorious. But there remains something more primitive, more powerful, more mysterious about poetry, and always will. I think it's really closer to the spinal cord, in evolution as well as present fact.

How has the role of poetry changed in the last fifty years? Does it have a more specialized role than it once had?

I don't know that it does. American poetry in 1934 was in a pretty weird state. There were some very, very fine poets writing in their prime. I would love to believe that there are today living in the United States poets as good, powerful and important as those poets then. T.S. Eliot was writing *The Four Quartets*. William Carlos Williams was writing, Ezra Pound, Wallace Stevens, and in England, Yeats; my God, they were all writing some of their very best work.

There are some who think we don't have figures like that today. There's nothing harder for a poet or critic to judge than his contemporaries. A poet seems a very minor and unimportant matter if he's in the next room. But from a distance of fifty years, not so little. The friends of Eliot and Pound and the rest of that list underestimated them rather dramatically, I suspect.

I don't know what the current place of poetry is, in other words. That has yet to be discovered. Poetry may very well be influencing our times in ways that we cannot detect, rather than following our times. I don't know that you can always tell.

What are poetry's prime tasks historically? What has it done?

It has expanded human consciousness. It has kept the language alive, which is necessary to the mental health of whole generations. I don't know that poetry is ever able to do that detectably at any one time.

Maybe that's what Shelley was trying to get at.

The "unacknowledged legislators"? Well, maybe they are. I know that the world is not the same because Keats and Shelley lived. They changed the nature of reality. They changed the ways that thinking people can feel and experience life. If it's true that poetry tells us how to live, if Matthew Arnold is right, Keats and Shelley taught us a good deal. And perhaps contemporary poets have done the same. Certainly those poets from fifty years ago and some contemporary poets have done that for me.

What kind of satisfactions do you get from writing poetry?

If you've prepared yourself to be a writer, if you've done the hard homework of heavy reading, have practiced your craft, have developed your strengths, and then if you've written a poem about which in sober, solemn retrospect you can say, "That is about as good as I can do," you will have very few satisfactions in life that match it.

It is a little like asking, "What are the satisfactions of love? What are the rewards of love?" They are the highpoints of life, and the same can be said for poetry. In my case, poetry and love not only resemble each other but very nearly equal each other in their richness, their complexity, and in what they can ask of you and what they can give to you. A poem will ask of you everything you have, and there will be room for much more, alas. And the same is true of love.

James Welch

JAMES *Welch's prose is as spare and elemental as the Highline country which is the setting and subject of much of his poetry and fiction. One of the foremost contemporary American Indian writers, Welch tells his stories from the point of view of Indian people. His novels* Winter in the Blood *(1974) and* The Death of Jim Loney *(1978), and book of poems* Riding the Earthboy Forty *(1971) explore contemporary Indian experience, while his most recent novel,* Fools Crow *(1986), recreates the world of the historical Blackfeet Indians.* Fools Crow *takes place in the 1860s, at a time when tensions between the whites and the Blackfeet were at their peak. The book details the daily life of the Blackfeet people, and records the horrible slaughter of a large part of the tribe at the hands of the white soldiers. It was after this slaughter that the Blackfeet laid down their weapons and sued for peace.*

Welch has as much Irish blood as Indian blood, but he has spent much of his life on Indian reservations in Montana, Alaska and elsewhere and identifies strongly with Indian people. His familiarity with Indians allows him to portray them accurately and to eloquently evoke their world.

*Born in 1940 in Browning, Montana, Welch attended schools
on the Blackfeet and Fort Belknap reservations before graduating
from high school in Minnesota. He received a B.A. in liberal arts
from the University of Montana in 1965 and went on to take graduate courses in creative writing there, studying with the poet
Richard Hugo, the fiction writer William Kittredge and others. After his apprenticeship at the university, Welch settled in Missoula,
Montana, where he now lives with his wife, Lois.*

*The interview took place in early September of 1985 at the
Welches' white and blue house on the banks of Rattlesnake Creek.
Welch is a genial man with dark hair and a light, musical voice. We
sat down in his living room where, accompanied by his golden re-
triever Frank, we began talking about his work. The dog proved
uninterested in the process of a literary interview, and without ob-
serving any formalities, promptly fell asleep on the rug, getting up
only once or twice to knock over the tape recorder.*

How did you get started writing Fools Crow?

I started with a few stories from my dad. His grandmother
lived with his family when he was growing up. She was an old
Blackfeet woman who didn't speak a word of English. She had
been in the massacre that the book ends with. She was a survivor
of that. She had been wounded in the leg, but managed to get
away. She told him about that, and she told him about the way
their lives were around that period of time.

That's what made me want to write a book about that period.
But when I came down to it, I finally had to go to some books. I've
only referred to five or six books, but they cover everything from
religion to practical things like how to tan hides. The hardest part
about writing the book was immersing myself in that period of
time in that culture. It took a long time to slip into that world.

When I started writing, I felt uncomfortable in that world for
the first thirty or forty pages, but after that I could get into that
world after fifteen or twenty minutes in my writing room, and then
I'd stay there for three or four hours a day. It was very important
that I could think the way they would be thinking, and look at the

world the way they looked at it. Their sense of reality was quite
different from the present sense of reality; their notions of religion
were totally different from Christianity. I just had to try to be
there, and finally I was there, and after that the writing became a
lot easier.

Do you use any of their old legends or myths?

I used some of their stories. And then there are two or three
stories I made up. I think that they would have been made up by
some Indian storyteller a hundred years ago. That was fun. I enjoyed making those stories up. I played around quite a bit. I didn't
strictly follow their stories.

One very important story to them was how they got the Sun
Dance. There was a woman who was partially responsible for this,
Feather Woman, who married the Morning Star and went up and
lived with Sun and Moon and so on, and did a wrong thing and so
was taken back to earth to live with her people again. That's pretty
much how it ends. She dies an old woman, still mourning the loss
of her husband who she sees in the sky all the time. But I go on
with that. After she dies, she goes to another world, which is
halfway between this one and the one she knew in the sky. She
shows my main character what's going to happen to the Blackfeet
people, so that he can tell his people, which he never does quite
get around to doing, because the vision is too horrible—after that
came starvation and general defeat.

At any rate, I make Feather Woman alive, and she has this
role of having to tell him this stuff. I know I've really overstepped
my bounds by doing that, but on the other hand, I thought, "Why
couldn't this have happened?" I felt that as a writer of fiction I was
within my rights to do this.

Do Indians resent it when people use or change the old myths?

It's happened. I know of some writers who have gotten into a
bit of trouble, for instance, Chuck [Hyemyohsts] Storm who wrote
Seven Arrows. A lot of the Cheyenne people didn't like that book.
It was supposedly telling stories that they didn't want to be told to
the outside world, and in addition it was telling them wrong. So
they jumped him on that. And a couple of other people I know
have gotten into trouble. There have been books that have had
trouble, and this book might have some trouble, but you just have

to write the way you see fit, and deal with the trouble down the road. You have to tell the story that you're telling, or write the poem that you're writing. If you let the anticipation of certain problems bother you, you're going to compromise your writing. It's best to get your writing done and then let what happens happen.

Do you think that reading the old stories gave you a new idea of what fiction was about?

I think it did. It helped to free up my imagination. I'm a product of this society. I think pretty much the way everyone else does. So I think the stories did help to get back into that world and think the way they did. Things happen in their stories that couldn't happen in our notion of reality.

Any time I could hear that Indian voice, whether by ear or in print, I knew that this was something to pay attention to. This wasn't Indians as perceived by the outside culture, which was bringing its own baggage with it.

So finding this voice was the key to writing the book?

Yes. It was important to establish that voice, that point of view, that tone, very early on, otherwise I suspect it would just be another historical novel. I think I had something to work with that most writers of historical fiction don't, and that was a pipeline to the Indian people themselves.

Did you grow up mostly around Indians and on Indian reservations?

Most of my early years, up until the seventh grade, I spent around Indians, and mostly on a couple of reservations: the Blackfeet, where I was born, and the Fort Belknap, where my parents lived. My mother was from the Fort Belknap reservation. Her dad was a rancher, and my dad threw in with her dad. They still live over there. My younger brother farms on the Fort Belknap reservation. So those were two places where I spent my earlier years, as well as an Indian school in Oregon, and an island up in Alaska on which there were native people.

Did you have any problems adjusting to the white world?

Just a few times. My older brother and I were just a year and a half apart, and so we hung around together. When we moved to a different place we'd sort of have to prove ourselves. Most people didn't have much of an opinion one way or another when they found out we were Indians, but a few kids did, and so we would have to battle them. But later it would be all right. They would become our friends. We would be playing baseball with them or whatever. I never had any real prejudice from the grown-ups, partly because I'm only part Indian. I'm a breed, a little over half. It's really the full-blooded people who look like your classic Indians who really suffer the prejudice.

Do you see yourself as primarily an Indian writer?

I used to be able to say that I'm an Indian who writes, and I still say that, but more and more my subject matter has been Indians. A lot of people would just say, "He's an Indian writer," rather than an Indian who writes. On the other hand since virtually all of my subject matter is Indian-oriented, I'm becoming more and more identified that way. When I was writing poems, a lot of my subject matter didn't have anything to do with Indians. So at that time I could say that I was an Indian who happened to write, but I seem to be becoming more and more of an Indian writer.

Do you like that idea?

I don't mind it. I used to think that it was a way to dismiss a writer, by saying he's an Indian writer. When Indians were first starting to write it was a condescending attitude, that they weren't as good as a lot of the writers in the general society. The writers in the general society had to live up to a certain standard, but the Indians could be somewhat below that standard. But then some of the Indian writers turned out to be such good writers, such as Scott Momaday and Leslie Silko and several others, that they've had to look at Indian writers in a different way, and judge them by the standards everyone else is judged by.

Do you see yourself as a spokesman for the Indian community?

I don't think I'm close enough to the Indian community to ever assume a role as a spokesman. To be a spokesman you have to be totally involved in their community, and I'm not. The only thing I've ever thought of myself doing is showing people a way of life of some Indian people, the positive and the negative aspects of certain Indians' lives and reservation life.

I'm just in my little house in Missoula, Montana, writing about Indians. A spokesman is somebody like Earl Old Person, the head of the Blackfeet tribe. He's a national figure; he can speak not only for the Blackfeet, but for a lot of Indian people.

What do the Indians think of your work?

Almost across the board they've liked it, which pleases me much more than if the New York critics like my work, because the Indians are the ones that know what I'm writing about, and if I were peddling a lot of baloney they'd be sure and tell me about it. I know that I'm pretty much on the mark when they say, "Yeah, that's the way it is." They know what that narrator in *Winter in the Blood* is all about, they know what Loney is going through.

I've had a couple of negative responses. I was signing books out here at the bookstore at the local mall. I was with another guy, and a couple of other people were sitting with us. We had our books out on the table and this one Indian woman came by. This was when *The Death of Jim Loney* came out. She didn't know I had written it. She picked it up. I thought she was going to buy it. She said, "I don't know how these people think they can get away with portraying the Indians as a bunch of drunkards and ne'er-do-wells." She read us the riot act and then just threw the book back on the table and walked out.

Are people like Loney and the main narrator in Winter in the Blood *representative of Indians in general?*

They certainly are. The narrator in *Winter in the Blood* is a readily identifiable Indian, and he suffers some of the prejudices that people have against Indians. Loney is a half-breed; he had a white father and Indian mother. There are lots of half-breeds on reservations and they suffer their own kinds of problems. They are looked down on by both whites and full-blooded Indians.

So you intended those characters to typify modern Indians?

Pretty much so. I wanted situations that almost any Indian would experience, especially an Indian young man, especially in his late twenties or early thirties. That's a period when a lot of Indian young men have been drinking and they have a crisis point about whether they're going to be drunkards falling in the gutter or whether they're going to pull themselves out. That's a transitional point for a lot of young Indian men.

Loney thinks a lot about his past. Is that a positive thing for Indians to do, or can it lead to self-destructiveness, as it does for him?

Well, probably both. It's positive for Indians to look back at their traditions, the way of life that their parents and grandparents had. It's good for them to know about that because it gives them a sense of their own identity, but quite often a person can dwell in that world too much and not see a positive way of dealing with the future.

Reservations aren't good places for young people to find opportunities. They just aren't there. The jobs aren't there, unless you can work for the government or do some farming or ranching—which very few people can support themselves doing.

I can't emphasize enough that there are not job opportunities on reservations. I think if there were, a lot of people would turn out all right. All you'd need is a little money coming in, the kind of respect that you get from going off to work every day. That really makes a great deal of difference in how you look at yourself. If you look at yourself as this person who's unemployed—you can't support yourself, you can't support your family, and maybe you're on some type of government relief—then you don't look at yourself as positively as you would if you were out there earning your way. That's not a problem only with Indians, but it's certainly one that a lot of Indians face.

Is there a way out for people like Loney?

Sure there is. One way out is to move away. His sister wants him to move away. His girlfriend wants him to move to someplace where opportunity exists, but for some reason he feels the reservation is his "place" and he might not be who he is if he moved away.

Is that often true of Indians?

Oh yes. They're always trying to relocate Indians. There was a big movement in the last few decades to relocate Indians to cities. To send them off to get some sort of training: Seattle, Chicago, Minneapolis or Denver or wherever. The feeling was that they should then go into a job in that area, and just forget about the reservation, just forget that they even came from the reservation. Some people have been able to do that. But a lot of people—I'd say the majority—their roots are in the country that they come from;

they have very strong cultural ties to that country. So a lot of them come back. They don't finish the training. They don't get the job. So what are they going to do on the reservation?

When you were growing up, did you go through the crisis that you talked about earlier?

I had to think about whether I was an Indian or not. Because I've got just as much Irish roots as Indian roots. Back in those days when I was growing up, if you could get away from the reservation, you were really encouraged not to tell anybody that you were an Indian, to just sort of melt into society. My mom felt that my older brother and I shouldn't tell people that we were Indians because it would only create problems for us. But we always did. It was a matter of pride for both of us. And it created a few problems, but people generally accepted us.

But personally I had to decide which culture I wanted to be identified with. And now of course I live off the reservation. I have a few Indian friends, but not many. But I still identify strongly with that country over there, especially the Blackfeet reservation. *Fools Crow* is about that area. Mostly I started writing that book for my own benefit; I wanted to learn as much about them as I could. And so I had to do a lot of talking to people, a lot of research. It's been really beneficial to me personally, even if a book hadn't come out of it.

So the book helped you to come to terms with what it means to be an Indian?

I think so. You have to make some commitments when you write, and one of them in my case is, "Whose point of view am I going to write from?" For instance, those first two books could have been written from a white point of view looking at Indians, and this historical novel could have been written from the point of view of white people coming into Indian country. But I've always chosen to tell it from the Indian point of view. This historical novel is told from within the Indian tribe. That's far more interesting to me. I feel more of a commitment to the Indians than to the whites. The whites are almost the puppet figures to me, the stereotypes.

There seems to be a real need to tell some of these stories from the Indian's point of view.

That's true. There hasn't been much of that, and I think it's important to understand the culture that the Indians had, and what they lost. To understand Indians today, you have to try to understand what their lives were like back then. In this book I'm really trying to emphasize their daily lives, their religion, how they hunted, how they prepared the hides, how they went about selling them—just little day-to-day things, as well as the more momentous things. The book takes place in the 1860s. At that time they were being really crowded. They were really at odds with white people. Many of them knew that something had to happen. There was always this feeling of impending conflict, which they labored under. My book ends on a historical massacre that happened to the Blackfeet. Soldiers rode up one cold winter day and at dawn they pumped thousands of rounds into these lodges where people were still sleeping. They killed 173 of them and burned up everything they could find so that the survivors who managed to escape had absolutely nothing.

That, and a smallpox epidemic that winter, took care of the Blackfeet, as the white people hoped it would. They laid down their arms against the whites as a group, but still some of the young men were out raiding on their own.

Weren't the Blackfeet one of the fiercest of the tribes?

They were. Even Lewis and Clark were scared of them. The one group of Indians they didn't want to encounter were the Blackfeet, and as a matter of fact they had a run-in with some Blackfeet. That was the only physical conflict they had with Indians. And so from Lewis and Clark's day on, people thought of the Blackfeet that way, but that massacre really took the heart out of them. They realized that they were no match for these people; they didn't have the firepower to fight them. They were the first Northern Plains Indians to lay down their arms against the whites. They went from the fiercest to the ones that no longer wanted conflict.

Does your book end with the massacre?

The book actually ends on a little more positive note than the massacre. It ends with a thunderpipe ceremony in the spring, and the people are going to go on, in spite of these things that have happened to them. But the massacre is very important to the Blackfeet people.

In this book, were you speaking to a larger audience than you were in your previous books?

This book is certainly broader. It's something I've always wanted to write. It's just been burning a hole in my pocket for years, but I didn't know how to attack it. But I figured a way to do it, and it's been very good to write it. I've really enjoyed this more than anything I've written. But from now on I don't know what I'll do. If I wanted to I could write two more historical novels about the Blackfeet. There have been a couple of other periods that have been very important to them. Maybe someday I'll write one or two like that. But right now I feel like writing poems again. So after I finish this I'm going to try to write some poems.

Where was the Blackfeet territory?

On the eastern slope of the Rockies near Glacier Park to over near present-day Havre, and they had all the territory north of the Missouri River. At one time they had about a third of Montana.

What kind of Indians were they?

They were hunters. The buffalo were just thick up there. Their accounts and white people's accounts described the hills as just black with buffalo; there were rivers of buffalo. Their life centered on the buffalo. Even before they had the horse, they had these *pishkuns*, these runs where they would run the buffalo over cliffs and then butcher them down there. When they got the horse, they really enjoyed the chase. The *pishkun* actually was probably a more effective way of getting a bunch of buffalo, but they liked the idea of running them and shooting them. The buffalo has always been their life. The government tried to transform them into farmers but that hasn't worked very well. They're hunters.

Maybe that's why they have difficulty staying on one spot, on the reservation?

They consider the reservation their home now. Most of the people, even the grandfathers and grandmothers, have known nothing but reservation life, so they really think that reservation is their home. The reservation kept shrinking by government decree or some agreement in which they'd pay the Indians a pittance for a part of the land, so the present-day reservation is just a little teeny place compared to the place they once had.

Are the Indians now speaking up more for their rights?

Oh yes. There have always been a few people speaking up, but it took something like the AIM [American Indian Movement] movement back in the very early '70s to get young people thinking of themselves as Indians, to take pride in the fact that they were Indians, and to try to get things that were due them. And they weren't selfish things; they didn't want money or their own farms, or whatever, they wanted reforms in education, certain government commitments to economic projects that would benefit the people as a whole.

AIM started with a splash. A lot of Indian people felt, "Okay, it is time to change things, time to stick up for our rights." And now they're doing it legally. Water rights is becoming a very big issue all throughout the West, and so the Indians are really examining their water rights, mineral rights.

How much of your work is autobiographical?

A lot of it has to do with people I have known. The bars I write about are bars I have known and can envision in my mind. The towns are real. I've never attempted to create an imaginary landscape; I've always used just what was there. I've always used the people that were there, though maybe not individuals. The whole novel will be a work of fiction, but it's based on real people, real landscapes, real situations. I make up probably three-fourths of the actual situations, but maybe a fourth of them are variations of situations that I have either experienced personally or have heard of other people having experienced.

Do you draw on other writers?

Not really. When I first started, I was reading novels like crazy to figure out how to write one. I would study them for their structure and the way characters started out and grew and how they ended up: technical stuff. I did a lot of studying. Like most male writers, I was really influenced by Ernest Hemingway. I liked his simplicity of style, his evocative style.

And being a poet helped me to know the value of language, how each and every word has to count, and how you can make a scene happen, not by explaining every single detail of the scene, but describing the significant details, so that the reader will see all of the rest of it in his or her own mind. So reading Hemingway and a couple of other writers who had that evocative style helped a great deal.

Who were the other writers?

There's an Italian writer named Elio Vittorini. He wrote a book called *Conversation in Sicily*. God, it's just a beautiful book. It's only 150 pages long, but there are 500 pages' worth of evocativeness in there. I really studied his structure. I patterned *Winter in the Blood* on that book if I patterned it on anything. Nothing much happens in the book, just incidents and situations, discoveries and so on. And in a sense, nothing much happens in *Winter in the Blood*. When he's standing at the grave of his grandmother at the end, not much really has happened to him. I wanted to convey the sense that he was going to go on with his life, and it might not be much changed from the way it was at the beginning of the book. I believe that not many of us learn from our mistakes. If we touch the stove we learn not to touch it again, but we seem to have a tendency to repeat our larger mistakes. So I wanted to write that book in a circular fashion, in which he starts off at the bottom of the circle in the beginning and goes around and then comes full circle at the end, and even starts on the upcline of the circle again.

You don't see him as changing much?

No. He had a few insights as a result of the things that happened to him, but the opportunities aren't great on a reservation and I think he would be probably searching still for something. And the girl—he's thinking of going after her again—is his way of continuing the search for something.

Did you start writing poetry before writing fiction?

I had written two or three short stories early, and then I had written pieces that I couldn't even identify. Maybe they were little prose poems or something. But it wasn't until I went into Richard Hugo's class when I started the M.F.A program here [University of Montana] that I had ever written an identifiable poem. And this was a graduate 500-level course. I had talked to him earlier and told him that I didn't know anything about poetry but wanted to learn. He said, "Sure, come on in." It was a good crash course. I learned a lot in one quarter. And then after that, I loved it so much I was writing a poem a day for the next year or so, and throwing most of them away, but trying things. About a year later, I took another course from Hugo, and by that time the poems were good enough so that he liked my poetry, and gave me a lot of encouragement. I wrote poems for seven or eight years exclusively before I decided to try to write a novel.

Did you find that writing a novel was a lot different than writing poems?

Yes, very much so. A novelist has to invent, which a poet really doesn't. It was hard for me to learn how to invent, and to make a plot and have the characters go through this plot and come out the other side. Even today, I'm a lousy plotter. I just can't make a plot, like so many writers can.

In some ways I'm not even interested in plot; I'm interested in characters and what happens to the characters, both inside and out. I'm more interested in what the characters are thinking about and how they're bouncing off each other than I am in what they do.

Do you try to make the fiction clear?

Well, I try to make it simple. I believe strongly in using simple sentences, simple words, simple situations that might seem simple on the surface, but as I say, if they're successful, it's because of an evocative nature. Even though they're simple on the surface, there's something going on underneath. So yeah, I love to write very simply. In fact in the rewrite for *Fools Crow*, one of the things I'm doing is getting it back to simple writing. There are words in there that I don't use, but I fell into a trap; because they were historical Indians I thought they had to talk in this highfalutin' way. But they don't.

How did Winter in the Blood *get started?*

I wanted to write about that Highline country in an extended way, and my poems just weren't doing it. They were like snapshots. They would get pieces of it, but never the whole scope of the thing.

When I first started thinking about a piece of prose writing, I thought it was going to be a travel piece. I always used to get mad about the fact that every time I'd mention that I was from the Highline country people would say, "Oh, God, I've been there. We drove all day to get through that place, to get somewhere that was interesting."

That was almost a universal reaction to that country. And that used to make me mad, and so I would fantasize about capturing a carload of tourists and making them look at that country. I'd take 'em and show 'em various things, 'cause it is rich, interesting country if you know what to look for.

I thought of doing this article where I hijack a carload of tourists and show them around. But then I thought, "Well, you're talking about characters and you're talking about a situation." And then I thought, "Why not just try a novel? Get a main character who is part of that country but is fairly sensitive, who has a good eye." I knew that I was going to tell it from the first person right from the beginning. I started writing and eventually came up with a draft of a novel. I took it to my friend Bill Kittredge.

I had always been successful in poetry; I never had any problems writing that. So I thought it would transfer over. But after Bill read that, God, there were red marks over every single sheet of paper. And one night he and I sat down together about ten o'clock or so and worked all night long. We went through it page by page and he showed me where I had messed up. I was really jarred. I went home and put it in a dresser drawer and just forgot it for about a month, thinking I couldn't write prose.

But later I pulled it out and started looking at Bill's comments, and felt, "There's still a novel here." So with the help of Bill's comments and some of the larger conceptual things he told me about writing, I was able to turn it into a piece of fiction, which it certainly wasn't in the beginning.

Why didn't you name the narrator?

Well, the simple truth is that for the first thirty or forty pages I didn't even think of him having a name. And it wasn't until then that I realized, "Either I've gotta name this guy or not." So I made up a little game for myself. I said, "We'll pretend that he's an old-time Indian and that he's going to have to earn his name." He just wouldn't earn his name, until maybe the time when he pulled the cow out of the mud, which is getting pretty close to the end. For some reason I didn't feel that he was really successful in that attempt, and so I just kept him nameless. It seemed like I fell into that, but after I realized what was going on, I just kept him nameless, and I couldn't even tell you why. It would have been easier to call him Roger or something, maybe a lot easier to name him than to keep his name from being used.

Was it more difficult to write The Death of Jim Loney *in the third person after writing* Winter in the Blood *in the first person?*

Not really. I just experienced one technical difficulty. I started writing that one in the first person, even though I knew he was going to get blown away at the end. I don't know what the hell I was thinking. How could you write a first-person novel about a guy who's going to die right on the scene? What do you do, just end with no period or whatever?

But for some reason I thought I could do it, and maybe I would have kept going and seeing what I would have come up with, but he was becoming more and more reclusive as the novel progressed, so pretty soon I was just inside his mind entirely, and these other characters were out there but there was no place where I could get to them. I wrote maybe a hundred pages and realized what was going on. I went back and changed it to third person, so I could follow him around, and then I could switch over to his girlfriend or his sister or somebody else.

Did you model the book after Under the Volcano?

In some ways that was a very important book to me, too. I read that when I was over in Greece in '73. This young Greek woman recommended it to me. I was really stunned by the whole book, the main character and all the other characters, the situation, the landscape—everything. It was just such an overwhelming, inexorable book and you knew the way it was going to end but you were fascinated to reach that point. I like that way of working. I love the idea of the secret being out, so the only reason that a reader would stick with a book like that would be to see how it's going to happen. I enjoyed thinking that the readers were in on the secret right away, but they didn't know quite how it was going to happen. I wanted his [Loney's] death to be really well-orchestrated so that it wouldn't be what they would expect.

Does he die in vain?

Not to his way of thinking. He does orchestrate it. He does plant all the clues and lets 'em [the tribal police] know pretty much where he's going to be. He knows that this cop still hates him, and wouldn't hesitate pulling the trigger, and he's counting on that. So he accomplished his own death. I'm sure that's not a very positive thing, but at least it was an accomplishment for him. And it was also a way out.

The landscape seems to play an important part in your writing. Is this a conscious thing on your part?

Yes. To me landscape is almost the main character in anything I write. I feel that if you don't convey the landscape to the reader, they're not going to really understand these people who live in that landscape. It's very tough country up there. It's hard country to get along in. For years people have been trying to make a go of it in that country. People fail, and they curse the country, and they curse the weather and yet they love it. It's a classic love/hate relationship when you live in that kind of country. I wanted a reader to gain that sense of that country. You love it and you hate it. It's awful to you, but most of the time it's just a force that is out there to be dealt with every day of your life.

Every time I start thinking about something to write about I just naturally wander over to that country. We visit a couple times a year, and I just get all charged up about it again. Every time I see those prairies, I can just envision so much life going on there. And here I look at all the trees and beautiful rivers around Missoula and I can't even imagine what kind of people would have lived here, and what would have been important to their lives. I know another writer could do that beautifully, but I just can't.

In one of your poems, "Riding the Earthboy 40," you wrote that, "I ride/ romantic to those words,/ those foolish claims that he/ was better than dirt or rain/ that bleached his cabin/ white as bone. Scattered in the wind/ Earthboy calls me from my dream:/ Dirt is where dreams must end." Are you suggesting in this poem that writing is making yourself better than the earth?

In some ways I was thinking of that. We're constantly trying to find significance in simple acts, in simple people's lives. That's necessary, that's part of writing, but I guess there I was making a little jab at those of us who try to find all this significance, and that a man like Earthboy would already know the significance of his life. There's a wisdom some people have that the others of us are searching for. We just don't know how to accept things. We constantly try to find other things. And a man like Earthboy maybe can accept this life.

Unlike somebody like Loney?

Yes. Both of my novel characters were frustrated. They were searching for something, but they didn't quite know what it was they were searching for. They just felt that if they searched they would find it.

Is there a certain danger in words and language?

I don't know if I would say that. It's just whatever people make of words and language. It can all be used very constructively, very decently. I would like to think that I'm using language to try to get people to understand Indian people. Because Indians have lived good, decent, civilized lives. They have very complicated beliefs, and their systems of survival were attuned to the way they lived.

A lot of people say that they didn't have a written language, they didn't have an alphabet, therefore they weren't civilized; but it's always been my belief that that kind of thing has nothing at all to do with a civilized way of living. It's more your systems, and how you're able to use them to reflect the way you live and the elements of the landscape—to bring them all together.

I don't know of another people who were more attuned to the way they should live in their surroundings than the Indians. That's the essence of what I would hope to convey: these weren't a bunch of savages running around half-naked.

Can whites learn from the Indians?

They could learn from the Indians, and they probably should, but I don't think many of them will, and I don't think many of them want to. I don't know why. Maybe it is that idea, "What do they know? They were running around half-naked all the time." But if they would take the time to learn some of the Indian beliefs and learn about their way of life, maybe they would get a better handle on their own way of dealing with the world. I sure did when I started learning about them.

What did you learn?

I realized that although they suffered many hardships, their lives were better than most lives today. Because it was all so carefully tied in to their natural world. You knew the things that you had to do to become a better person, and you strove to do those things. Everybody did. It seemed very simple. It seemed something that anybody could do. There were ways of expiating your guilt that made a great deal of sense to me. In spite of their very spiritual belief system, there was something so down-to-earth about it that I could really see how they could have adhered to these beliefs.

Whereas I look at the Catholic church, for instance. I was raised a Catholic, and I can't grasp anything. They want me to accept everything, but they won't give me anything to grasp onto. The Indians could grasp everything. And yet they knew there was an overriding mystery. They knew that Sun Chief was watching over them. There was a certain mystery involved, and yet there were enough things that they could touch, so that they knew they were living decent lives, or they knew when they were straying from the decent life. It wasn't an abstract thing for them.

Have you been able to put some of this into practice?

I guess I'm more like the narrator in *Winter in the Blood*: I repeat my mistakes. But I know that that way of life and that way of believing is there, and that's pretty comforting. It's not so much that I'm going to believe that way, but just to know that a group of people, the people I identify with, really had such a beautiful way of living and believing.

Raymond Carver

RAYMOND Carver writes with uncommon power about commonplace things and commonplace people. His short stories operate by implication; every word, every gesture is fraught with significance. By choosing details judiciously, he endows objects as seemingly insignificant as a kitchen chair with startling power. In his hands, colloquial American English achieves such concision that a whole world view or moral condition can be summed up in a single sentence.

Through meticulous rewriting and revising, Carver gets underneath the veneer of ordinary lives, exposing the workings of the human heart at its best and worst. His stories concern people pushed to the edge—of bankruptcy, divorce, separation, eviction—people forced to reveal themselves through speech and action. Once he gets his hands on them, he can be absolutely pitiless in his examination of the nooks and crannies of their characters, but he does not condemn them. He approaches them with sympathy, and respect for their inherent mystery.

Carver portrays the American underclass with accuracy and compassion because he was once a part of it. Born in Clatskanie,

Oregon, in 1938, he spent much of his early life in Yakima, Washington. At age eighteen he married Maryann Burk, and by the time he was twenty he had fathered two children. To support his young family, he worked a succession of what he describes as "crap jobs," including pumping gas, picking tulips, sweeping hospital floors, cleaning toilets. After years of such jobs, of family troubles, of problems with alcohol, his life hit rock bottom. Only after giving up drinking did things turn around for him. Gradually, Carver got his life back on track, and the memories of those troubled years made him better able to bear witness to those who have not yet found a way out of their difficulties.

Carver is the author of four collections of short stories: Will You Please Be Quiet, Please? *(1976),* Furious Seasons *(1977),* What We Talk About When We Talk About Love *(1981) and* Cathedral *(1983). He is also the author of* Fires: Essays, Poems, Stories *(1984),* Dostoevsky: A Screenplay *(1985) and five volumes of poetry:* Near Klamath *(1968),* Winter Insomnia *(1970),* At Night the Salmon Move *(1976),* Where Water Comes Together with Other Water *(1985) and* Ultramarine *(1986).*

In 1963, he received an A.B. from Humboldt State College. He went on to study at the University of Iowa, and eventually taught there and at a number of other universities around the country. Before coming to Port Angeles, Washington, Carver lived in Syracuse, New York, where he taught at Syracuse University. He has received numerous awards, including the prestigious Mildred and Harold Strauss Living Award, 1983; the National Book Critics Circle Award nomination in fiction, 1984, and the Pulitzer Prize nomination in fiction, 1984, both for Cathedral.

The interview took place in the summer of 1986 at Carver's house in Port Angeles, which he shares with the poet Tess Gallagher. The house is in a quiet, residential neighborhood, and overlooks the Strait of Juan de Fuca. Carver is a tall, soft-spoken man, shy in manner, who is very meticulous about getting his wording right.

Why do most of your stories take place indoors?

I don't know. They do though, don't they? That's probably partly due to the fact that I spend most of my time indoors, and really the stories have something to do with the engagement or involvement between men and women, and these moments or little dramas are better played-out indoors than outdoors. It's healthy out-of-doors, and there are always some vapors hanging around indoors—fetid air.

Could most of your stories take place in almost any town in the United States?

Sure, and have.

The physical place, the city and so on, isn't quite so important?

No, those kinds of landmarks and guides aren't terribly necessary in my stories. There are always certain spins on these things, but you could say that men and women behave pretty much the same whether in Port Angeles, or Bellevue, or Houston, or Chicago or Omaha or New York City.

And I don't know if this is a good thing or bad thing in regard to my stories; there's no way to judge. I was rootless for so many years and didn't have any real *place* or location, some of the things that are so nurturing for a writer. I seem to have lost them in some great cyclone back in the '60s.

Where did you grow up?

I grew up in Yakima, on the other side of the Cascade Range. I was born in Oregon, and my parents moved to Yakima when I was two or three years old. I went to grade school and high school over there. My childhood was given over to fishing and hunting and baseball and those kinds of activities. And then I began going steady with this girl when I was seventeen. We were married about a year later and moved to California. I still have some relatives in Yakima, and I still like to go back there now and again. It's very different from this country over here, but it has its own particular beauty. My heart lifts up when I see the Yakima Valley.

I don't know what else to say about Yakima. I'm glad I left; it was much too small a place when I was a teenager, and I had to leave. I wanted to get out and see the world, where things were happening, where I thought things were happening.

So pretty quickly you moved to a larger city?

I just knew I couldn't live there forever, and I was very anxious to get away. But I don't think that's any different than what happened to a lot of other young people. I wanted to go places that were not familiar and do things that I was not in the habit of doing.

Were you ambitious?

I suppose I was, in a sense. I knew I wanted to write even then, but I was quite lazy in lots of other ways. I didn't want to work. I was offered a job in a hardware store in Yakima. It would have been comfortable; I'd just got married and it would have secured our life. I didn't take it. Furthermore, I've never liked physical labor; I've had to do it but I've hated it.

So I was ambitious in regard to the things that interested me, and extremely lazy and lackadaisical about the things that didn't. [Laughs]

Was writing one of the things that interested you?

Sure. I've wanted to write for as long as I can remember. When I got married, that life seemed to take over to a large extent, because we started having children early on and my family became the central focus of my life. I still wanted to write, but we had to cover the rent and the groceries and the school clothes.

Before you were married did you have plans of writing a novel?

Frankly, I was never all that much interested in writing a novel. I liked to write short stories. And the circumstances of my life dictated that I write the shorter forms, the things I could finish up in a few sittings. I like to read novels, but I've never been that interested in writing one.

My reading tastes were very unformed during this time. There was no one, absolutely no one, to give me directions or pointers in this; no one to tell me what or who I should be reading. So I sort of followed my nose. I used to go to the library and check out anything that interested me—fiction, of course, along with books about cattle drives and searches for buried treasure, history books of all kinds. There was less time to read, of course, after I got married, but I always liked to read in those early years. And it was during this period I felt I wanted to try to write. I made some half-hearted tries at it.

Was it poetry first?

I think it's poetry first with everyone; and it certainly was with me. Those first poems were awful, of course. Later on when I began writing more seriously I started sending the work out. Along in there somewhere I had a story and a poem accepted by two different magazines on the same day.

Did this happen a long time after you had started writing?

The acceptances came when I was twenty-three, and I'd been wanting to write since I was seventeen or eighteen, but I didn't have any serious work habits in those days.

Did you find it hard to reconcile family responsibilities with writing?

Yes, of course. It's harder when you're unformed and untried and untested yourself, and then suddenly you have certain heavy responsibilities like raising children and earning a living and all of that. It was difficult and it remained difficult until we all parted company.

It struck me in reading your stories that somebody couldn't have written them without going through a lot. Could you have written those stories without going through the things you did?

Well, probably not; I'm certainly a product of the things that formed me. Certain events made a very deep and abiding impression on me, but who's to say what I would have written had I not lived the life I did, given the fact that I wanted to write as badly as I did? I'm sure I would have found something else to write about.

The stories and poems I've written are not autobiographical, but there is a starting point in the real world for everything I've written. Stories just don't come out of thin air; they come from someplace, a wedding of imagination and reality, a little autobiography and a lot of imagination.

But the stories have taken a particular turn or are cast in a particular way because I know what I'm writing about; in that I'm no different from any author whose work you might admire. What you look for in a writer is someone writing with authority about his subject; you want to feel you can trust him, and put yourself in his hands, so to speak, and go with it.

Had I not had the life I did have, I wouldn't have written the particular stories I did, but I want to think that I would have written stories of equal interest and of equal merit. But who can say?

I asked that question because in reading your stories I noticed that you seem to have a lot of compassion for the downtrodden.

I hope so, I hope that comes through, because I cast my lot with those people a long time ago. Those are the people I grew up with and know best, and they still seem to be a source of most of my imaginative interest. I haven't written that much about people who haven't found it necessary to be tried in some way or another. I've been around academics off and on, and I've spent a lot of time on college campuses, but I've never once written anything about a college campus or about school. Never. That life simply never made a lasting emotional impression on me. I do know something about the life of the underclass and what it feels like, by virtue of having lived it myself for so long. I do feel more kinship, even today, with those people. They're my people. They're my relatives, they're the people I grew up with. Half my family is still living like this. They still don't know how they're going to make it through the next month or two. Believe it or not, but it's true.

Do you see yourself as a spokesman for these people?

I'm just bearing witness to something I know something about. Most things in the world I don't know anything at all about, and I couldn't care less. I'm bearing witness to what I can.

Did you feel compelled to write those stories?

Yes, or I wouldn't have written them.

Was this compulsion building up in you over the years when you didn't have much time to write?

If you look at the copyright dates of the stories that are in my first book of fiction, *Will You Please Be Quiet, Please?*, the first story was published in 1963, and the last story was published in 1975, and the book was published in 1976, so it took about twelve or thirteen years to put those stories together. I wasn't able to apply myself all that much, all that steadily.

The stories in *What We Talk About When We Talk About Love* were written between 1976 and '81, and the stories in *Cathedral* were all written in eighteen months.

So the stories in Cathedral *came a lot more quickly?*

Right, within eighteen months. And the first book took twelve or thirteen years to put together, partly because I was out of control for several years, and partly because of the vicissitudes of trying to earn a living and raise a family and write stories and go to school.

As an editor at The Seattle Review, *I read a lot of stories submitted to the magazine which are Raymond Carveresque stories. Are you aware of how influential your style has become?*

I was thinking about an anthology I saw recently. There are two parodies in it, good-natured parodies, parodies of my stories. And they recently had a Raymond Carver Write-Alike Contest at the University of Iowa. It was good-natured enough, but it was a real contest.

I'm aware of the fact that a lot of young writers are trying to write more or less the way I write. But a lot of young writers try to write like somebody else. It's not all that bad if they're trying to write like me; they could have worse models. Some of the economy in the stories is good for young writers, and some of the care for what's being said. It's okay to try to write like somebody else. A lot of people used to try to write like Don Barthelme. Barthelme is a wonderful writer in many respects, but he isn't always the best kind of model for young writers. What he can do well, young writers who are not as smart and talented as he is would botch. And the results are usually pretty terrible.

Did it take you a long time to evolve your particular style?

It took a while to develop my style, sure. It took from the 1960s into the 1970s, writing stories and then rewriting them and continuing to work on a story. I was not all that anxious to send a story out, because if I sent it out I'd just have to write another story, and stories were hard to come by in those days. It was a conscious thing and it just took a while. I didn't just start writing stories like "Feathers" or "Cathedral."

I think the newer stories are similar to the other stories, but different. And that pleases me, because you can't keep repeating yourself. This is not saying anything against the earlier stories, but the new stories are sufficiently different from the earlier stories that I'm pleased with the difference.

When you were starting out, did you learn by imitation?

I didn't, at least not in the way you might be thinking. I've heard stories about Frank O'Connor trying to write like Guy de Maupassant or studying de Maupassant's stories to see how the stories worked, and even copying them out. Somerset Maugham would do things like this, copying out whole passages of writers he admired, in an effort to improve his own style and assimilate what those writers could teach him.

I never did this, but there were certain writers who meant a lot to me and still do, writers like Chekhov, Hemingway, Tolstoy, Flaubert, to name a few. I read their books, novels and stories, and while I didn't try to write like these people, I certainly wrote more carefully, and better too, I think, because those were the kind of people I admired. But I never had any one particular writer over and above all the other writers, unless it was Chekhov. I think he is the best short story writer who ever lived. Isaac Babel is another wonderful writer. He could take two or three pages and make the most wonderful little story.

Were you always a perfectionist, I mean in your writing?

My life was very sloppy. I guess I was looking for perfection in some area. As far back as I can remember I couldn't abide the sight of a messy manuscript. In those days I didn't have access to copy machines and typists and all that. I did all of my own typing. A story would come back from a magazine that I had submitted it to, and if I changed a few words or crossed something out, saw a paper clip mark on it, or a coffee stain, I would end up retyping the whole story. I might type twenty copies of a story, just trying to get it right, getting it where I wanted it to be. So I suppose the answer's got to be yes—a perfectionist in the writing, not the life.

And you don't send out anything until it's just right?

I'm in no hurry. I wrote a lot of stories this spring and the first part of the summer, but the stories never went out in a hurry. I have a story up there in a drawer right now that hasn't gone out. I'm working now with a typist who has a word-processing machine, so I can give her a manuscript and she can spend time with it, and give it back to me; and at the same time I found myself working on another story. So, often I find myself with two stories in the works at the same time. I like working that way.

Do you ever leave stories for six months or so?

I've never left them that long, but even recently I have left them for two or three weeks. It's good if a writer can do that because the story cools down a bit and the writer gets a bit of distance on it, and the emotional heat isn't as strong as it was earlier. I like it when my stories cool down enough that I can look at them very coldly.

Who was the first person to recognize that you had talent?

I suppose every beginning writer has to feel like he has talent, or he wouldn't be able to do what he has to do. You need something to sustain you, so certainly you have to believe in yourself. But I was just flying blind for the longest time, and without question my life changed when I found John Gardner as a teacher. He made a vast impression on me.

Did you pick up things from Gardner's style?

Not from his style, no. But I had never had anybody look at a manuscript of mine the way he did. And let me say I believe that things can be passed from one person to another. The association of a maestro and an apprentice is age-old: Michelangelo had a teacher, so did Beethoven. They were apprentices at one time or another, and then somebody showed them how, taught them their trade. If someone you knew had the desire to study the violin you would try to engage a really distinguished teacher to teach this person, you wouldn't put the person in the room with a violin and some sheet music. So certain aspects of writing can be taught.

Gardner was a wonderful teacher. He could show you things. He could take a story and tell you, "This is working and this isn't working and this is the reason why."

I was simply electrified. I'd never met a writer before. I was nineteen or twenty years old, and I'd never laid eyes on a writer. And he was a writer; even though he hadn't published at the time. He was cut out of different cloth from anyone else I'd ever met. He was very helpful. He showed me things, and I was at that particular point in my life where nothing was lost on me. Whatever he had to say went right into my bloodstream and changed the way I looked at things.

He made me understand that if you can say something in ten words, say it in ten words rather than twenty words. He taught me to be precise, and he taught me to be concise. Taught me a lot of other things, too; I learned a lot from him. My life was still pretty boxed in, but I'd learn things from him and even if I couldn't put these things into practice immediately, the things I learned were long-standing and abiding.

Did you see him outside of the classroom?

No, not really. He wasn't much older than I was. I was nineteen and he was probably twenty-five. But he was very busy; he was trying to write his own books, and *was* writing his own books, even though some of these books never got published for another fifteen years or so. *October Light*, for instance, was written when he was in his twenties but it wasn't published until six years or so ago. That's why it seemed he was so prolific; but much of the stuff that was published in the '70s was written in the '60s.

I associated writing with a high calling, a thing to be taken very, very seriously, and he was very important in strengthening that, but there was very little off-campus association with him. Once in a while he would come to a party with the students but other than that I never saw him socially. I was just a squirt, and he was a grownup with grownup friends.

We resumed an acquaintanceship which became a friendship during the last year of his life. In the course of seventeen years we probably exchanged three or four letters, and then we got to know each other again after not seeing each other for a long time, and it was nice.

To what extent are you writing moral fiction as Gardner would define it?

For a long time I didn't want to read Gardner's book on moral fiction; I didn't want to find out that I was writing *immoral* fiction. But what Gardner was asking for was that writers be more serious in their approach to their work; you just didn't know what effect your works might have on somebody; somebody might be sick and dying of cancer, and your work might give them some kind of support or succor. There's enough stuff around that diminishes the human spirit.

John Cheever said the same thing to me once. He said that fiction should throw light and air on a situation, and it shouldn't be vile. If somebody's getting a blow-job up in the balcony of a theater in Times Square this may be a fact, but it's not a truth. There is a difference. Maybe some of my later stories would be considered life-affirming, linking us all together in a great enterprise, etc., but there are writers who will tell you that the act of writing itself is a moral act, and that that is enough in itself.

You said in one of your essays that moral fiction had a lot to do with being truthful and accurate in your writing.

Yes. In the same essay, I quoted Ezra Pound, "Fundamental accuracy of statement is the one sole morality in writing." That's as good a starting point as any; and then you go from there. But you can't say, "I want to write a moral story." You have to write what's given to you. And then there's the melody that comes out of you and comes out in the story too, if you're lucky; the story should certainly be a connecting up emotionally first, and then it should be an intellectual connecting up.

When I read and am moved by a story by Chekhov it's similar to listening to a piece of music by Mozart and being moved by that, or being emotionally moved by something by Edith Piaf. When something can reach across languages, and hundreds of years even, and move you, that's all you can ask.

Do you try to avoid making explicit statements in your work?
Yes. I'm incapable of doing that; I wouldn't know the first thing about making statements: the peach pickers aren't getting paid enough for picking a box of peaches, so put a character in there who shows that. No, nothing schematic or programmatic.

But there does seem to be a point to your stories. A reader comes away from them thinking someone has behaved badly, or somebody has behaved well.

Yes, absolutely. Many people behave badly and some people behave well in my stories but I'm not out to make a point, or illustrate anything.

So what you want to say is contained by the story?
Yes. The meaning of the story comes out of the story itself,

and is not imposed on the story. I don't want to sound like a dope about my own stories. But sometimes I'm surprised by the stories, sometimes they veer away from what I had in mind and felt as I was writing them.

Is it more the emotional effect that you're interested in?
Yes.

In Chekhov, it seems that the meaning arises out of what is implied by the story.

Not something that was imposed by him. Of course he was in the driver's seat because he was giving you the information about these people in a given situation, so he took you where he wanted to take you.

Would you say that that's true of your stuff too?
I think so.

How do you go about writing a short story?

When I am writing, whether it's poetry or fiction—and I mean this—virtually everything suggests itself as a story or as a poem. Something that's said, something I see, something I overhear, an image or even a line or dialogue, transfers itself to an image, and I feel a necessity to start writing.

When I start writing, I tend to write very quickly. And of course at that time I'm looking for someplace quiet, someplace where the phone isn't ringing. And then I try to write the story as quickly as I can. I don't think I've ever written more than two or three stories where it's taken more than two days to write the first draft. Usually I just plunge on, even though I don't always know what I'm doing, and try to get something out on the page.

And then when I feel like I've exhausted it, that's the time I'll go back and type it up and see what I have. Sometimes I'm quite surprised, even when I read the story in longhand and am typing it up. Sometimes I won't know what's coming next. I'm quite surprised to see what I've written. I'll be reading something, and think, "Oh, that's interesting. What's going to happen now?"

I'm not saying the early drafts are written unconsciously, in a trance or daze, but they're written in some kind of condition whereby you've taken leave of normal things, and the stories have kind of taken over and directed me somehow.

I don't have very many wasted stories, or stories that don't work or come off. I know a lot of writers who make a lot of false starts. That rarely happens with me. I have a few that I've finished that are drafted that I don't have much interest in, but I don't have very many stories that I feel I didn't know where I was going or what would happen.

And then, after the story is typed up and I have worked on it for several drafts, I'll show it to Tess, get a response from her, and then it's usually back to the typewriter again. Eventually that story will find its way to a typist, she will type it up, and then the real work begins: the rewriting, the tinkering around, that kind of thing.

Does that usually mean compressing the story?

In the past it's always been compressing and taking out, but lately I'm putting in as much or more than I'm taking out. It used to be that the story was ten pages long in manuscript, but when I first wrote the story and had it typed up it was twice that long. I just rendered it down. Now a story is twenty pages to begin with and twenty pages in manuscript, though the substance might have changed. I'm putting in as much as I'm taking out. Cross a line here, and add a line somewhere else.

Why are you adding more things to the stories now?

That's hard to say. I feel it's necessary or I wouldn't be doing it. The stories, most of them, are larger somehow and I'm simply putting flesh on more things, putting color in the cheeks, rather than trying to take all the color out. I'm sure this has something to do with my own frame of mind and getting older, etc. But now I'm adding to the characters, and adding to the situation itself, making it larger, making the stories give more, making them more generous.

Are you moving toward writing a novel?

I don't know. All the stories I'm writing these days seem to be 5,000 words or so, which is certainly longer than they used to be. I'm not consciously moving towards a novel. I could get a contract to write a novel tomorrow if I wanted—I'm under contract to write this book of stories—but I waited to sign the contract to write stories until I felt I wanted to write stories again. And for two years I didn't write stories; I wrote poems and some essays. My agent was very perturbed with me, I think, because I wasn't writing any fiction, but maybe I'll write a novel someday, and again maybe I won't. It's no big thing. I'll either write a novel or I won't. I'm not going to worry about it. I don't have to write a novel for money or for glory or anything else.

It seems that together the stories create a world in much the same way a novel does.

I've been told that. I'm always interested in hearing such things. I don't know if that's good or bad or simply a matter of interest. There are more things in this life that I don't have an opinion on than I do.

In these longer stories are you trying to show more sides of your characters?

Yes, and the characters' relations with other characters.

I really noticed that with the stories in Cathedral. *The characters seemed to be more sculpted.*

True, and that's good. That, too, was a conscious thing. It wasn't part of a program, but I felt I wanted to get back in the world more.

To what extent are your characters general types?

I don't think that there are any types. In fact when I'm talking about characters in stories, I tend not even to talk about characters, I tend to talk about the people in the stories; they're individuals, after all.

Many of them seem recognizable, as if they were people you would know.

That's good.

So you're trying to create specific personalities for your characters?

I try to write them as individuals, sure. If I weren't trying to write them as individuals, I don't think you'd have this feeling that you do. If I somehow failed to make them believable, I don't think you could have made the remark you just made. They're not types, they are individuals.

Physically for the most part, you don't know what they look like. I'm not good at, or very interested in, physical description, how somebody wears his hair or her hair, or if they're pale or ruddy or have hair on their forearms or what they're wearing. But emotionally I think I struck them right, and that is what you recognize. I was never interested in great long descriptions of characters in Victorian novels, page after page of how he was dressed or how she walked and held her parasol.

You were more interested in what they were thinking?

Not so much what they were thinking, but what they were doing, what they were saying to each other, what they *weren't* saying, what they were saying as opposed to what they were doing, and what they were doing and not saying much about. People's actions seem to be of most interest, finally, than *why* they do things.

I'm not really interested in what makes torturers in Chile or Iran do what they do. As far as the psychology of what brought them around to become torturers, I don't care. The fact is that they're torturers; that's what's important, and so awful.

So that through their actions they show...

What they are. Who cares what made the Green River killer kill thirty-five people or however many? The fact that he killed thirty-five women because of something in his past is of little interest to me. What could bring someone to do this? I don't even want to know. The fact is people do things, people commit terrible acts, acts of public or domestic violence. I don't need to go back on a twenty-year expedition to what brought this man to punch his wife in the eye, or this woman to hit her husband with a skillet.

How do you come up with your stories?

Ideally the story chooses you, the image comes and then the emotional frame. You don't have a choice about writing the story. I think that writers reach a point where they realize most areas of experience are not available to them—through lack of interest, lack of knowledge, lack of emotional involvement. I would be quite incapable of writing a story about young politicians, or even old politicians, or lawyers, or the world of high finance and fashion.

There's a filter at work which says this is or is not a story. And maybe there will be some little something, the germ of an idea, which will strike some kind of chord and begin to grow. I think a story ideally comes to the writer; the writer shouldn't be casting the net out, searching for something to write about.

In one of your essays you talked about how short stories offer a glimpse of life. Do you try to pick incidents for your stories which can sum up a whole life?

Sure. Again it's not part of the program, it's not a conscious thing, but readers are certainly free to draw inferences from certain fictional situations, and do. I've been beaten over the head by some critics, mainly conservative critics. Someone wrote a long essay against my work in the *The New Criterion* a year or so ago, saying that the picture I portray of America is not a happy one; that my characters are not real Americans; that they should be happier and find more satisfaction in this life; that I'm concentrating on showing the dark underbelly of things. This was a real political interpretation of my stories. They said I didn't know anything about the workingman; that I've probably never held a blue-collar job in my life, which is amusing.

Then I have some people, especially foreigners, tell me that my stories are without question an indictment against the American capitalist system, because they show the failure of the American capitalist system—people out of work, people drinking too much, and so forth.

I'm not following any kind of formula or program for myself. I don't have any goals, and I don't have any plans worked out; I'm just writing stories.

Somebody was trying to give me a strange reading on one of these *New Yorker* stories recently. You get the strangest kind of letters in the mail; people write and tell you what your stories mean. I named a character Bud in one of the stories, and someone told me it really must be short for Budweiser and the good times. [Laughs]

Has Port Angeles been a productive place for you to work?

Yes, it's good to work out here, especially in the winter when the days are short and there're no interruptions, and there's nothing to do but work, and everything is at a great remove—from about December to March. It's good to be here then. We're isolated, and that's good when you're working. But for myself, I get cabin fever if I'm here too long. I need to get out every now and again. It's a little different for Tess because it's her home; she grew up here and has family here.

Did your writing change as a result of moving back here?

Well, it changed a lot in that book of poems. I wrote that book in Port Angeles when I was out here by myself, during that time when Tess was back in Syracuse, teaching. I've never had an experience quite like it in my life. I wrote one, two, three and sometimes four poems a day. I wrote from sunup until sundown. I did this every day for six weeks. I wrote the whole book in six weeks. I've never had anything like that happen in my life. When I had finished the book and was ready to go back to Syracuse, I felt like I'd been through some kind of astounding experience, something I'd never been through in my life.

The poems came in this burst of energy and activity, and they were a real opening out for me. I hadn't written any poems in quite a long time and there was nothing I wanted more at the time than to write those poems. And so, of course, it helped to be here.

That was January of 1984. I came out here with the expressed intention of writing fiction. *Cathedral* had come out that fall and there was still so much happening in connection with that book that it was very hard to get back on the track and writing again; there were a lot of distractions. I came here with the intention of being out here for a couple of months and working in utter quiet and solitude on fiction. I didn't write anything for a week, and then I started writing poems. I can't imagine I would have written those poems had I stayed in Syracuse or had I gone someplace else. So it's changed my writing in that regard, yes, and also my life.

My fiction I don't know, maybe so. I'm not the best judge. Maybe if I were in San Francisco the stories would be the same, but maybe not.

Why did writing poetry appeal to you?

I hadn't written any poetry in a long time, as I said, and I was beginning to feel I wouldn't write any more poems—ever. And so the poems were just a great gift and completely unexpected. Whatever the merits of the poems, and I think that some of them are pretty good, they allowed me to write something every day and something I wanted to write more than anything else. They satisfied my storytelling instinct; most of the poems in there have a narrative line to them. And it was just wonderful to write them;

there was just nothing else like it. And I did it because I wanted to, which is the best reason for doing anything.

And the same thing with the second book of poems?

Yes. I had some poems left over that were not going to be published in the first book, and some more poems that I wanted to write, and so in that instance I sat down with the intention of writing poems. I wrote poems and more poems and pretty soon I saw another book taking shape.

Was it a relief to get away from writing short stories?

No, it was a relief just to be working, and to be working on something I wanted to work on. Had I been writing stories I'm sure I would have been just as happy. It felt good to be working again and it felt wonderful to be writing poems again. When I was writing those poems, I felt that there was nothing in the world more important than writing them. I didn't know if I'd ever write another story or not, and it was okay, it didn't matter.

Do you and Tess help each other with each other's work?

We're the best readers that we'll ever have. I read her stuff with a very cold eye and she reads my stuff the same way. As I said earlier, I'll write four or five drafts of a story and show it to Tess and usually I'm back at my typewriter the next day; she has made some good suggestions. She's a very good reader.

Has she changed the direction of your writing?

I'm quite sure of it. There is more of a fullness as a result of Tess's good eye and encouragement. We met, and then with her encouragement and suggestions and my own sense of my life and what I wanted out of it, my life began to open up.

Are you happier now?
Than when?

Ten or twenty years ago.

Oh, sure. There was a long period in my life when I was writing and had children and so forth; it was hard, but it was a life, it was my life, and even though it was hard, I was, I'm sure, happy. And then there was a very dark period for several years of emotional assaults on each other before the marriage ended.

There's no question that I'm better off now, but comparisons are difficult to make, and I'd rather just say that I've had two lives:

one life that ended when my drinking ended, and another life, a new life, that started after I quit drinking and met Tess. This second life has been very full, very rewarding, and for that I'll be eternally grateful.

Carolyn Kizer

CAROLYN Kizer's poetry is written to be read aloud. Her mentor, the poet Theodore Roethke, used to say, "I teach a beat," and Kizer has followed his example. Poetry for her is "an intensely physical act, involving all parts of the body, every orifice, and each of the five senses." She sees her work as continuing the oral tradition in poetry which dates back to Sappho and Homer. Her poetry readings are public performances, bravura displays of wit, personality and a finely tuned intelligence.

The politics of love has been a persistent theme in her work, and the interplay between public and private lives remains of especial interest to her. It was for this reason that she found an affinity for the Chinese poets of the T'ang dynasty, for whom these were favorite themes. In adopting and adapting the forms of Oriental poetry, Kizer has amplified her own voice, and has still retained the vigor, rhythm and musicality of English verse.

Her works include: The Ungrateful Garden (1960), Knock Upon Silence (1965), Midnight Was My Cry: New and Selected Poems (1971), Mermaids in the Basement (1984) and Yin (1984).

Kizer was born December 10, 1925 in Spokane, Washington.

*She received a B.A. in 1945 from Sarah Lawrence College, and
later did graduate work at Columbia University and the University
of Washington. She married Charles Stimson Bullitt in 1948. They
had three children, and were divorced in 1954. In 1975 she married
architect John M. Woodbridge. Kizer was a founder and editor of
Poetry Northwest, and has won a long string of prestigious
awards, grants and appointments which culminated in the Pulitzer
Prize for poetry in 1985.*

*The interview took place in the summer of 1986 at the
Centrum Writers' Conference in Port Townsend, Washington,
where she was teaching. Kizer and her husband were staying in
what were formerly the officers' quarters at Fort Worden. They
had just recovered from a bout with a bad batch of oysters, but
were both very welcoming, and we were soon talking about her
work. Kizer is a statuesque woman with blonde hair, a rich, engaging laugh and a penchant for large, theatrical gestures.*

What did it mean to you to win the Pulitzer Prize?

It was a terrific surprise. I didn't know I had been nominated.
When I got the phone call from the newspaper I thought they were
referring to the award from the National Academy and Institute of
Arts and Letters, which had come in three weeks earlier. They
asked me for my reaction, and I said, "Isn't that old news?" They
said, "Old news? It just happened."

I called my husband at the office and he came racing home.
He tore out to the front porch and roared, "Carolyn just won the
Pulitzer!" Windows opened all over the neighborhood, doors flew
open. Everybody within two blocks knew about it.

The next day was pretty crazy. A newspaper woman rang the
doorbell before seven a.m. She said, "I wanted to make sure I got
you first." Then all the television people started coming. There
were cables twisting all over the floors, and lights on top of
stepladders. Then the phone would ring and I'd trip over one of
the cables or I'd disconnect somebody. And then the doorbell
would ring. It was madness.

I had no idea it was going to be such a big deal. I'm not knocking it, you understand, but even though I try to write about a dozen letters a day, I'm always two or three cartons of mail behind.

Are the letters from people who have read your poems and want to tell you something about them?

Not really. I wish that were true more often. It's people who want you to read their poems and tell them what you think of them. And people sending you manuscripts, usually without a return, self-addressed, stamped envelope. And people wanting you to read, and people who knew you years ago who are getting back in touch, and several gentlemen who claim to have known me rather well, of whom I have no recollection. That sort of thing.

But as far as affecting my work is concerned, I think that I'm fortunate that it happened when I was too old to spoil. I know young writers who have won a number of honors who have been thrown very badly off base. But I'm too set in my ways to change my patterns, and I have too many things in my head that I'm working on that I want to do. I have all these big and unfinished pieces that are still in progress that I can go on picking away at. And that really takes the heat off. I'm not sitting around saying, "Oh my God, what do I do now?"

And the other thing that's always a help is that I continue to translate from the Chinese. I've been translating a young Chinese poet. Her name is Shu Ting. She's thirty-four. In the spring I toured around California with her, and then she and I read together in New York. And that was a good resource, because if there's a moment when you are a little uncertain about what you're going to do next, then you translate another poem. It's very important, not only to keep you working, but because you really learn something about the resources of English by translating. You find out what your language can and can't do.

When you started writing poetry did you expect to win anything like the Pulitzer?

That's very hard to say, because like most women of my generation I didn't take my own work very seriously for a long time, because men didn't take our work seriously. So you hardly thought of yourself as a professional poet. I was middle-aged before the idea really penetrated. It was just something you did and you

hoped that editors liked it and that your men friends who wrote
poetry would give you a passing grade. But as far as long-range ambition is concerned, I can only think of a couple of women poets
that had it. Sylvia Plath had it very strongly. And I think Adrienne
Rich has always been ambitious. But for most of us it's almost a
question of being given permission to be a serious writer. In my
case I felt that Theodore Roethke gave me that permission. Ted's
the person who said, "All right, when are you going to send your
stuff out?" And my answer was, "Who, me?" And then I sent a
poem to Delmore Schwartz at *The New Republic* and he took it.

You grew up in Spokane. Why did you move to Seattle?

It was largely because when my father came back from China,
where he had been administering United Nations relief, he had a
job at the University of Washington. He was the Walker Ames
professor, lecturing on China. It was just after the Chinese Revolution. So we had a house in Seattle. I met my first husband in
Seattle, and that's how I happened to settle there. My parents
moved back to Spokane after my father's professorship ended.

Was your father a professor?

No, he was a lawyer and one of the founders of the American
Civil Liberties Union. My parents were very liberal people in
Spokane, which was a very conservative town. We were considered rather freaky and unreliable. My childhood was marked by
the fact that we seemed to be very different from most of the
townspeople, who were prosperous and conservative. We were
Democrats, we were supporters of Roosevelt. My father wouldn't
join any of the clubs because they wouldn't allow Jewish or Negro
members. I wouldn't join a high-school sorority for the same reason. So we were not pariahs exactly, but we were set apart.

Did you fit in more easily in Seattle?

My husband's family, although very wealthy, was very liberal
and still is. And I couldn't possibly have married into a family that
wasn't, with my background. I remember when I was fifteen or
sixteen I said to my mother, "I will never kiss a Republican," and
as far as I know I never have. I was a political animal from a very
early age. When I was twelve my father had me out behind an
orange crate with a petition saying, "Repeal the forty-mill tax
limitation measure." My parents were very active politically and I

was too, and always have been. I'm less so now partly because I'm older, but when I got the Pulitzer Prize I thought that I'd been going along minding my own business and writing poems long enough, and it was about time I got politically active again. So I have been trying to pay my dues in that sense.

Do you keep the political and the poetical separate?

Not entirely, no. Once after a reading somebody said, "Oh, I love that political poem you read." And my husband, who was standing next to me, said, "Which one? They're all political." I guess it depends pretty much on what your definition of political is, if it includes a humanistic view of life, the kind of thing that makes Jerry Falwell shudder. And love's political too, in its own way. Everything is. Much of the best poetry being written today is. I've been working on an anthology of poetry of social concern from the end of World War II to the present, and the thing that I've found surprising about this collection is that it is awfully good stuff—Denise Levertov's poems about Vietnam, Marge Piercy's anti-"Pro-Life" poems—very strong, powerful stuff, which I think surprises people because it is generally perceived that when good poets write political poetry it is never their best work. But you can't do it on demand, you can't sit down and say, "Now I am going to write a poem about something that is terribly important." It either happens or it doesn't.

How did you come to know Roethke?

When I separated from my husband I went and signed up to take Roethke's class. I had published a bit before I was married. I published a poem in *The New Yorker* when I was seventeen. I had a poem in *The Atlantic* during my marriage, and I'd had a few poems in small literary magazines. I'm very grateful that I had a little bit of publishing before I married because it meant that I kept my own name. Many of my women friends, long divorced, are still having to publish under the names of their ex-husbands, simply because that's how they made their reputations. So I was fortunate in that I was able to keep my family name.

When I left my husband and signed up for Roethke's course I'd evidently been storing up an immense amount of psychic energy. It was like taking the cork out of a champagne bottle; it just went whoosh! And you could say I've never looked back.

He was a great teacher. It's sinful that although the electronic age was certainly capable of recording his lectures or his classroom conversation, it wasn't done. It's a great tragedy, because he was an absolutely incandescent teacher.

I won the Pulitzer Prize exactly thirty years after he did. I was in the classroom when Ted got called out of the room. When he came back a few minutes later looking rather odd, he tried to pick up the thread of his talk. But then he stopped dead and said, "I've just won the Pulitzer." We all leapt to our feet screaming and hugging each other and jumping up and down. This spring I gave the Roethke Reading at [The University of] Washington. It seemed awfully nice and symmetrical that it happened like that.

What part did Roethke play in your development?

He made a serious writer out of me. I hadn't known the essential thing that you have to learn, which is how to make a good poem out of a bad poem. At Sarah Lawrence I studied with Genevieve Taggard who was one of the minor woman poets of the '20s. She used to say, "This, my dear, is a good poem. You must send it out." Or she would say, "This is a bad poem, my dear." And she would drop it in the wastebasket.

Roethke on the other hand would tell you what was wrong with it and give you a rough idea of what you ought to be doing about it, not by dictating to you how to change it but just by saying, "This part's good, this part isn't, now get to work." That is the kind of teacher you learn from, that's how you learn to write. The teacher should supply you with the critical discrimination that you need. You can learn it on your own, but it's an awful waste of time. A good teacher can save you ten years. You can't teach creativity, you can't infuse people with psychic energy, and you certainly can't give them a good ear, which is a gift of God, but you can teach people critical distance, how to look at their own work objectively as if it had been written by somebody else.

While studying with Roethke, did you decide at some point that you were going to commit yourself to writing poetry?

The big step was to start sending things out and to stop being the amateur housewife. But I just slipped into it. I can't think of a moment when I suddenly said to myself, "Well, that's it." I can remember isolated episodes when I felt good about it, when *The*

New Yorker took the poem when I was seventeen, or when I was still studying with Roethke there was a great magazine called *Botegha Oscura*, in Italy, an international magazine that appeared in three languages. It was run by an American, Marguerite Chapin, who had married Prince Caetani, of the oldest family in Rome. I sent her five long poems, hoping she would take one. Then I got a cable that she'd taken all five. Nothing will ever equal that! The Pulitzer was nothing compared to that.

Really there isn't that kind of thrill about getting published anywhere anymore. When we were young we all wanted to be in the big important quarterlies, like the *Partisan Review* and *The Hudson Review*. Now you don't even send them your work. They're all ossified. They've gone on too long. They ought to creep into the ground and throw dirt on themselves.

How about The New Yorker?

The thing about being in *The New Yorker* is that you get read by people other than other writers, which is comforting. You get letters from lawyers and psychiatrists and dentists. That's nice. But there's so much bad poetry in *The New Yorker* nowadays that that's not so thrilling either. You have a poem taken by *The New Yorker* and you feel pretty good about it, and you pick up the next issue and there's some poem I would have rejected instantly had it been sent to *Poetry Northwest* when I edited that. So the thrill is gone. But there again it's a magazine with a poetry editor who has edited it far too long. I don't think anyone should edit a magazine for longer than seven years. You get stale.

What influence did Roethke have on the poets and writers out here?

One of the great things that Ted did was to keep any of us from imitating him. If we tried, he would mock us and tease us so mercilessly that we never tried that again. In contrast, a friend of mine, Richard Hugo, turned out students who wrote like him. I can spot them a mile a way, or a continent away. I was at a conference at Stony Brook and a girl got up and read a poem to me, and I said, "When did you study with Dick Hugo?" She was just floored. But I spotted the formula.

But if you think of those of us who studied with Ted, like Hugo, Jim Wright, and Dave Wagoner and me, we don't write anything like him, and we don't write like each other. That is the hallmark of a really great teacher. To encourage you to find your own voice. And he often said such wise things. One of the wisest things he ever said I try to remember in dealing with students. I can see Ted and me and some male standing in the hall in Parrington [Hall] and the other person was talking about a line of mine that he thought was overwrought or overwritten, and Ted said, "Now you want to be very careful when you criticize something that seems excessive and extreme, because *it may be the hallmark of an emerging style.*" That's a very profound remark.

I had a student at Columbia a couple years ago that made me feel much as one of the professors at Pennsylvania must have felt when he had Ezra Pound in class. I didn't understand what this kid was doing, but I didn't necessarily think that that was his fault. I went the extra mile with him to try to figure out what he was trying to tell me, and whether or not it was my own age or density or lack of intellect that was preventing me from understanding what he was doing. One of the other teachers there who is very, very bright simply dismissed this boy out of hand. "I don't understand it, therefore it's no good." You have to be careful about that kind of thing, as you get older particularly.

How did Roethke make a difference in your education?

By his teaching. He made an enormous difference in the whole university, for that matter. It struck me both there and other places I've been how very few people it takes to give distinction to a large school, or even a moderate-sized school. At Sarah Lawrence it was Joseph Campbell, who was my don. I can't imagine my life as a writer if I hadn't had Campbell. My history and philosophy teacher was Charles Trinkaus. That was the school: two people. And I doubt very much if there's any school that has more than two or three or four. I don't care if it's Oxford or Cambridge or the Sorbonne. That's why I think it's so important for a school to try to have a couple of really distinguished persons around. Who you learn from is far more important than what course you take.

How did you meet the painters Mark Tobey and Morris Graves?

One morning early in my first marriage the doorbell rang. I went to the door clutching a small baby to my milk-stained bosom, opened the door, and there was Jesus Christ: this tall, gaunt man with a beard was the most striking-looking person I'd ever seen in my life. It was Morris Graves. He'd just come to pay a call. I reeled back, and had presence enough of mind to invite him in. That was the beginning of our friendship.

I can't remember the first time I met Tobey. Maybe I just looked up Tobey on my own. We became very, very close friends almost immediately, which was lovely, because he was my parents' generation; he was an old man when I got to know him as a girl in my twenties. My parents were old enough to be my grandparents. And when I persuaded my father to sit for Tobey, they were both in their seventies. Tobey did this magnificent portrait of my father.

Do your parents still have that?

No, I have it. You bet I have it. I have an incredible collection of Tobey, things he gave me or things that I bought. My mother gave me a tiny allowance which I was supposed to spend on a cleaning lady. It was something like twenty-five dollars a month. Well, I bought paintings on time from Tobey, like everybody else who bought him then—young lawyers and professors. The wealthy people of the town weren't buying anything. I remember trying to sell some paintings for Mark, who was in terrible straits at that point. Morris was doing well in the '40s and '50s, but Mark wasn't. I took a load of priceless paintings in the back of my car to show to a prominent society woman who had good taste, I thought. She came to the door wearing a $400 suit, which would cost $1,500 now, and looked at some of these great masterpieces and said, "Yes, they're beautiful. I wish I could afford them." And he was selling them for $200 or $300, less than her clothes allowance for a month.

People didn't really do anything for Mark, or care anything about him until he became internationally famous, and then all of a sudden they were all his old friends. If that sounds bitter, it is. He got tired of it so he left. And he got tired of fighting to save the Public [Pike Place] Market. Now when you consider the reams of publicity about the Market as the focus for the town, and the ef-forts to tear it down all the damn time, it was crazy. The whole area around it was a wasteland, but the only thing that had any character or any color, or meant anything to the farmers or the

Orientals and the artists, was what they wanted to get rid of. When Mark won his last battle I think it wore him out and he said, "The hell with Seattle." And he went to Switzerland. But he was a remarkable person and a beautiful man. I have pictures of him in my house and people come in and say, "Is that your father?" And I say, "Yes."

Did you talk about poetry and painting with him?

Oh, yes. And I read aloud to him a lot. My best friend Jan Thompson, who still lives in Seattle, was closer to Morris, and I was closer to Tobey. But it was a circle. We used to go to wonderful parties at Morris's beautiful, exquisite house in Edmonds. There were memorable parties at that house. There were wonderful intellectuals at the University of Washington, too, very eminent men, like Arnold Stein and Jackson Mathews. There was a great infusion of scholarly brilliance as well as creative brilliance, people who loved William Blake, who liked to read us. We could talk to them about Blake, Homer, Garcia Lorca; who was good and who wasn't. It was infinitely livelier and more stimulating than the atmosphere I now live in in Berkeley, which is the center of a great university.

In what sense did Roethke and his students constitute a school?

I don't think they did at all, unless you call learning your trade a school, or the emphasis on craftsmanship and on things like punctuation. He spent a lot of time on punctuation, because poetry, unlike music, has such a limited system of notation. You've got commas, periods, colons, semicolons, line breaks, dashes. In music you've got literally hundreds of ways of indicating how you want something played or sung, at what speed, how long the rests should be, how long you should hold a syllable—it's marvelous! I've often wondered why we poets don't do more with that. But of course one of the great things about somebody like Alexander Pope, about whom I've been writing recently, is that he shows you how to make a line run rapidly or how to slow it down, which is of course part of the whole craft, too, which people don't pay nearly enough attention to any more.

How did you become interested in Pope?

There's just been a good biography written by Maynard

Mack. There are several things in there that are just wonderful. Mack understands how a poet works, which very few biographers know anything about. He speaks of "the gift that Pope had of charging his lines with sounds and rhythms felt as much upon the tongue and teeth as heard by the ear." We don't just sit at a typewriter, or in a chair with a pencil and a notebook. It's something you do with your whole body.

But what I was really going to talk about was revising. I quote, "Pope was quite aware, as most working poets are, that the lines which seem to the reader or critic most spontaneous, graceful and natural are often the ones laboriously revised, far into the night, with an obligato of curses, and an outpouring of sweat. When Pope was praised for his powers of fancy and imaginative vision, he chose to emphasize the process of revision, once calling it, 'the greatest proof of judgment of anything I ever did.' With practice, revision itself becomes a creative act, not simply drudgery, but accompanied by the same excitement with which one sits down at the first draft. One learns dispassion, judgment, and a certain limited faith in one's powers of discrimination." I believe that with my soul, and I think Roethke did too. It's at the heart of the whole process of writing.

So you're not a member of the spontaneous school like Jack Kerouac?

Oh, yes, there are many poets from Byron to the present who accept the romantic notion that equates spontaneity with poetic genius. Your first impulse is so wonderful you don't do anything to it. In the words of a student I just had at Stanford, "That would violate the integrity of the poem." But what you try to do through revision is to *find* the integrity of the poem. I've always had this superstition that the poem inside here is perfect [points to her forehead], and I have this very clumsy retrieval process for getting it out. It's like trying to get out a baby with a lousy pair of forceps. Bring it out without bashing its head in or knocking off one of its ears.

You revise a lot, then?

Yes. Pope also said you should keep a poem for two years before you send it out, which I do. Any serious poem I keep for two years—at least. I have poems around now that I've read in public, because you can learn things about the poems by reading them aloud, particularly to a good, interested audience. You can sense if they lose interest, or even if one phrase or word seems to be dead. So I often read things a lot of times in public before I publish them.

Do you write your poems to be read aloud?

Absolutely. That's the way poetry began.

Not so much so that somebody could pick up a book and read them?

Nope. Oral tradition. Homer. Sappho. They're to be *heard*.

Do you think that tradition is alive and going strong?

I was at a literary festival in Yugoslavia a few years ago with many internationally famous guests, and I was at the end of the line to be interviewed. The interviewer had one question, "If you had to choose between having your poetry heard and having it read, which would you choose?" I said, "To be heard, of course. That's the way poetry began, as a sacred ceremony, with dance and song." He looked at me in absolute amazement and said, "You're the first person that's made that choice."

Something else I automatically assume is that the poem is going to last. People say to me, "How can you keep poems so long? Aren't you afraid they'll date?" And I say, "Well, if they'll date, then they're no good, so the hell with it." I can think of poems that are dated that were written twenty minutes ago. A lot of the Beats have dated terrifically, not the best of Ginsberg, but a lot of other people. And I think some of the classical poets of my generation have dated pretty badly, too, because the diction now seems so artificial and mannered. But if you keep something around long enough, some of that becomes clear to you.

The good writers don't seem to date so much. Mark Twain, for example, seems very contemporary.

Well, hell, you can go back a lot further than that. We were at Ashland a couple of nights ago, seeing one of Shakespeare's worst plays, *Titus Andronicus*. But lines come out that sound as if they were written yesterday. And the interesting thing about Shakespeare is that the rhythms never get mechanical. You wonder with Shakespeare as an example how people could go in for automatic stressing: da-dum-da-dum-da-dum-da-da-da-da. It never happens. The rhythms sound like normal speech, yet they have such wonderful variations.

And then you get into a lot of nineteenth-century stuff that is deadly. Browning. I can't read it. The psychological insights are fascinating and the whole narrative and dramatic structure of the poetry is interesting, but the rhythms are deadly. And I don't understand how you could be educated on Chaucer and Shakespeare and George Herbert and John Donne and have your ear turn into a player piano.

Maybe it was deliberate.

Maybe they thought that they were better. "Poor old Shakespeare, he just didn't know how to swing a line."

Yeah, he was just too crude.

Well, I thought that about Chaucer for a long time, that he was just sort of clunky. And he's heavenly. He's wonderful. And talk about fresh and contemporary, and a great student of human psychology!

And that gets us to where I am as a poet: I am interested in *character*. That is my subject. And that is one reason why I've been interested in writing about Pope, because character was his subject: the impact of one person on another, or one person on society, or how even in the most casual kind of meeting between two people, the whole chemistry of a relationship changes. It's like what Heisenberg says about subatomic particles: by looking at them you alter them. That's the way human relations are too. You and I will never be quite the same after this interview as we were before. And that's my subject.

Character is usually more the subject of a fiction writer. Have you ever written fiction?

I've written one or two short stories, but I think the music is too important to me. If you write for the ear, then poetry's your means.

Why does Oriental culture seem to influence so much of the writing and painting from the Northwest?

We just seem closer to it somehow. Even in Spokane, which was so remote, I was always interested in it. I guess the fact that my mother read me Arthur Waley as a child has a lot to do with it. And Vachel Lindsay, who lived with us, had a sister in China who was a missionary. He used to get letters from her, and he'd read them to us. He wrote what I think was his best poem, "A Chinese Nightingale," on our sofa.

The atmosphere of the Orient seems so much closer than in fact it is. I guess it's just the pioneer habit of looking off to the west. It's called the East of course, but it isn't. It's the East from the point of view of the English, but for us it's the west. We kept looking that way instead of looking back over our shoulders at the East Coast and at Europe.

One of the things that struck me forcibly about Australia, where we were last summer, is that they're still looking over their shoulders at Europe. They're not influenced by Asia at all, as far as I can tell. They aren't even influenced by their own aboriginal culture, which is extraordinary. The poets want to make sure that you know that they've been to England and have sat in a Paris café. So it's not very interesting.

It's very fortunate that we Western writers care about the Orient. It gives us something very special. You see it very clearly in Gary Snyder, and certainly it's been very important in my writing, getting involved with the poets of the T'ang dynasty, for whom I seem to have a great affinity, partly because their minds worked dialectically and partly because friendship is a serious subject in Chinese poetry, a serious element in Chinese life, as it is in my life. It seems to me the influence of China and Japan in the West has been nothing but good. I wish we could say the same thing about our influence on them. We export the worst, and they seem to export the best.

When you were writing poems based on Oriental models, did you find that these models fit what you wanted to say?

Oh, yes, or otherwise I wouldn't have done it. Sometimes I think there are certain kinds of life crises like falling out of love where a classical poet can give you a vehicle for expressing your feelings that would be difficult for you otherwise.

Such as "A Month in Summer"?

Yes, exactly. That's one example. But all the imitations of

Chinese poetry, too. "A Month in Summer" of course is based on a Japanese model.

Do you think that this Oriental influence is confined mostly to the West Coast?

Except for a few people like William Merwin, and Charles Wright. Charles and Bill are the only ones I can think of who have a serious interest in the Orient.

Do you think that it's proximity?

Well, in some cases I think it's subject affinity. Zen Buddhism has had a lot to do with it in the case of both Merwin and Snyder. That hasn't been my interest at all. I'm an Episcopalian myself. I was very amused when I was touring around with my Chinese girl whom I was translating. We were in Santa Cruz where they had invited all the local writers in to meet her. There was a whole table full of them, a lot of minor poets. And typical of Santa Cruz, a lot of them were what I call Zenophiles. One of them said to her, "Would you care to discuss the influence of Buddhism on your poetry?" And she said, "Well, actually I have been much more influenced by Christianity." I wish I could have had a picture of their faces. I got a big kick out of that.

How much of your poetry is autobiographical?

Very little of it. Almost none. There's a poem in the Copper Canyon book of 1984, *Mermaids in the Basement*, called "Where I've Been All My Life," that's an autobiographical poem. That's it. Now I'm doing stuff that's directly autobiographical and no bones made about it, but that's something unusual. I am not a confessional poet. Of course there are universal experiences that happen to everybody, death and love and work, and so on. You use the experience of your life but it gets transformed and changed out of recognition.

The other day I read something which alleged that my poem "Bitch" was about my first husband. It didn't have anything to do with my first husband. It doesn't have anything to do with any man I ever knew. I thought of this metaphor that we all had some kind of an animal inside of us, the id of course, and I've always thought of mine as being some kind of tiger. But I thought, "Well, suppose I had a dog inside of me and I ran into somebody I used to be in

love with, then what would happen? Let's keep it to one metaphor, just push it as far as we can." And this is what came up. It
isn't based on anything, except an idea that I had.

*When you have an idea like that, how do you decide on a form
for it?*

You don't. When you've written a first draft, you see what the
predominant meter or shape of the most important lines is, and
then you bring the rest of the poem in line with that.

Would you describe yourself as a feminist?

Oh, yes.

And what does feminism mean to you?

Equality with men in every way. The damage done to women
writers in their adolescence and young womanhood by reading
about the poet "he"—all references to artists being put in masculine terms, as if there wasn't any such thing as a woman
writer—is so damaging. I happen to be a pretty strong person so I
don't think it harmed me.

I don't want women to have to be superwomen. I want them
to be able to be talented and good at what they do, and not have to
be the perfect wife, the perfect mother, the perfect job-holder,
and crochet besides. I just want women to have a fair shake. I want
them able to make money commensurate with their efforts. I want
them to have flex-time so they can take time off for their children
in emergencies, and not get hysterical if they have to take someone to the dentist or the hospital. I want them not to get fired if
they get pregnant, and to have husbands who help out, not because they have to but because they want to.

I'm not particularly angry at men. I don't think anybody likes
relinquishing power. If we lived in a matriarchy I wouldn't like to
give it up either. The division of power is one of the things that
makes marriage a very complex relationship—trying to keep
things in some kind of reasonable balance. It never reaches stasis;
it either deteriorates or you work at it. And I think that's what happens in the life of women and men in society. Constant attention
has to be paid to the balance of forces.

James Mitsui

JAMES Mitsui is a native Northwesterner, but the "gray continent" of Asia looms up in his poetry like mist rising from the background of a Chinese landscape painting. The son of Japanese immigrants, Mitsui was born in 1940 in Skykomish, Washington. After a year, he and his family were moved to the Tule Lake Relocation Camp in California. The family stayed there for a year and a half, and then were permitted to move to Lamona in eastern Washington where his father had found a job working for the Great Northern Railroad. Mitsui barely remembers the time he spent in the camp but the experience there has become a persistent theme in his work, giving his often personal and private poetry a larger political context.

His first book, Journal of the Sun, received the Pacific Northwest Booksellers Award in 1974. His other books are: Crossing the Phantom River (1978) and After the Long Train (1986).

Mitsui attended elementary school and high school in Odessa, Washington. In 1963, he graduated from Eastern Washington State College where he played football and baseball. He received an M.A. in English from the University of Washington in 1975, *where he studied with the poets Richard Hugo, William Stafford, David Wagoner, Richard Blessing and Nelson Bentley.*

For the last twenty-two years, Mitsui has taught in high schools around Puget Sound; at present he teaches English in Renton, Washington. He lives in Seattle in a brick apartment building on the west side of Lake Union. The interview took place there on March 10, 1986, just as the cherry trees outside his window were beginning to bud. Mitsui is an introspective man with dark hair and a trim athletic build. He sat on an overstuffed couch below a Zen-like ink painting and the interview began.

Why did your parents move from Japan to the U.S.?

My father was not the eldest son, and in Japan there is a tradition that the oldest son is the one who gets the farm or whatever the family earns their living off of, and the rest of the sons have to go fend for themselves. So my father took off to Toyko. He was kind of a...the Japanese word for it is *yan-cha*, which is not really playboy, not really a thug or a rowdy, but somebody with a lot of spirit and stubbornness and bravado. He left there when he was seventeen, came over here.

Why did your parents come to the Northwest?

It was probably the easiest route at that time. My dad got a job originally in a sawmill, and then he got a job in the railroad. He ended up working on the Great Northern Railroad for fifty-seven years.

I was born in Skykomish. Then the war occurred and we moved to Tule Lake. Right before the war ended we moved to eastern Washington because we could reside 100 miles away from the coast. As long as you were 100 miles away from the coast and there was a situation where you could earn a living, you could stay there.

So I ended up growing up in eastern Washington wheat country, Odessa. That's really out in the scab-rock and wheat fields. It was a mixed part of my life. It was kind of nice but I don't like going back there. I've only gone back to eastern Washington three times in twenty years. Literally.

Was the experience of immigration any different for Japanese Americans than it was for other nationalities?

I don't think it was that much different. Maybe the only difference is that people are real simplistic, and they can discriminate or identify Chinese or Japanese just because of the physical characteristics, whereas if you're German or Italian or even Spanish you can blend in. Other than that I don't think that there was a whole lot of difference.

The same thing is going on with the Vietnamese. You start way at the bottom working on the railroad, you save enough money to buy a farm or a shop. It's a cycle. In my generation, the Nisei, the second generation, there's this huge difference in what parents did versus what kids ended up doing. Part of it is that there's a real emphasis on education with all Asians. In our family there are three college graduates out of five.

How did it affect your parents to be sent to the internment camp?

They wouldn't talk about it much. I have to believe that it was pretty upsetting and traumatic. They hid a lot and just kind of suppressed it. I was never really aware of too much anger.

So they didn't tell you much about it?

No, even in later years you really had to pump them for information. And then you get busy, you do other things and all of a sudden you discover it's too late. And you lose a lot of information that shouldn't be lost.

When you wrote the poems about the Japanese relocation, how did you research them?

I looked at pictures and I travelled through there, and I talked to my sister. She was in high school then. There's a lot of retention.

Did you feel a responsibility to write about that situation?

Yes, I felt outraged. It wasn't because of anything that was done to me personally, but to my family and just the whole idea. And for a while it wasn't getting in the history books. It wasn't being publicized or acknowledged. In fact I felt it was being suppressed.

Did you feel discriminated against because you were Japanese American?

Not a whole lot. When I started school it was awful, but I think that maybe was based only on a day or two days, or at most a week of harassment, because, God, it was right after the war. I was different from all the other kids. They were yelling at me and making fun of me and whatever. But I think it had to be two or three days. In my memory it seems like a year or years of that, but I think it was a very short time. And then after that I was accepted, partly because I found or created an outlet for myself through athletics. I was good in athletics so that kind of overpowered any kind of problem. And socially I didn't have too much problem, except a couple situations where parents felt things were getting too serious and they felt uneasy, but that probably would be true in a lot of cases anyway, regardless of what race you were.

In many ways it was nice to grow up in eastern Washington. And I liked it because it made me somewhat independent, not feeling like I had to have a crowd or find comfort in groups. When I came over to the U [University of Washington], all the Japanese students ate lunch in a reading room and they clustered together and hung out together. I felt different. I felt really excluded. They excluded me more than any whites would, especially the ones who were from Seattle, because they were so tight, and here I was the country Japanese from eastern Washington. In fact there were a couple of quarters when I was catching a ride with these guys that I felt really shut out. But that was okay, too, because I didn't need a crowd or group.

I think sometimes that's a mistake. I see that at schools with the Vietnamese students or black students or any kind of ethnic race that tends to group and cluster. It's natural to do that, necessary and logical and everything, but I'm glad I was forced to be isolated, because it affected me in maybe not a positive way but a way that I like.

Do you think that most Asian Americans resist getting absorbed into mainstream American culture?

It really varies. Sometimes it almost alternates from one generation to the next. The generation after mine wanted to get back to their roots a little more, and wanted to take Japanese classes and wanted to find out more about the customs. I'm kind of young to be a Nisei; I think the older Nisei didn't want to deal with that.

They wanted to drop the curtain on that and get into being successful and businesslike, and almost materialistic. I don't think that is exclusively Japanese. I think that's a real common pattern.

Does your Japanese-American ancestry influence the kind of poetry you write?

Maybe it does a little with family and heritage and history, but I don't feel like I'm catalogued with Asian American poets. In fact sometimes I feel not included. This is getting into almost a political thing.

I've always wanted my poems to be published and accepted and printed because they were good poems, although I think there were a couple of situations where I was the token Asian poet to be included in an anthology. In most situations I don't like that; it makes me uncomfortable. There would be certain situations where I would withdraw my poems or not be involved. I think poetry should transcend any kind of race or heritage or whatever.

When did you start writing poetry?

I started late. Most writers and poets start in fifth grade or high school or whatever. But I didn't start till I was twenty-eight. I was going to have to teach this creative-writing class one fall back in '68 and I hadn't done any poetry at all, but I could always write pretty well so I decided I better take some classes. That summer I signed up for a class.

Over at the University of Washington?

Yes, with Nelson Bentley. And that's how I got started. I found out that I could write and I liked it, and it kind of stair-stepped.

What were your first poems like?

They were pretty bad. [Laughs]

Short?

Yes. In fact the first poems I took into the workshop were haiku, because that seemed pretty simple and something I could handle, three lines. My first poems looked a lot like Williams's poems because I liked William Carlos Williams. They were real skinny and kind of linear. In my first book there are some of those skinny poems.

Then I started reading other people and eventually I developed my own style or voice. Everybody at the beginning is influenced by whoever they're reading or whoever they like. When I discovered Hugo, I found that the lines of my poems started getting longer and the poems got longer and denser.

Is your poetry still influenced by the poets you read?

Not so much any more. I change around the format of my poems. For a long time they were solid blocks of writing, but lately I've been writing a lot in two- or three-line stanzas.

What are the reasons for these changes in form?

Well, I haven't been writing much lately. In my workshop—I have a little workshop I belong to—we always set up an assignment for the next workshop. And the assignment was to write in two-line stanzas because one of the poems that night happened to be in that format. And I'd seen some poems by a friend of mine, Bill Ransom, and they were also in two-line stanzas. And I've been working with my students with two-line stanzas, and so I tried the two-line format and it really worked. In fact I wrote two poems really quick, in an hour, and I haven't been writing much. Part of it was that I could go two lines at a time, whereas if I was in my old format writing a whole block of a poem, I was feeling intimidated or like I had to sustain something. If it bogged down I had trouble getting it started again. But with the two lines I could kind of increment my way down the page.

Do you find that there are some things you can say in the two-line stanzas that you couldn't say in another form like the sonnet?

It's just a matter of proportion, I guess. The one thing about the two lines is that you can really make jumps between line one and line two or between stanzas, which is good. Instead of sustaining a plot line or chronological narrative, you stop. You can continue to run it on into the next stanza below or you can stop and make a jump.

Who were some of the teachers that helped you with your poetry?

Well, initially Nelson for inspiration, and then after that I was lucky because the summers I was going to the U, Bill Stafford came and Dick Hugo, and later on in graduate school I was able to work with David Wagoner and Richard Blessing. So I had a nice variety.

Did these teachers make a big difference in your writing?

Yes, very much so. Different personalities, different perspectives. Some people work better with certain kinds of teachers. Some students would not work well under Wagoner but would thrive under Nelson. Maybe the best teacher I had was Hugo. He was critical but nurturing and had a lot of good practical suggestions. He was a nice blend of styles.

How do you choose the subjects of your poems?

You can cause poems. You can write poems for people or to people. You can write a letter or note. But mostly I just write in response to some kind of need, to what's going on, things that are bothering me. Because poetry for me is therapeutic. It's personal and it happens to be something that some people like to read, and I have found that I have a little bit of talent or ability to express myself, so I send poems out and I get them published, but I think the main thing is just writing because I need to.

How do the individual poems start?

Sometimes it's an image or a line or a title, some kind of irony. Once in a while something in the newspaper. Usually it starts with some kind of interchange or reaction to people.

Do you have to rewrite a lot?

Not as much as I used to. I have one poem somewhere I have twenty-seven drafts of, retypes, spread out over a year and a half. That poem finally got published in *Poetry Northwest*. It seems lately I go through at most about eight drafts and sometimes as few as four because a lot of it gets done in my head now. It used to be all on the page. A lot of it now is subconscious. I'm not conscious of the poem sitting in my head but it's there and something triggers it and it comes out.

I'm going through a process of becoming single again. I've written five poems in the last two weeks and they all either deal directly with that situation or allude to it.

And you find that writing about something helps make sense of it?

Yes, the poems are like little ceremonies. This time it isn't real traumatic like it was before. It was almost a beneficial decision for both parties. So this time there isn't the trauma and sadness and unhappiness. And in the past I've found that I've written poems that were clearance poems or closure poems. They were ceremonies I had to do to free myself emotionally. And this time it's more a looking ahead. It's not really a release or a letting go or a regret, but, "Let's get on with it." I suppose they are like little records of a period of time in your life. So most of my stuff is fairly personal. I don't think it's personal to the point that it's too personal. I deal with real issues and real things. I'm in a workshop but I don't have a teacher giving me assignments or writing exercises.

You're in a workshop?

With some friends of mine. We get together once a month because you need feedback. Artists need feedback, all artists. Otherwise you don't improve. You never really know what's going on with yourself.

Why do you sometimes dedicate your poems to individuals?

A lot of times it's just because it's an excuse to write a poem. I'm really fond of dedications and epigraphs, little quotations. When you're a writer or a poet you find pleasure in little silly things. I have a book coming out in May and the typeface that the printer chose is called Californian and it has a real neat ampersand. I like ampersands and so I can really get excited about that.

When you dedicate a poem to a person, is it as if you're writing the poem to that person?

It's like a target or excuse or a reason to write the poem. Frequently the poem is sent or given to the person. They're like gifts or presents. People really like to have poems written for them. It personalizes it, and yet if you write the poem right, it doesn't exclude everyone else.

And how do you do that?

You try to stay away from being real personal, otherwise no one really understands what you're talking about. The stuff should still be universal. You have to be aware of not being melodramatic or maudlin or too personal. It wouldn't be that you would write something that would embarrass you, but you don't want other people to feel embarrassed reading something that you've written because it is too personal. As long as you stay away from that I don't think that there's any problem.

Why is it that you write poetry rather than another form?

One reason is that my short stories are really awful. [Laughs] Part of it is just time. I can work on a poem in bits and pieces. I can finish something in one night. There's something masochistic, too, in doing something well that goes unappreciated or unrecognized or unread by, say, the majority of the population. Maybe it's a little affirmation of the fact that I do it because I need to do it; it isn't that I need an audience or the publicity or the recognition or whatever.

I know that with writers, with poets, the question invariably comes up, "Are you writing?" And if your response is, "Yes," then it's understood that things are going well and you're feeling good. But if you're not writing it's a bit of a worry. It's not like you're never going to write another poem again, but it's like something is just a little off kilter.

Are your poems fictional?

I don't think that there are any that are fiction. They're all basically true or they're philosophically true. They don't say anything that I personally disagree with.

How is poetry different from ordinary speech?

I don't think that it's that much different. Some of my favorite poems are conversational poems. I just taught a workshop yesterday and I used a poem called "Three A.M. Kitchen, My Father Talking." It was written by Tess Gallagher, but essentially her father wrote it and he's not a poet. He was talking and she just wrote down what he said. It's a great poem.

One mistake that a lot of students and beginners make is that they sit down to write a poem and they think they have to sound like a poet. They think that they have to sound poetic. So they change their natural speaking voice. It doesn't ring true then.

Poetry is a lot tighter than ordinary speech. You pick and choose stuff and it's more evocative than just regular conversation because we ramble and use a lot of clichés in conversation that you wouldn't get away with in a poem. But I think that there are phrases and pieces of conversation that are pretty much true to what a poem would be.

Do you count out the rhythm of your lines?

No. I've just deliberately refused to even think about or learn scanning lines. I've tried to stay away from it. I just try to develop a good ear. Writing poetry is a form of music. A lot of trial and error.

It seems that contemporary poetry tries to stay away from a formal style or rhythm. Is that true of your poetry too?

I think so. In many ways it's more complicated. I was teaching a workshop yesterday, and I was talking about that comment by Frost that free verse is like tennis without the net. One way you could look at that would be: "Yes, it's like playing tennis without the net, but you still have to imagine that the net is there and you still have to judge whether the ball has cleared the net or not. And that's harder than having the net there." So you can turn that quote around.

Contemporary poetry is a lot more subtle in its rhythms, its momentum, its sounds: you really have to be aware when you're writing a poem now. It has to sound good, but you don't have standard rules to help you decide, or grade or evaluate the sound. And it differs. It depends on what kind of poem it is, what the subject is, if it's serious or funny.

Is it tough to know when you've finished it?

Sometimes it is. Sometimes you just know. I used to have trouble with stopping. I think there's a tendency to go past the ending. There's also a tendency to start poems too soon. The more you write, the more you pick an ideal place to start. The ideal place is not standing still, then accelerating and shifting gears until finally by the second stanza you're going forty miles an hour. The first line should be travelling, pulling the reader into it pretty fast. And if there's background information you need to give the reader, you can do that with flashback or later in the poem.

So you start after the beginning?

Yes, in mid-incident and then you can go back. The other thing is you need to let the poem happen on the page as you're sitting there working on it, not having it plotted out ahead of time knowing what you're going to say and especially how it's going to end. I don't think you should really know how it's supposed to end.

I think all writing should be a process where the discovery happens during the creation of it, working on it, not beforehand. Which is hard because I think our whole system of education and writing instruction implies that you already know what you want to say, and you just have to figure out arrangement, that basically you have your thesis and your proof and you go get your facts. But that kind of writing isn't very creative. I don't know how much discovery goes on in situations like that; I don't care how many books you check out of the library.

It sounds as if your poetry proceeds by associations.

Yes, it's a loosening up of your consciousness, stream-of-consciousness, making jumps, coming upon realizations about associations and connections and relationships.

I don't know how well I do talking about stuff like this, because I don't really think about it much. Something in me resists formalizing it, or thinking about it or analyzing it too much.

Even though you're a teacher?

That's a big conflict. Because in class we frequently are discussing poems and novels and whatever, and yet as an artist, as a writer, I know a lot of books that English teachers have just murdered because they've got into symbolism and kids hated it after a while. Shakespeare said, "Explanation is death to art."

As a teacher you must have to struggle with that.

Yes, because writers need to be aware of their audience and how their audience is reacting, and how they're going to read things and what the connotations and symbols are, so you have to do some of that.

Why is it that most of your poems are serious in tone?

I think they've gotten less serious. My first book is very bad that way. Really serious. I still like some of the poems in there, but. . . . My second book has a few semi-humorous poems. I guess I've become aware of it at readings. There's nothing worse than a poetry reading where all the poems are philosophic or serious, so I have some humorous poems interspersed. And actually that works well because it's like going to a good movie. At a good movie you're crying and then a few minutes later you can be laughing. It's examining the whole range of human emotion. Maybe you can't do that in one poem, but maybe you can in a collection. I'm aware of that, and try to lighten it up.

The five poems I've written recently, they could be dreary

and heart-wrenching, but I don't think they really are. They've backed away from it and have treated it in a lighter fashion than I would have ten or fifteen years ago.

That was one thing I liked about your second book. The humor in it was refreshing. So much poetry seems so deadly serious.

That's a real mistake. But it's hard not to do that, because if you feel good about something you feel like going out to a tavern and having some beers and going dancing. You feel exuberant. You don't necessarily feel like writing about it.

Is it important to you to address public as well as private issues?

I think so. That's always kind of a struggle. You feel some responsibilities, and then you hear echoes of teachers telling you not to write "cause poems." I don't know of any good poems that came out of the protest years or the Vietnam War. Just because you get so involved in your cause that your emotions overpower what you want to say and the effectiveness of that. But there are things I feel almost obligated to write about. I wrote about relocation. I haven't so much any more, but maybe that's because I used up a lot of material. These latest poems talk in a real general way about relationships and why they don't work as well as they should—trust and stuff like that. Those are little causes. Those are where you have strong feelings.

I hate politics but I have very strong feelings about the current administration and I sometimes have to be careful. You can almost sense it. You can almost feel a point where you can just let it go, but you know the writing isn't going to be very good because it's too emotional. The best way to do it is to sit back and report objectively, show a situation and let the reader arrive at some kind of reaction, rather than trying to tell the reader how they're supposed to feel about an issue.

The poem in which you described the young Japanese-American kid holding the U.S. fighter plane was effective in that way.

He was holding it upside down, like it was topsy-turvy and mixed-up. I wanted the detail of the image to be a metaphor for the situation and the time, and then the irony of a U.S. fighter plane.

I think it said a lot without shouting.

Yes, it's a real mistake to shout, and use explanations and get carried away. Because regardless of how people feel about the issue, they almost instinctively turn away from it when it's treated in that manner. Nobody likes to be yelled and screamed at. Usually the people who read the poems are not the ones who need to be yelled and screamed at anyway.

Why do you write about paintings and photographs?

I'm not sure. It used to be that whenever I got into some kind of a writer's block I would do that. Partly because it forces you to be imagistic, use concrete details. I like painting. I have some artistic ability. So there's some connection.

Do you paint or draw much?

A bit. I like to go to museums. I like paintings, bookstores, posters, cards, movies—visual things.

When you write a poem about a painting, do you try to get the same effect that a painting would have?

It's more that you report the physical details of the painting but you try to capture some of the spirit, or the stuff that's off to the side, off the margin.

Are your poems more lyric than dramatic?

Probably lyric, although it varies. My poems are never very long. They hardly ever go beyond a page. I don't know why. I think that's just a style or personality type. I know that it's popular or has been popular for some poets to write page after page and they're still on the same poem. Then it becomes like writing a short story.

The shorter something is, there's more challenge in making it good, just because it doesn't have the length and content to carry it through any kind of mistakes or errors. If you really get down to it and write a five-line poem, it's got to be perfect.

Do you read much Oriental poetry?

Contemporary, hardly any. I like some of the novelists who were writing in the '30s. I mostly read poetry.

Li Po?

I like that and most of Rexroth's translations and Pound's.

They were writing in free verse and they were very imagistic. The only problems with those poems is that the poems tend to be descriptive and lack tension. But they're really nice pictures.

How close are those translations to the originals?

Well, that's always a big problem. When people talk about haiku I don't even want to recognize or acknowledge it because I don't think you can translate it. Haiku in English is totally different from Japanese haiku. I can't read Japanese but I know that. It's real simplistic to say haikus are seventeen syllables long and it's five, seven and five and there has to be a metaphor in the last line alluding back to something that's artificial.

Do you pattern your poems after Oriental models?

Not deliberately, but I think there's some influence there with my heritage. Even though I grew up in eastern Washington in a real white environment, I still had parents who spoke at least half Japanese, and the food, and just the conversations talking about family, about Japan. I think some of the sensibility is still oriented toward being precise and things like that.

Is it difficult to use a Japanese literary model when writing a poem in English about Americans?

That seems real artificial or contrived. In any kind of translation, you lose. Like if you translate from the Spanish or French you're going to maybe capture the detail and the images, but the sound, no way.

Do you have any desire to visit Japan?

At some point. I feel a little uncomfortable with not knowing the language and having everyone over there assume that I do. A good friend of mine, Garrett Hongo, is also a poet. He grew up in Gardena. He went over to Japan and he knew the language fairly well, he thought, but it was so fast and there were times when people would be real rude and yell at him because he was standing under a sign telling him the information that he was asking them for.

Are there things about the Northwest that are similar to what you know of Japan?

In a lot of the Japanese paintings and poetry there's a lot of water and evergreen trees. Tom Robbins talks about the similarity of the Skagit Valley to China and Japan. Probably the landscape has a lot of similarities. Probably there's some connection to the fact that my parents ended up in Skykomish because the landscape in Skykomish is very similar to the landscape in Japan where they came from.

Seattle does have traces of Asian influence, but it's real subtle. You see a lot more cherry trees here than you do in Spokane. In Spokane you see lilac bushes.

Why do you stay in Seattle?

I really like Seattle. I like water, I like the size of the city; it's not too big yet. Even though you can get stuck on the freeway and go through all that, it's still not as bad as other places. I would have a hard time leaving here permanently.

Do you think that living here makes a difference in your writing?

I think I'd be writing the same poems if I were living in Paris, it's just that the names would be changed, but the same types of things would be happening.

People say, "You have a salmon and a seagull in your poems so you must be a Northwest poet," but I travel to Mexico and to France and England and when you're there you write about the trees, the flowers, the pastries. I don't know that there are Northwest poets, I think that there are poets that live in the Northwest. There is a group who likes to foster that idea of regionalism. "We're better than you are. We're writing the poetry." But that's politics again.

Do you see yourself as part of a community of writers out here?

I don't actively pursue that. I have friends who are writers and poets. I get involved in readings and workshops, but a lot of my friends are not writers. I don't hang out at the workshop at the U like I used to. For a while I did, after I graduated. I used to go back there. There's kind of a tradition where Nelson's [Bentley] old students drop in and get involved. I haven't done that much lately, and I think it's almost consciously not wanting to be part of a group or clique or establishment. For years I didn't join our teachers' union. I don't like clubs.

Does it ever bother you that you can't make a living writing poetry?

It doesn't really bother me. I would like to be able to just write, but I'm not sure how successful I'd be. I know that part of having a job like teaching is that you come into contact with people. If all you did was write, you'd have to hang out in a coffee place, go out and have breakfast.

I'm kind of lucky because I have my summers off and I teach creative writing. The only time I don't enjoy it so much is with my freshmen, when I'm just teaching standard freshman English and the kids hate English and don't understand poetry and they're immature.

You have to be kind of a warden.

Yes. It's the only time I'd rather be doing something else. But my older kids, the juniors and seniors, are great. I really enjoy doing that. And it's a chance to use my writing in a different way. I feel I know what I'm talking about when I talk to them about writing, or a story or a poem. So it's a nice supplement.

I think I've evolved to the point where I tell people I'm a poet who happens to teach English out of necessity. But it used to be the other way around. And for a long time it was, "I'm a teacher." No mention of the poetry.

Do you plan to continue writing and publishing poetry?

Yes. Probably forever. Somewhere in the back of my mind I think I'd like to work on a novel. If I did that I know I'd write about the camps or about my family. There are fragments of stories I would like to save. But I always feel I need a lot of time to do that. Poetry, you have to write 200 or 300 poems before you start writing *poetry*. And maybe with fiction you have to write seventy-five bad stories and then they'll start getting better.

Unless you have some natural aptitude.

Yes. I don't conceive of myself as a natural poet. I conceive of myself as somebody who has to work hard, has learned a few tricks and for a long time was really compelled and driven. I owe that to Williams. He was a doctor and he was doing all this stuff and he was also doing this huge body of writing. He was talking about this in one of his books and I felt guilty because I wasn't writing while I was teaching school. Here he was delivering babies and working late at night, and he was still doing all this writing. He talked about compulsion, about being driven. I think that's really important in the arts. It almost transcends talent. You have to have a certain amount of talent but.... I know several people who graduated with me from the writing program who I thought were better writers than me, but who maybe haven't gotten books published, and a lot of it is just persistence or drive. After a while it gets real wearing, sending those poems out and getting rejection slips. You want to get them back out there, but it's easier just to say, "Don't worry about it," and go to a movie.

A.B.
Guthrie, Jr.

*T*HROUGH *his many novels and stories about the West, A.B. Guthrie, Jr. has been instrumental in helping Westerners define their sense of themselves and the country they live in. His first novel,* The Big Sky *(1947), presents the West in its unspoiled state, when mountain men such as the book's main character, Boone Caudill, roamed freely throughout the country—hunting, trapping, trading with the Indians.* The Way West *(1949) chronicles the settlers' journey by wagon train from the Midwest to the Oregon Country.* These Thousand Hills *(1956),* Arfive *(1970) and* The Last Valley *(1975) concern the settlement of the new land. In addition to these novels, Guthrie has written screenplays for the movies* Shane *(1953) and* The Kentuckian *(1955). He is the author of* The Big It *(1960), a book of short stories, and several other novels, including* Wild Pitch *(1973).* The Blue Hen's Chick, *his autobiography, was published in 1965. He is now working on a more complete version of his life story, as well as a whodunit set in England.*

The author was born in Bedford, Indiana, on January 13, 1901. Shortly thereafter, his family moved to Choteau, Montana.

He graduated from the University of Montana in 1923, and at-
tended Harvard University in 1944-45 as a Nieman fellow. He
served as a reporter and editor in Kentucky on the Lexington
Leader from 1926 to 1947. In 1950 Guthrie won the Pulitzer Prize
for fiction for The Way West.

Guthrie lives with his wife, Carol, twenty-five miles outside of
Choteau. Their house stands on rocky, wind-swept ground in the
foothills of the Rocky Mountains. The interview took place there in
the fall of 1986. Despite his eighty-six years and a fringe of gray
hair around his head, Guthrie's blue eyes still blaze with anger and
his voice becomes grave as he talks about the beauty of the land
and what men have done to destroy it.

What did growing up in Choteau teach you about the West?

When I was a boy, Choteau was still pretty much a pioneer
town. We had no automobiles; it was horse and buggy, saddle
horses and buckboards—things like that. I can remember booted
cowpunchers with their spurs, going in and out of saloons. And all
around Choteau were hunting grounds for ducks, sharp-tailed
grouse, rabbits. It was a wonderful country to grow up in—then.
The town was almost as big as it is now, but the surroundings were
not cultivated, and there hadn't been the sprawl there is now. We
always had a pony and a cow. Many families had cows in those
days. There were no dairies. You couldn't buy milk, so people kept
cows. And we always kept a flock of chickens, too.

How did you first become interested in the history of the
West?

My father developed an interest in the West. As the first principal of schools though, he was busy, so he couldn't pursue it. Neither did he have the money to buy the original sources that he
needed. Neither did I of course, until later. But through him I developed an interest in the West.

When you were growing up, were there people around like the
characters you later wrote about in your novels?

Somewhat, but I haven't ever written about actual characters.

The characters I write about exist in my mind. I think it's
treacherous work to write fiction about someone you know or
know of. I don't like it.

*Were there people around like Boone Caudill or Jim Deakins
or Dick Summers?*

Only in the vaguest sense. Now in Kentucky, in certain
mountaineer types, there is a deep strain of violence, and that in a
sense is Boone. I don't know where Jim Deakins came from. I just
had fun with him. I don't base characters on anyone.

Did you hear a lot of stories growing up in Choteau?

No, I didn't. I read before I could go to school. I was always a
great reader. My father used to read aloud to us—*The Jungle
Books*, Dickens—those were the stories I heard.

Why did you become involved in journalism?

We assumed it was the way to becoming an author. My
brother majored in journalism, so did my sister, and so did I. That
was my father's doing. He wanted us to know a trade that we could
fall back on.

I spent my high school years, after school and in the summer,
working in the *Acantha* office. I got to be a two-thirder, as the professionals call an apprentice, a two-thirder to being a pro.

Did you like the newspaper business?

In the beginning I liked it very much. It seemed exciting. But
as the years wore on, it got to be the same old story over and over.
I tired of it. My feelings toward it became as jaded as my excitement had been in the first place. It helped me, I suppose, but I
could wish, looking back, that I hadn't spent as long in journalism.
You see, the techniques of journalism and fiction writing are far
apart, though newspapermen tend to think that because they can
handle language in one medium, they can in another. That's false.
That's like saying you will be a good bricklayer because you're a
good carpenter. Newspapers deal with surfaces, by and large. Fiction doesn't. Good fiction goes much deeper.

Did you learn much about writing as a journalist?

I made myself learn. I didn't have any special instruction. I
just learned by trial and error and determination.

Had you wanted to write novels since you were younger?

Yes, I can't remember when I didn't want to.

When you were growing up, who were the writers you admired?

When I was a young man, I was far more rebellious than I am now, and I enjoyed Henry L. Mencken. I thought he was great. But just recently I bought his selected writings. You know, I can't stand him. He's so self-important. He knows everything.

I used to like Sinclair Lewis; I wouldn't go back and read him for anything. I don't think he could write well. He was a sort of trailblazer, but he wasn't a good writer.

How about Hemingway?

Hemingway was a good writer, in his early years especially, and in his short stories especially. I don't like his novels much; his short stories are great. He will stand as one of the people who taught us a lot about fiction writing. In his dialogue especially, every sentence, every word, goes somewhere. Hemingway will endure. I think in most of his later life he was kind of a hoax.

What about The Old Man and the Sea?

It's a little too moralistic for me, but some of it is fine writing. And even in his early writings, his best writings, some of it doesn't hold up anymore. I just reread "The Big Two-Hearted River." That doesn't hold up at all. Whereas it's still there in "The Short Happy Life of Francis Macomber." And "The Killers" is a damn good story, and so's "The Capitol of the World."

So he was a writer who you admired.

At his best, you bet. But even in those early stories, he was always a frightened man. He was always afraid of the gentler passions. The gentler side of life scared him, so he had to be the big macho kind of a guy. You can't see any tender emotions in anything he's written. Someone remarked, "His life was fitting, the final thing he killed was himself."

Were there Western writers whose work you liked?

I liked and still like James Schultz's *My Life as an Indian*. It stands up very well. One time my father was talking about Schultz's success in his writing and he said something I didn't understand. My father said, "He knows how to tell a story." That just went by me. And there's the whole craft of fiction: how to tell a story.

But back then, my reading was not informed reading. I knew what I liked and didn't like but I had no idea of what constituted good writing. I didn't arrive at any definition of good writing until my Nieman year at Harvard. Then I began to grasp the differences of viewpoint, the differences in technique, so then I began to understand.

And it was then that I developed the practice that I follow faithfully to this day: I hate the author on the page. That's why I can't read Hardy any more. I just despise the author on the page. I don't want to be reminded of the author. I don't give a damn about the author. I'm interested in his characters. As Ford Maddox Ford said, "The object of the novelist is to make the reader entirely oblivious of that fact that an author exists, and indeed of the fact that he is reading a book." That expresses my philosophy about writing entirely.

Did you come to this conclusion as a result of your study at Harvard?

Partly, but mostly it was because I ran into a terrific professor of English, who is my friend to this day. His name is Theodore Morrison, and he opened the doors of knowledge for me. A very fine man. Knows more about writing than I will ever know.

Was it there that you started The Big Sky?

I had started it earlier. I had two or three chapters written. I don't know how he endured me, it was so bad. We just kind of hit it off. He wasn't a New Englander, but he had the mannerisms of one. He was restrained; the criticism he made was always very mild. And here I was, a sort of breezy Westerner.

He went over those chapters and talked to me. For a long time I didn't know what he was saying; for six weeks I was just puzzled as could be. Then one night my wife and I went to a double-feature movie in Boston. The second movie was a Western in which everyone was pounding his chest to show the violence of his emotions. I said, "That's it. I've been hamming it."

And from then on it was as if a curtain had been lifted. I rewrote those chapters. I didn't finish the book then; I went on to

Breadloaf that summer and then back to my job. They gave me a lot of leeway on the job; I just had to make sure that the newsroom was running all right. I spent afternoons working on the novel. I sent every chapter to Ted for his criticism. He had none. He'd just say, "This is good, Bud." But you see, as restrained as he was, good was excellent to him.

When did you start writing The Big Sky?

Early 1944, while I was still in Kentucky. I started writing it because I thought no honest story of the mountain men had been told. The books all made a hero of the mountain men—romantic stuff. I wanted to tell an honest story.

How did you come up with the title?

The publisher and editor Bill Sloane and I had been at a loss for a title. Sloane had said, "Never mind, write a little biographical material." So I started writing about my father and his first day in Montana. My father had come from Indiana. And I said, "On his first morning, he got up early and went outside, and under that big sky a little shudder shook him, and he said, 'By George, I'm free.'" I sent that to my publisher and he said, "You've got the title: *The Big Sky*." I hadn't even thought of it.

How long did it take you to write the book?

It was a good two years; much of that was spent in research. Harvard had a good library on the subject, and also I was able to buy a good many prime sources. I took an awful lot of notes. I still have them.

Was Boone Caudill there early in the book?

Well, your characters grow. You introduce them and see what they make of themselves.

Was he originally the main character?

Yes. There are three main characters, but Boone is the protagonist.

Did you intend him to be the epitome of what the mountain men were about?

I don't know that I do things like that. I made him out to be himself. And if he happened to be the epitome, then that was that, but I don't work in that kind of a framework at all.

What did you feel about him as a character?

I was half sympathetic. But I knew at the end of *The Big Sky* that Boone Caudill was done. His life was bound to be anticlimatic and downhill. It seemed implicit in the book.

In the course of your research, did you come across a lot of men like Boone who couldn't get along as the West changed?

There's a theory that the West was settled by neurotics who couldn't get along in civilized society. And it's partly true, but it's not altogether true. We had a lot of people who were resistant to laws and order and who wanted to be away from society entirely. Boone was that type of person.

In writing The Big Sky, *how did you familiarize yourself with the territory?*

I had seen a good deal of it, but I hadn't seen as much as I wanted, and so I got some of it from books and letters. I had never been to Jackson, Wyoming when I wrote it, but I got the pictures and all through the Park Service and studied them until I felt I had it.

It was different with *The Way West*. I traveled the Oregon Trail as nearly as possible, by car, on foot. I felt I needed that. But I don't know. You can imagine yourself in another time if you read enough about it, and study enough. When I finished *The Big Sky* my wife said, "Thank God you came out of the last century."

Is there a bit of wistfulness in the book for the way things used to be?

I suppose there was some of that. And yet if I'd actually been there I'd probably have hated it: the savagery, the dirt, the cruelty to animals.

Was it difficult to dramatize that historical material, to make it into a story?

All writing is difficult. Don't make any mistake about it. Writing is a hard row. I don't know if it's harder to discipline historical material than it is to write in any present-day plot. I doubt it.

Did you conceive of the first three books as a trilogy?

Not to begin with, but after *The Big Sky* came out, I felt I ought to do this chronologically. The Oregon Trail came naturally then. Then the cattle country in Montana. There are some skips. I had nothing to say about the Mexican War except maybe a refer-

ence. I haven't dealt with gold-mining days in any degree, or with
the homesteading times, so there are some gaps, but by and large
this is a steady progression from 1830 to the end of World War II.

*In dramatizing the history of the West, did you think of your-
self as doing a service for people?*

No, I didn't think of doing a service. Anyone who pursues that
idea becomes a pamphleteer. I thought of being successful.

Was the westward migration inevitable?

Yes. I regret our treatment of the Indians, but that was inevitable, too. I think history has no case where a vigorous, domi-
nating people don't overcome the local inhabitants. You can look at
the Picts and the Saxons in England, or the Normans and Vikings.
It was one push after another. So I think it was inevitable. There
was so much cruelty and injustice that was involved, but it was in
the books that that would happen.

How is the Northwest different from the rest of the country?

Here in Montana, Wyoming, Idaho, especially, people are far
friendlier than they would be, for instance, in New York. I think
this sense of community is strongest when people live some distance apart. You can live in the same apartment building for years
without knowing your fellow tenants. But here, if we were in
trouble, people would come. Bud Olsen lives four miles away.
Chuck Blixrud is six or eight miles up in the canyon. He'd be here
immediately if we were in trouble. Similarly, we would go to their
aid.

I do not like the typical New Yorker at all. New Yorkers are
the most parochial people on earth. New York is it. Nothing else
counts. I hate that insular attitude. You find that in the Eastern
press. Unhappily it is New York and the whole Eastern seaboard
that dictates our reading tastes. That's true of the magazines, that's
true of the newspapers. A writer writing about the West has a hard
time getting much attention. The Eastern establishment tends to
ignore us. It's only the occasional person who gets much attention.
The New York Times alone is better about that. But take *The New
Yorker*, which in many ways I dislike thoroughly, or *Time*, or
Newsweek, or the Boston papers, the Washington papers. They
haven't time for us. They think the West is unimportant.

Is that attitude changing at all?

I haven't observed it. I do not think it is.

Do you think the fact that the West is less settled makes a big difference in the attitude of the people out here?

That's true. Our greatest asset is space. I hate to see this crazy development, to the detriment of natural beauty. Pollution of the watershed, damage to the air: this is what development means to me.

People are so thoughtless. The Teton River used to be excellent fishing. I used to walk out just a mile from Choteau when I was a boy and catch a mess of trout. There's no water there now, for several reasons: clearcutting in the headwaters, overgrazing, plowing and irrigation. We're apt to have a spring freshet and then the water goes down to hardly more than a trickle. And west of town it's nothing. I can't believe that's good for the country.

Did you move back to Choteau so that you could be close to the mountains?

Yes. I like to have mountains within easy access, but also I like room for my eye to roam, so we're ideally situated. I don't like to be right in the mountains.

Was growing up here important to your writing?

I think it was very important. I think that is one of the reasons I've chosen the subjects I've chosen.

Is landscape one of the most important subjects of your writing?

Oh, yes. This country has shaped me as it shapes all of us who live here long enough. We develop a sort of unacknowledged kinship with it.

In what ways does it shape you?

That is a question that permits no answer. I don't know. I just know it does shape us.

How did you come to write the screenplay for the movie Shane?

Total accident. I was in Kentucky and my agent called me and said, "How would you like to write a screenplay?" And I said, "I don't know. I never have. I don't know what it's about." And he said, "Well, there's a director named George Stevens and he wants a person who can write Western language and I told him you could, and he wants you to come."

I didn't know a thing about movie writing, not a thing about Hollywood, but I got along fine with Stevens. We hit it off. I didn't have any great difficulty.

Did you know at the time what a good movie it would turn out to be?

I knew Stevens was trying to make it a fine movie, but I didn't see it in total until a year later. They kept it in the can, so to speak, for a year because *High Noon* was doing so well. They asked me down to Hollywood a year later to see it, and it just knocked me over, it was so good.

The phone rings in the kitchen. Carol Guthrie takes the call. After she hangs up, Guthrie asks, "Who was that, honey?" She says, "He wanted to know if you had seen the Acantha. *There's a letter in there from a person who wants to shoot all the grizzly bears and you." Guthrie says, "Tell him I've got a couple of guns myself."*

We've been engaged in a great controversy. Not that I sought it, but I seem to be the spokesman of the people who are on the side of the bears. That's all right. A little controversy never hurt anybody.

Why is it important to protect the grizzly bears?

Because they're symbolic, because they're the greatest animal that North America has produced, because they have a place in our history, because I hate to see anything extinguished. We have had a lot of regrets about species we've extinguished already.

It's in the nature of man to think that the planet was made for his benefit. It's not true at all. It's made for the benefit of all living creatures, if there's any purpose in it, which I sometimes doubt. We've chivvied that great bear from the Mississippi, across the long prairies, across the high plains, to his last refuge in the Rocky Mountains. Christ, let's let him be.

So animals should be protected whether they're useful to men or not?

Hell, yes. I don't go for this thing that the earth was made for man, that man was the favored species. That's just not true. It's anthropocentrism at its worst.

When you were younger, did you read the Bible?

I read it, I went to Sunday school. I've rejected all that. I think organized religion is damn foolish. I'm not even sure I'm a Christian. I don't think I am.

Did the Bible have much of an effect on you?

Probably made me more rebellious. The only thing that you can get out of the New Testament we've already developed in ourselves to a degree—qualities of compassion, mercy, honesty.

When it comes to talking about animals, do you think the Bible was misinterpreted?

No, the Bible, the Old Testament especially, is very much at fault. "Go forth and populate the earth. It was made for you." Nuts. That's foolishness. That's probably our first trouble. There are too many damn people in the world. The Bible has to bear a lot of responsiblity for our present predicament.

Richard
Hoyt

NOVELIST *Richard Hoyt imparts a twist to every story he tells, finding humor in even the most serious of subjects. His main characters see themselves as actors in a kind of global theater of the absurd. Journalist Jim Quint and CIA agent James Burlane romp through the world of espionage and international intrigue, defying superiors, disdaining authority, ignoring protocol and succeeding generally because they don't take the circus of the world too seriously. Detective John Denson takes cases because he "feels part of a tradition of freelance wise guys." Denson is a gumshoe of the '80s: he can crack wise with the best of them, but he doesn't carry a gun, eschews violence, and triumphs more through wit and imagination than brawn and brass knuckles.*

Hoyt is the author of the thrillers Siege *(1987),* The Dragon Portfolio *(1986),* Head of State *(1985),* Cool Runnings *(1984),* Trotsky's Run *(1982) and* The Manna Enzyme *(1982). He has written four John Denson mysteries:* Fish Story *(1985),* Siskiyou *(1983),* 30 For a Harry *(1981) and* Decoys *(1980).*

The author worked as a counterintelligence agent with Army Intelligence from 1964 to 1966, as a newspaper reporter from 1967 to 1972, and as a communications professor from 1972 to 1982. He received a B.S. in journalism from the University of Oregon in 1963, an M.S. in journalism from the University of Oregon in 1967, and a Ph.D. in American studies from the University of Hawaii in 1972. He was born in Umatilla, Oregon, on January 28, 1941.

The interview took place in the summer of 1986 in the work-room of his house in Beaverton, Oregon. Hoyt is a tall, lanky man with silver-gray hair and a whimsical lilt to his voice. After pouring me a glass of John Denson's favorite beverage—screwtop red wine—Hoyt settled into a chair and began talking about his work.

All of your books are topical. Does this have anything to do with your background as a newspaper reporter?

I think that's true. You think of a hook or a lead or some kind of peg. What the hell, I want something that's a little bit topical. My books start real fast, and I work hard at it. Just like you do in a newspaper story, you want a lead that will hook 'em in the first couple 'graphs and get 'em going. Don't give 'em any reason to stop reading or to have to reread. Go to the end. That's what I do in my books—if I can.

So you really start out fast?

I jump right into the story, first paragraph. Start right out and go. Lay smoke. Don't wander in. That's dumb. That's a problem that beginners have; they think they can put in all kinds of detail and background and narration and doo-dah, and then it's actually twenty or thirty or forty pages before you actually begin the story. You can't do that, because you won't get published.

Did you want to be a writer from early on?

That's really hard to say in retrospect. If you're a farm boy, the idea of being a writer doesn't occur to you. It's like wanting to be an astronaut and walk on the moon. It's in another world. But somehow I've popped through some sort of warp. Here I am. It's fun. I guess I wanted to write. Why else?

Why did you start out by writing for a newspaper?

With a newspaper you could get a job, hey, and a salary. You could earn your living on a typewriter. It's an achievable ambition to be a newspaper reporter. Most intelligent people can master the elements of the craft. It is a craft. It can be taught. That's why there are schools of journalism.

But fiction is in another realm. It's not necessarily an achievable ambition for everybody. That's the difference. You can aspire to be a magazine or newspaper journalist or write non-fiction books, and achieve that, whereas the odds against earning a living writing fiction are long.

Did it help your writing to work on a newspaper?

Definitely. Writing for a newspaper cuts the fat out of your writing. You're required to write simple, straightforward standard English strong on verbs. And also the notion of getting a reader started on a story, and keeping his or her interest. Those are the essential skills I learned on a newspaper.

But every writer will tell you the best way to learn is the way *he* learned. I'm just like that. I learned to write on newspapers, so I think, "Hey, that's a great way." But there are other ways, probably just as good or even better.

Did you want to write novels while you were working on a newspaper?

The ability to write novels very largely has to do with your personal circumstances. I get involved in these stories and I don't come up for air. Day and night I'm thinking just about these stories. I'm very self-absorbed in that sense. Just thinking constantly, constantly, constantly, constantly, constantly, constantly. And it's hard for somebody. It really is.

I'm twice divorced. With my first wife, when I was a newspaper reporter, it would have been impossible. Plus the fact, when you write for a newspaper all day, to come home and face that typewriter and keep on truckin' is pretty hard. When I got a job teaching at the University of Maryland, then I had summers off, most of December and a week in March. When you teach journalism there's not a lot of intellectual substance there, hey. It gets pretty repetitious. So I was able to start writing fiction. But it wasn't really until I had split from that woman in January of 1978 that I just dove in and wrote, in this order: *Decoys*, *The Siskiyou Two-Step*, which was later published as *Siskiyou*, and *30 For a Harry*. But they were published out of order.

So you write a book a year?

Yeah, but I say again, it's all-absorbing and consuming to be able to do that. I could write one of those books and take two or three years, but if I did that, I'd have to teach again. Last year I made, by writers' standards, good solid money. But it makes business people smile, because it's not much by their standards. But I want to write these books; there's nothing else I want to do. I'm happy.

When you started writing fiction, why did you choose to write detective novels?

That wasn't very well thought out. I'd just been reading some early Dick Francis, *Enquiring Bonecrack*, and a man named Reuel Denney who was my professor at the University of Hawaii said, "You can write as good as this guy. Why don't you try it? Do it. See." Francis was the last writer I read before I launched out writing *Decoys*. So for whatever reason, I sat down with a private detective and gave him my background, just to see. That's a good little book. People like that book.

Yes, it's funny.

But it was an accidental book, because I didn't know what the hell I was doing.

How many revisions did you have to make?

I don't remember. I didn't have the woman character at first, and she made the book. My editor suggested I come up with a woman. So I came up with that bet. I just ran it through my typewriter again.

Did the editor help you much in writing the book?

My editor, Fred Graver, made the suggestion. It was a good suggestion. I haven't had editors who've tried to write my books; their suggestions have been mostly constructive. I appreciate their help.

I have a woman editor now. She's good. I think it's better for a man to have a woman editor and vice versa. For me it means in this last book that I took more chances. I came up with a real good woman character, a female spy. I'm proud of her. I took more chances than I would have if I had had a man editor, 'cause after all what does he know? He doesn't know any more about women than

I know, for Christ's sake, and it turns out I probably don't know very much.

Was it easier to get a detective novel published than a serious novel?

I thought that was the case but I don't think it is. I was thinking small because I didn't know what I could do. If I had to do it over again I'd probably start out with something else. But you never know.

Are you going to write more Denson books?

My publisher wants me to write an occasional one, but I'm trying to shake the label of mystery writer; I don't want to be considered a mystery writer. These thrillers are satiric and sardonic. They're really congenial. I like doing them. They're much harder to do; they're much more complicated and sophisticated. I get a lot more pleasure out of them, and I'm making more money off of them.

There still is a demand for the others, and occasionally when I have a superior idea, I'll do a Denson. But I don't want to have to do Denson after Denson after Denson after Denson like detective writers do because it would drive me wild. Then you're stuck looking at the world out of this detective's eye.

Did you read a lot of detective novels and thrillers when you were growing up?

During the summers I drove a wheat truck up at Pendleton [Oregon]. I'd be sitting there, waiting for the wheat truck to come by. It would come around and dump. Then I'd wait, then it would dump again. Then I would drive down and dump it at the elevator. The hired man had a great big cardboard box of Shell Scott mysteries, so I read all of those, and Mickey Spillanes. Mickey Spillanes were real sexy for the time.

But it was almost by accident that you started writing detective novels?

You see, I wanted to be a professional and earn my living at it. I didn't want to be subsidized by a college and have to teach, because I found it hard to deal with teaching. I wanted to be independent. I wanted to live off book royalties. I didn't want to be beholden to institutions. I know that a lot of good writers, who are

serious writers, who write novels primarily of character and understanding, don't make very much money, don't sell very many
books, so they're forced to teach. I didn't want to do that. So I
thought, "Well, if you get going as a mystery writer, there's a possibility of building up enough people who like your character, and
you can do it." That's why I started with Denson. So now I've gone
off in this other direction and it's working for me. Whereas if I decided to be real serious and win awards, I'd still be teaching. And
instead of being able to write all day and all night long, or go anywhere in the goddamn world to write, I would have the fall semes-
ter coming up, classes to prepare for and all that bullshit. I just
don't want it.

Is Denson a kind of Sam Spade for the '80s?

Denson's a good private detective and I'm proud of my books,
but I'm wary of those kind of comparisons. Besides that, the whole
business of Sam Spade kind of tires me anyway. What the hell?
There are a whole lot of good detective writers around.

How is Denson different from Spade?

He's of a different generation, different entirely. He doesn't
believe in violence, doesn't carry a weapon, and I guess is far less
of a traditional man in the way that Sam Spade was. But he has certain things in common. He believes in certain codes of honor, and
correct and civilized behavior, and justice—the kinds of themes
that run through private detective novels. He deals with people
differently than Sam Spade does. He deals with women a lot differently. Times have changed. Detectives have to change too.

What's the difference between a detective novel and a thriller?

Usually the thriller is bigger in scope. The classic definition of
difference in structure is that in a mystery you're working through
what is known, to some sort of solution. You ask the question,
"Who killed him?" And you go through all you can find out and you
solve it.

A thriller is where you go through the unknown to some sort
of climax.

What makes thrillers distinct as a genre?

Tension is the key, and story. But good ones have good characters as well, although the characters don't dominate. I try to do
my best to have good characters, plus good stories. But these are

novels of knowledge. You find things out. What's gonna happen? Who did what? More serious fictions are novels of understanding. Why did they do that? These are stories of character and people more.

I write entertainments. I entertain people. They want a story, that's first of all. Hey, they don't want to work, they want to be entertained, right? Good time when you read? Sure. They don't want all that heavy duty doo-dah stuff. I try to write for a literate, sophisticated reader, somebody who's hip to all kinds of things, but irony especially, right, and who likes an interesting little bit of history thrown in, exotic locations with some good details and stuff.

So I go out there and hang out with Rastaman in Jamaica. Hey, it was fun. And I went and wrote for five months in the red light district of Amsterdam for *Cool Runnings*. And I rode the train across the Soviet Union. Then I hung out in Hong Kong and Macao to do the book that's coming up.

How well do your books fit into the categories of detective novels and thrillers?

They don't fit well. That's one of my problems. I'm a hard sell for a publisher because I don't do spy stories like, "This is what it's like to be a spy." The real world realism. I don't do that, but I try to get the little details right.

In all good books, the author has to have something to say. So I always try to have something to say in my books, various kinds of themes I work around. Like that anomaly business in *Cool Runnings*.

I also try to give my readers real characters, with their quirky little identities.

But you don't write straight realistic stuff?

No. If John Le Carré is the Balzac of spy stories, I'd be the Jonathan Swift.

Are your books parodies in any way?

No, I don't regard them as parodies. I just set up to tell a story with my guy; I don't think about other people's books.

Why do you write thrillers in the third person and detective stories in the first person?

You can write thrillers in the first. But it limits you. You have to follow that one character around. So if you write in the third person you can go from person to person and you can keep a lot of tension and suspense going.

Do you find the detective and thriller genres limiting?

With the private detective one, sure, that's limiting. For one thing, you're stuck with the first person. Second, you're stuck with a serious character.

Why are you stuck with the first person?

You're not exactly, but if you want to do a classic private-eye book it's the first person.

But the thriller genre doesn't limit you?

No. Heck, I can explore all kinds of things. In the one coming up I'm exploring greed, and I've given the reason for the Chinese economic turnaround. *The* reason, impeccably logical. So I can roam and play all over the planet, with all kinds of themes, stories, ideas, characters. Whereas mysteries are much more confining, especially if you have a character who is confined to one city or one area, which Denson is—to the Pacific Northwest.

Would you like to write books outside those two genres?

Maybe some day. Whatever. See, you have to write a book that comes out of you naturally and spontaneously. You're driven. You want to do this book. That's the way I do it, rather than trying to say, "This is what the market wants, or this is some sort of fad or fashion." Mostly that doesn't work anyway. The hell with it. I just come up with an idea that strikes my fancy, take off and do the best I can.

Are there rules that you go by in writing a book?

No, I don't have any rules. There are things I try to do, mainly keep the reader turning pages. If you get too rule-bound, then there's a sameness. I try not to write the same book twice. There have been some well-known private-detective writers who've been accused of writing the same book over and over.

How can they do that and still keep interested?

They have some sort of genius to be able to do that, and do that, and do that. You have to admire them. I know how much work it takes.

What do these books have to do with good and evil?

Most books have to do with good and evil in some way. That's what gives books their tension.

But in detective novels and thrillers it seems more pronounced.

That's because they're plot books more than character books. You're dealing with things that happen, more than with ambiguities of the spirit, confrontations of good and evil, marriages gone bad and middle-aged men wondering what they're going to do with their lives—all that crap.

But you're aware of the tension between good and evil when you're writing your books?

That's Manichean though. The story's the thing. I want a story that interests me. When you tell a story that has tension and drama and you can get the reader's interest, questions of good and evil will be involved, questions of civilized and uncivilized behavior. I don't think in the abstract. Everyday at the typewriter, I'm thinking concretely, "How can I advance this story?" and make it so it's not redundant, so it's interesting, so that my reader hasn't come across it in one of my books in the past.

It has to have characters which the reader can identify with, and characters which people believe. But I never think in English-professor terms in how I approach it.

Would you say that a lot of your books are tragicomedies?

Yeah, sure.

Is that true of most thrillers?

Some, but not most. See, that's part of the marketing problem with my books. How do you describe them to readers? It's hard. But once I get readers to read one of my books, they buy more than one. So if I just stick with it, writing a good one every year, one that won't fail to get a sale for one of my other titles, then it will grow and get better and better. You build up readers just by word of mouth and by extending your body of work so that there are a whole bunch of titles out there, good ones, quality books.

It took Dick Francis a long damn time before his books were up there on the bestseller list, but he'd been writing good books for years. Same way with Elmore Leonard. They had the capacity to keep writing good books, and the determination and the discipline not to stop, and the confidence to keep going. And they did that, maybe the hard way, but they still did it.

Do you admire those two writers?

Sure. They're good writers. It's not just that the recent Dick Francises or the recent Elmore Leonards were better than *Fifty-Two Pick-up* or one of his early ones. No, no, no, no. They're not any better. This guy's been writing good books for a long time. It's just that people just got around to discovering him for one reason or another. But you just can't get your reputation on a book every three or four years.

So you have to write a book fairly often?

Sure. You don't have to pop 'em out like farts, every three months or something, but you should be able to write a good book every year.

How well does humor fit within these genres?

The book's the reflection of the tastes and the personality and character of the writer. Hey, it's us. We can't write them any differently. This is the way it is. I started *Head of State* determined to be real serious but I couldn't maintain it.

Is it difficult to make a book suspenseful and funny?

You mean to maintain tension and have it be funny at the same time?

Right.

I don't know. I just write the best books I can. It's not like I'm trying to do this or that; I just write the book. I don't always have a lot of control; I do the best I can. I'm always conscious of story, and of pacing. But at the same time I like to screw around and have fun. And I like the erotic and I like the sardonic. So that stuff just comes out. No stopping it. I guess you could say that I couldn't take this seriously as a kind of book. I'm having fun with it; I'm not parodying it, mind you. I'm just writing these entertaining stories.

I don't revere institutions, period. It's a circus. There are clowns and acrobats and fucking lion-tamers, and everything else. It's a zoo. But I don't take them seriously. I'm not a true believer. I'm not any kind of *ist* — socialist, communist, Republican, Democrat. I don't like to identify with groups. I don't have a lot of respect for 'em. I'm just loose about it.

Do you think that writing about violence and terrorism in any way encourages it?

No. There are violence and terrorism for political and ideological and religious reasons. It's not going to go away. So stopping writing about it certainly won't stop it.

Will writing about it have any effect one way or the other?

I don't know. I don't write to change people's minds, anyway. I just write to write entertaining stories and have some fun. If they're changed by it, I guess that's good, but that's not the reason I'm writing them. I write 'em the way I write 'em because that's the way I believe. I don't write 'em because I'm trying to educate, or anything. I don't look at it that way. It would be insulting to the people attracted to my books. They wouldn't like it; it would put them off. They would sense that, and say, "Well, screw you. I'm not reading you. I've got my own opinions, thanks." But I do have opinions. They're opinionated books.

Is it harder to set a crime novel in a place like Seattle than it would be to set it in L.A. or Chicago?

Listen, they've all been done before. Seattle has the advantage of not being done quite as much as the others. So it's a good city. That's part of the reason I set my guy up there.

Why did you set the Denson books in Seattle rather than Portland?

It's a bigger city. It's got that Sound, got Canada right there, got Vancouver, got Victoria, got mountains all around, got big-league sport franchises. Portland is a small town. It's a nice place, but in the imagination of the larger country, Seattle is much more visible. It's stupid, folly, dumb to write books and expect to earn a living off readers from one section of the country. You can't just do that.

Was the region important to the Denson books?

Well, I wanted to get a sense of realism. I've grown up in this area so I know it a bit. Physical detail gives your book believability. People like that. People in the Northwest like the Denson books because they like to have books set in their area of the country.

Is a detective novel written about the Northwest going to be much different than a detective novel set in another area?

I guess not. It ought to be a little different because of the area of the country you're dealing with, but what makes it different is the telling of the story and the attractiveness of the detective. I have to like the detective and want him to succeed. And then the writing and telling of the story has to have a little fizz to it, a little style. Because there are a lot of writers out there who tell an okay story, but the writer doesn't show any particular grace of expression or felicity of phrase, or intelligence. It's okay, it's all right, it's quite well done, all the basics of the story are there, but there's just no spark.

The most colorful geography can't make up for that. You can have a guy down there with all that L.A. sleaze and have him talk about it and write about it and describe it, and it's okay, but it has no snap or life or fizz to it.

A lot of people who are best-selling novelists, and very successful ones, are not good stylists but are good storytellers. Dick Francis is no great stylist, but man, he's a helluva storyteller. You buy his book and you expect a good quick story with maybe some class difference, and this guy sort of head-down and plowing through all this stuff, these villains lurking in the background. It's well done; it's professional.

Who are the stylists among detective writers?

There are a lot of them out there—Ross Thomas, Elmore Leonard, that guy Thomas Perry, the Englishman Gavin Law, and Bridget Connor—fabulous writers who are respected among their peers and earn money. All of them are steady producers of stylish books. They're stylish writers. Smart guys. Witty. With a sense of the ironic, the outrageous and the absurd. And it's reflected in their books.

But good writing doesn't necessarily equal great financial success and fame and celebrity. Once in a while it does. It's good when a guy like Elmore Leonard is recognized by *Newsweek*. Good for him. He deserved it. He's worked hard and writes good books.

How do you get ideas for your books?

I don't know. I just get 'em. It's not anything you set about to do logically, the process of deduction or induction. It just wells up out of your subconscious.

How do you come up with the names for your characters?

Sometimes I pick them off the back of book spines, sometimes out of a phone directory.

Is the name important?

Well, I have to be comfortable with it. It has to be something that is easy to pronounce, so that the reader is not put off by that word. And it has to be appropriate for the character, obviously.

In what ways do your main characters resemble you?

They're me, but I'm not them. John Denson's probably one version of me, James Burlane's another, but the one that's closest to me is Jim Quint out of *Cool Runnings*. He's in this next book. He's going to be riding in a camel race.

How do you plot your books?

As I go.

Do you start with the first chapter and then ad-lib?

Me, I get a broad idea of the story and then just start in and rewrite to make everything fit. So it sort of builds. I discover ideas as I go along, subtract some, add some, move around. I've got a system worked out on my computer that enables me to know what I'm doing.

What relation do the characters bear to the plot?

You add what characters are necessary to the plot and no more if you can help it. You want a cast of interesting people, people with some passion or beliefs, something that makes them interesting; you don't want a bunch of dullards. The people that read these books want to escape from reality anyway, and they want something funny, something they're going to learn.

What is your work schedule like?

Usually I start writing at seven-thirty in the morning and go till about twelve-thirty or one o'clock in the afternoon. Then I'll knock off and start in again at eight or nine at night and go to eleven or twelve. So I've got two writing periods.

What is the purpose of your books?

That's tough. I guess to entertain, enlighten, instruct, amuse readers of sensitivity and intelligence. If people just want fucking and strangling, other writers will give them more of that. I don't think they're reading mine for that reason, which might limit the amount of readers I can ever collect.

So you write them primarily for people to enjoy?

Sure, that's why they buy them. They don't want to suffer, right?

Why do they enjoy them?

A book is different to everybody that reads it. When you read one of my books it's a different experience for you because you have a different background. It's a creative act each time out, on your part as well as my part. I suspect that my readers typically are fairly well-educated people who like stylish writing but who don't want to get heavy-duty and philosophical, who want to be entertained. But it's very hard to say, because we don't run surveys, we just guess.

Why do men like to read about a bachelor, a free-lancer?

Because of that freedom. Men are settled in, have families, and all kinds of responsibilities. It's a form of escape for them; they can have adventures, too. It's the same for women. They have this romantic ideal, and they're married and after a while the sex loses its poop, and their husband is not very damn romantic, he's tired. So they're reading those kinds of romances.

It's perfectly understandable. People get the same kind of escapist entertainment from television, only it's not as well done. Its story lines are simple, its characters are predictable. Whereas I'm writing escapist entertainment for literate, intelligent people. They read, too.

How do women figure in your books?

I like them to be independent and intelligent. Readers are crazy, though. I was in Miami and I was talking to this lawyer who had read *Cool Runnings*. Almost everybody just loves that book. He said he didn't like that book. And I said, "Why didn't you like that book?"

And he said, "Well, your woman wasn't good-looking enough. She wasn't a beautiful woman."

When I wrote that book I purposefully gave her some physical flaws, so she wouldn't be perfect. And it annoyed him. Isn't that amazing? I couldn't believe it. I asked him, "What about the rest of the book?"

"It was a wonderful book," he said, "but I wanted her to be better-looking, and she wasn't."

There's no accounting for taste like that.

Also in *Cool Runnings*, I deliberately didn't have Jim Quint or Mad Marty Spivak save the day. I did that deliberately as a comment on heroes. They don't always win. Sometimes they're late and they don't make it. So it's dangerous to have bombs and stuff around; somebody's gonna fuck up sometime and something's gonna happen. That was the whole point of the book, right?

Okay. So I got this letter from a woman in New York. She said it was a wonderful book, but she was sore because of that very reason—the heroes didn't save the day, which is a convention for thrillers. She didn't like it.

People want to have closure. Enter the hero, the problem comes, the hero resolves it. Another closure: hero meets girl, there are problems, they come together. They want that sort of closure, a feeling that things are going to work out. They read escapist fiction partly, I'm convinced, to be reassured. In fact the term thriller is a misnomer, because they're not thrilled at all. They're satisfied. The good triumphs and the bad. . . . We all know that's bullshit, right?

Tess
Gallagher

TESS Gallagher builds her poems from the bits and pieces of everyday experience, often speaking through poetry for those whose lives might not otherwise find literary expression —loggers, longshoremen, a quiltmaker, a woman dying of cancer, and others. She says of her poetry, "When I was a young girl salmon-fishing with my father in the Strait of Juan de Fuca in Washington State I used to lean out over the water and try to look past my face, past the reflection of the boat, past sun and darkness, down to where the fish were surely swimming. I made up charm songs and word-hopes to tempt the fish, to cause them to bite my hook. I believed they would do it if I asked them patiently and with the right hope. I am writing my poems like this. I have used the fabric and the people of my life as the bait."

Her collections of poetry include: Stepping Outside (1974), Instructions to the Double (1976), Under Stars (1978), Portable Kisses (1978), Willingly (1984) and Amplitude: New and Selected Poems (1987), all published by Graywolf Press. In 1986, she published her first collection of short stories, The Lover of Horses, with Harper and Row. Her book of essays, A Concert of Tenses

(1986), was published in the University of Michigan "Poets on Poetry" series. She has written essays for various periodicals, screenplays for television, and has collaborated with Raymond Carver and Michael Cimino on two screenplays, one of which, Dostoevsky (Capra Press), was recently translated into Italian (Monadori Press).

Gallagher was born in 1943 in Port Angeles, Washington. She spent much of her early life in and around the forested foothills of the Olympic Mountains, helping her parents with the business of logging, and keeping house for a family of seven. At age sixteen she began working as a reporter for the Port Angeles Daily News. *She later attended the University of Washington, where she studied with Theodore Roethke, obtaining a B.A. in 1968 and an M.A. in 1970. She received an M.F.A. from the University of Iowa in 1974.*

Her awards include a Guggenheim Fellowship, a National Endowment for the Arts Award, two Governor's Awards from the state of Washington, and numerous other prizes for poetry. She has taught at the University of Montana, Kirkland College, St. Lawrence University, the University of Arizona, and currently teaches at Syracuse University where she has been awarded the Chancellor's Citation for her teaching and writing.

The interview took place in the summer of 1986 at the house she built outside Port Angeles where she lives with the writer Raymond Carver. "Sky House," as she calls it, sits on a bluff overlooking the Strait of Juan de Fuca, within earshot of surf breaking below on the beach. Over a bottle of Tsingtao beer, Gallagher, a dark-haired woman of unflagging good humor, talked of the journey that led her away from Port Angeles and finally, in recent years, back again.

After living on the East Coast for so long, why did you decide to move back to Port Angeles?

This is a love affair I'm involved with out here. It doesn't let me go, it wants me here. I have to obey. I've traveled everywhere—China, Brazil, lived in Ireland and England—but Port Angeles is my home.

My family is here. I still have a strong connection to family.

My mother is one of my best friends. I see her usually for tea every day. She's a widow now, so our relationship has gotten even more important, because I'm the one she confides in. She inspired a lot of my stories. One thing that began to develop between us as we began to spend more time with one another is that I could make use of her stories to create something new.

I love this body of water out here. I've always felt a closeness to water and to these mountains. I never feel far from this place, no matter where I've been, and I'm always waiting to get back here.

There are a few lines in a recent poem of mine which describe both me and my poetry:
"Likewise find me
   dependent on starlight and other crude
   fluctuations of the marketplace, troublesome to
   extract, and, like a jade coffin, impossible to move from my
      kingdom."
Poetry's the kingdom that has allowed me to return to my physical kingdom which is this peninsula, this town. This is a small community, and it's a community I've had an ongoing relationship with ever since I was a child. The values here were a part of the tensions in my life from the start. It's a very young, fresh part of the world, and yet it has some things which aggravate me—the pioneer attitude of, "Let's see what we can get from this place." It has its destructive side. There have been a lot of mistakes made, and attitudes toward resources are still pretty primitive. I'm thinking of the timber industry and the hunting and trapping policies of the area. Still there are some very good things that have happened on this particular peninsula just because it's a peninsula. Many elements of this natural environment have been preserved here against the odds.

In the East, you take your measure more often from the community of man, but here you're constantly aware of a very different kind of space and time. If I look at that tree [points to a Douglas fir tree], the tree tells me to slow down. That tree and those mountains are enforcing an alternate attitude. I watch the tides come in and go out. I know there's a force at work that's very mysterious and which is doing its thing, all the time I think I'm doing my very important thing. I'm aware of wildlife and space given over to that because of the Olympic National Park.

Does the spirit of the place get into your poetry?

Well, I'm not a naturalist in the activist sense of the word, though perhaps writing with a feeling of the sacred about a place is a kind of activism. I'm really perhaps more interested in human relationships. But nature comes into this. You take a poem of mine like "Boatride," where I'm talking about an experience where nothing happens. The characters just go out and ride around in a boat on the water, and these two different times come together: the time in which the father is already dying, and the time when he's out there in the boat trying to catch fish which they don't catch. That's a very Zen poem. And yet it had some of that pioneerness of my father, who wants to catch the fish, who wants to "use the resource," as they say in the fish and wildlife management lingo. What can be done? These fish must be caught. And yet, we experience the recalcitrance of the environment: the dogfish keep biting the line. And the father keeps slashing their throats when they get on his line: the violence of the pioneer.

Really, this pioneer attitude is so strong here. Unless that kind of strength, insistence, that kind of violence, had been a part of those men and women, no clearing would have been made, I suppose. You need a certain amount of determination to make a life in a wilderness, though this doesn't conscience continuing to flaunt what has to be a trust.

Are you using the resource too, in a way?

Not in the way you might expect. Not in a vigorous outdoor sense. I don't even hike now as I did when I was a kid. I go for walks into the woods or along the Strait. There's a spiritual nearness I have with the area now. There's a solitude I'm getting in this portion of my life, while my East Coast life seems to be an involvement with that literary community. My students are there and many of my friendships, though the longer I'm west the more I enter into the activities here, like the readings at the Elliott Bay Book Company.

How important is the natural world to your work?

It's very important. It's important to keep in your consciousness that you came from that ruthless but strangely calm world. And you're going back to that. It has a language, too. Part of what you're doing as a writer is to make that silent language of mountains and trees and water part of your language. It's speaking all the time, and I hear it speaking.

It's very important because it affects my sense of what it is to be human. Looking at trees or a shell or a fish, their difference tells me something about myself.

So it's important for you to live close to the mountains and water?

Yes, the magnitude of the mountains, and knowing that wild creatures exist there. And I don't have to take pictures of them or even see them for them to be meaningful to me. It's not a commodity, that mountain. It has escaped the commodity orientation of this country, except as it becomes a tourist attraction. Even if I never go up there, if I just sit here and know that those mountains exist and that there are mountain goats and cougar and bear and deer, that's important. Just like Wild Horse Annie who wanted to preserve wild horses. She hadn't even seen a wild horse when she became involved with saving the horses. She knew that there were wild horses in the Prior Mountains, and the *idea* of wild horses, herds of wild horses, was important to her idea of the West. The horses were a part of some spiritual entity that needed protecting. I have a similar connection with these mountains.

Is your attitude toward the natural world more of an appreciation?

I feel it's a kind of companionship. I feel like these elements are with me, and I am with them. I'm not *at* them, and I'm not *in* them; I'm *with* them. They accompany me. So I'm always looking to see how I'm feeling about them, what they're giving me.

There's a kind of transparency in the relationship, too. Some days when I'm not really aware, I'm getting these little glimpses of trees and water. They're nourishing me in ways that I'm not even aware of.

I'm very conscious of sky because I have these seven holes cut in the roof of my house and I often see a gull flying over, or the reflection of a bird floating onto this glass coffee table, or an eagle flying past along the beach. If Ray's here, he'll call out, "The eagle's passing." And I'll run up to the highest point of the house to catch a glimpse of the eagle because it's a spirit sign: good things are afoot, the eagle has passed, the eagle has blessed us. We've seen him today.

What was it like growing up in Port Angeles?

The important things to know are that I come from a family of five children, and that my father came here and began working as a logger, and that he sent for my mother who had been working as a cook in Denver. They had been writing to each other and seeing each other for ten years. I've written about this in the essay "My Father's Love Letters." She was a farm girl from Missouri. They got married and began a logging operation together.

I was the oldest of five children. There were no babysitters, there was no such thing as day care in those days, or if there was, we couldn't have afforded it. So we were raised in the clearing where the logging operation was taking place. My mother once had to save our lives because a tree was heading in our direction. She threw us into a ditch, my brother and I, and then protected us with her own body. Only the upper boughs thrashed down on us.

It was a life of striving, a life out in the woods, and your playthings were what you could find or make. I didn't have toys to speak of. I didn't play with dolls. I built structures, camps. I dug. I collected. [Laughs] I pretended I was an Indian. I pretended I was a horse, neighing and pawing. I think most children go through that but maybe they don't remember it as being important.

Was Port Angeles still pretty small when you were growing up?

It was small, but you don't have much sense of size or scale as a child. I went with the Girl Scouts to Seattle. We went to Victoria once. Those were the only ideas of cities of any size that I had.

Was your family close?

Very close. At a certain age I began to help with the logging. I marked the trees to be cut up into pulp wood. Everybody had chores. Eventually the family bought a little stump ranch outside of town, and because my parents were both from agrarian families in Oklahoma and Missouri, they had us working out there. Everybody had their thing to do. I milked the cows, I remember, and fed the calves, gardened, weeded and hoed. There was a sense of space in this life, a sense of the seasons, the feeling of having to live by the sweat of your brow, a sense of wildness from the struggles just to have a home and get food.

When did you become interested in writing?

When I was about seven. My mother had a typewriter in the house and I taught myself how to type with one of the books she'd used in business school. Then I decided I'd have a little neighborhood newspaper. I tried to peddle it for five cents a copy. I made up stories; it was just a kid's scheme.

I became fascinated with poetry in high school. We were asked to memorize large chunks of Shakespeare by one of my most forceful English teachers. This woman is still a very good friend of mine. Her name is Margaret Matthieu. She lives in Port Angeles and I see her pretty often. She gave me everything I needed by way of teaching me how to do research, how to use the library, how to pose a question and then pursue it too.

Very early I was fascinated with libraries. When I was ten I began to help the librarian at my grade school. I worked with her all through my grade school years. I was always going to the library and checking out books. I read continually.

I think that's the beginning of your writing. When you start reading in a certain way, that's already the beginning of your writing. You're learning what you admire, and you're learning to love other writers. The love of other writers is an important first step. To be a voracious, loving reader. Most of the writers I know, for instance Ray, also had this love of books and a need to read. And we were in families where reading wasn't encouraged, was considered a foreign activity. You'd be in the bed with your book, squirreled away in this household of loud activities, and you would be rousted out and made to do your part. An errand would be thought of. Something to spoil your dreaming.

Did you begin writing poetry at the University of Washington?

I went there to study journalism. I had worked from age sixteen on the newspaper at Port Angeles, and it was very exciting to be at the center of your town. There was a lot of gossip and you could affect how people saw what was happening. It was an intriguing place to be for a sixteen-year-old. Suddenly, by working there,

I saw my town from an entirely new perspective.

I worked there until I went away to college. I thought, "This is what I would like to do." But in the back of my mind I had these other writers whose work went into books, and was not wadded up and used to start the fire in the morning, so I wasn't totally satisfied.

When I got to the University of Washington I had the fortunate experience of having a teacher who really believed that no one had any prospects to become a journalist. All the good journalists had happened in his generation and weren't likely to happen in ours. He impressed this upon us quite ferociously.

I disliked his boot camp methods, and I was bored by reading *about* journalism in text books, because I'd actually done it. I'd been spoiled. I wanted to be out there getting stories, not being told how to do it. I knew how to do it. So it was the wrong place for me, luckily.

Finally, I didn't want to be in journalism. I was realizing that the people who were around me weren't interesting enough to me; they had a rather shallow idea of experience. I was tired of who, why, when, what. I wanted to get into the reasons for things in a different way. Into the mystery.

All this time I was writing poems. And I had the idea that I wanted to talk to somebody about these poems. I heard that Theodore Roethke was there. I had read his poems. And I'd had a course from Nelson [Bentley] who was very close to Roethke as a man and close to his writing. He encouraged me to try to get into Roethke's class.

I submitted some poems, was accepted, but I was suddenly terrified. I went to Roethke and asked if I could please come back the following year in the fall, because I didn't think I was ready, I didn't know enough. This was after sitting in on the initial class where he told us he was going to have to weed some of us out. He was only going to have twelve in this class. So when I found I was one of the twelve, I thought I didn't belong, and that some mistake had been made. I set about to correct it, but luckily he didn't let me off, because it changed my life to be with somebody who was that devoted to his craft, and who could communicate that to students.

So Roethke was very helpful to you?

Very helpful. I was only in his class for the spring quarter. He died that summer, so it was very lucky I hadn't delayed my time with him. It was important to have those other writers around and to feel how much I didn't know, and to feel this immense task in front of me—to learn all I could about poetry and to try to write something that mattered. That seemed to be my assignment.

Did you enjoy crafting poems?

My writing was often connected early on to reaching my father and reaching my sense of origins. I must have been taking my cue from Roethke's greenhouse poems. My writing was also very class-oriented at an unconscious level. I had come to college with no scholarship, even though I had done extremely well in high school. Other members of my graduating class whose fathers were doctors and lawyers or who worked for companies or whatever— their families were of such stature in the community that they got scholarships.

But I was a logger's daughter and I didn't get scholarships, no matter how well I had done. I came to college understanding that I was going to have to work for everything I got. I had three jobs at one time just to be able to attend classes. My family could have helped me, but money wasn't seen as a part of what should be volunteered. It had to do with my being a woman. My father didn't volunteer money, and he wept about this later on, after I had gone to school and had worked so hard. He said, "If I had known, I would have helped you." He hadn't realized who I was, that I really was willing to undergo extreme sacrifices to pursue that dream.

I did manage to make it through almost to the end. I didn't get my degree, though. By that time I was in a rather perverse mood, and I almost didn't want a degree. Maybe I was angry for how costly it had been—the sacrifice, the work. Not only did I not want to take my place in the adult world of earning money, but I didn't want to be sanctioned.

I was in love. I married a man I'd met at the university and followed him to the South; he was being trained to be a jet pilot in the Marine Corps. All this time I was trying to write. Once I got married, the writing kept trying to make contact with my selfhood as apart from family, but even so, the strongest poems of that time had to do with my family relationships.

The first poem that I remember feeling was successful was "Black Money," in *Instructions to the Double,* where I made contact with my father and his life. I was again writing out of my class-consciousness because my father was a workingman, and those working-class lives seem to evaporate; there's not much residue left in the way of literature when those lives are gone. I kept thinking, "This life matters. He's never going to speak for himself." It was my responsibility somehow to witness that life, that life which hadn't paid for my education, but which had kept me going and given me the dream until I could pursue it for myself.

In "3 A.M. Kitchen, My Father Talking," I finally tried to use my father's voice. I said to the father inside me, "Well, you can't write poems, but I can write you. I can give you voice." That seems an important function of poetry and fiction, to give voice, to give witness to lives that otherwise won't be recorded, though your actual reasons for using the voices are probably more selfish than that.

How did you go about speaking for your father?
You become the camera.

That must be hard to pull off.
It's hard to speak for those things which are closest to us; they're obscured in a certain way because of their closeness. It took some time for me to be able to do that. It was a very simple poem when it arrived. It caught me off guard. I almost didn't trust it. I was on a bus and I thought, "Well, I shouldn't be writing this on this bus; it's too important a poem." Yet I began to write it and wrote it.

Do you often borrow someone else's voice when you write a poem?
I don't speak often in a monologue like I do in that poem. I will usually let the voice come into a poem, have its moment, then go on. Very often I'm a witness; I am present and recording. But there's an important sense of my presence in the poem too.

For instance, the poem in *Willingly,* where I visit the woman who's been making the quilts, "Some with wings, some with manes." The woman has arthritis in her hands. Nonetheless she's trying to make this quilt and she's doing a beautiful job. I record the conversation and I record my dilemma: here's someone who wants to have a relationship with me and I'm in the American mobility scheme: I'm there for a few months and I'm going to be gone. And here she is making this thing she hopes is going to last, this beautiful quilt, against odds, with these arthritic hands. I will let voices come in, more like Yeats does, rather than do entire monologues like I did in the father poem.

So in some ways you're still a reporter?

I suppose I'm a reporter who's allowed to feel things. Everything was supposed to be objective in the reporter's life. You weren't supposed to have opinions, but we do, and it's important that we do. So in that way I'm not the same kind of reporter I started out to be. Cocteau said that it's unlikely that he would have continued to be interested in poetry in a world that is so insensitive to it except for the fact that poetry is a morality. This was important to him and it's important to me too.

Did it take you a while to develop your own voice?

That just evolves as you find your subjects.

And is it still evolving?

Yes, you change and the writing evolves. People noticed a change after *Instructions to the Double*. The poetry changes as the events of your life change. *Instructions to the Double* is an agonizing book, so much pain in there, so many questions, the hardship of what had befallen my life. That book is full of turmoil and questions.

In *Under Stars*, I reach a place of looking back on all that. It's not that I knew all the answers, but some sort of calm had come to me, some kind of equanimity had been allowed, so I could go out into the world again and I could take some of the pressure off "self" as I experienced it in *Instructions to the Double* where I keep trying to define how to live in a world where the instructions are alien to one's sense of being. How do you decide what life is about when people you love can be killed in the night for no reason as my uncle was, or when the man you love is taken away to a war you don't believe in?

When you wrote Instructions to the Double *was your husband in Vietnam?*

He was preparing to go to Vietnam during the writing of some of that book. But most of the poems were written after he returned, even after the marriage had ended. The whole prospect and his preparation for going to Vietnam was part of the energy that formed the antagonistic core of that book.

The fact that he went to Vietnam really put me into my writing life a lot sooner, because there was such an extreme need for making meaning out of things. Also I was thrown back on my own resources when he was gone and I no longer had that relationship with which to define myself, which is the way women have so often defined themselves in the past: in terms of that married structure. They don't do it in quite the same way now, even when they marry—the way of defining in that partnership is eroded now, changing—but that structure had been there for a long time when I was reaching that age.

When my husband was in the war, I had to live alone, and I had to manage everything for myself. It gave me a self-sufficiency that I hadn't realized I had. Of course I'd had it all along, but I hadn't taken possession of that self-sufficiency yet.

Instructions to the Double *seems to be struggling with a lot of things.*

Well, womanhood was right at the center of it. Because I had been made to understand that to be a woman of my class was to get married, raise a family, etc. Yet that wasn't going to be possible for me. I was just seeing that I needed solitude if I wanted to be an artist, and I could see that if I began to have children, I wouldn't be an artist. The odds were against it. Still are. I realized there might be no one to help me take care of this child. No man was likely to say to me, "I want to raise a child for you so you can write." There aren't many male "enablers" around. If I had been a man I would doubtless have had children and shared that experience.

My sister had been born when I was thirteen, so I knew that raising a child was not a romantic occupation; it was hard work. And you really had to give yourself over to that for some years. And I gradually just realized that I wasn't going to do that, especially when the war came and all the women around me whose husbands were in the war began to have babies in case their husbands would be killed. I didn't want to have a baby that the father would never see. So right then something penetrated the dream of our lives. When he came back it had somehow vanished, the idea of having children. That whole thing had gone.

Was it hard to get over the idea of not having children?

Not really. I guess I had a singularity of purpose, and my brothers were having children; it seemed as if the world wouldn't want for children. I didn't have any egoistical idea that I could produce someone who would be of immense value, although I might have. Who knows?

Right now I really love my life with Ray, and in a certain way my not having children made that possible. He didn't want more children. He had raised his family when he was so young. It was not a pleasant experience for him to have been a father at nineteen.

So you had a strong commitment to writing poetry?

I did. It was the thing I wanted to do more than anything. I left that marriage to do it. My family thought I was crazy. "What are you doing? You're not in journalism school any more, you didn't graduate from college, you went off and got married. You've left this perfectly good man, and now you're going to write poetry? You're going back to school to study poetry?" You see how it wasn't a very sane scenario for this family.

Did your family expect you to be different from the other kids?

There was a sense that I was different, but there weren't enormous concessions to it and I'm glad about this. I was treated very much like children were treated in any working-class family in this town. But the family's one luxury was my being sent to piano lessons. Other than that, I spent a lot of my time doing chores. Since I was a girl, I was made to iron, wash dishes, wash clothes, mop, sweep, straighten the house. The main involvement became the house, once that rather idyllic logging time had gone out of our lives. Then I was anchored, like most women and young girls of that time, to the house.

Housekeeping is pretty hard work when you have seven people in the family. I remember often feeling thwarted because I'd just fix it up nice, everything would be where it belonged, and then the other children would come through like a hurricane and it would all be undone in a manner of minutes. So there's a sense of futility associated with those childhood chores.

Did you become philosophical about it?

Well, I'll tell you one thing, I don't iron anymore. Ray took a picture of me ironing a couple of years ago because he thought it might never happen again. He had to get proof of this rare occurrence.

Why did you begin writing the short stories?

I wrote the first story in *The Lover of Horses* just to see if I could, and also because I had material which I didn't think I could handle in a poem. Mind you, I had written stories back in 1969, 1970, but I had given it up to concentrate on poetry.

I was also frustrated with the kind of poetry I was reading, and the eternal focus on self. It's true that when the best poets say "I" they are speaking "for the cosmos," as Cocteau puts it. But I felt some degeneration from that aim had taken place. If you're writing fiction, you can't just write about yourself all the time. Otherness is what you're involved in, because you don't get those stories by just sitting around looking at your navel; you're involved with people. You're listening and watching. You're much more of a collector again, an arranger, a conductor.

I get that sense too with contemporary poetry. Often it is a kind of intense self-examination, whereas fiction has to do with the self, but the self reaching outside of itself.

I can't seem to fictionalize in poetry the way some poets do. I tend to want to work with the actual experience, and to retell it in my own way, but to use those elements in a way that's fairly close to what happened.

In fiction of course I distort all kinds of things; that's part of it, the distortions; that's the art. But in the poetry, how something happened, how it really was, is what I want to give. I'm much more a naturalist or a scientist in the poetry. I want to get it right. In writing fiction, getting it wrong is how I get it right. By getting it wrong, by telling it wrong, some rightness evolves.

Is that part of the fun of it too?

It's like the surprise I used to get when I churned butter with my mother, having this substance which is completely liquid, before your very eyes, after this extreme exertion, turn into butter before your very eyes.

There's this unsuspected quality in the fiction. How it yields, without seeming to yield, different kinds of knowing than poetry does. I always feel in poetry that the poem is saying, "I'm going to make you feel what this life is about." Fiction is much less frontal in this way. And I feel more protected when I write fiction, less personally exposed. My perceptions are reduced or amplified by the terms of my characters. Chekhov said that he hadn't any firm opinions. That they changed from day to day, and that's why he only could know what his characters knew.

So fiction is more oblique than poetry?

It's more presentational and cumulative in its methods perhaps than poetry is. Eudora Welty was on TV the other night and she said she likes to present the people in a story in such a way that the reader comes away with the same conclusion she had. So that when readers get to the end of the story, even though she hasn't told them what she thought, they arrive at the same feelings.

Are there things that fiction allows you to do which poetry does not?

One of the reasons I like writing stories is that it's easier to have a cast of characters and to move them about in a larger space, and to allow incidental actions to have more of a play in the scene. Poetry doesn't have much patience for the incidental; it wants to know what's important and it wants to know right now. It's an extremely compacted form. And its rhythms will dictate a lot more of what's possible within the scheme of the poem than prose rhythms will in a piece of fiction. As a result, you can be a lot more lost out there in your prose writing.

Prose is maybe connected to my exploratory ambitions, going back to that logging clearing; allowing yourself to get lost for a while and then trying to find your way out. I love prose for that lostness. I don't know where I am in it. I could go one way, I could go another. Then having to make a decision to go, and follow one possible direction out, the consequences of having made that decision.

And then also revising. I revise a lot more in fiction than I can remember doing in poetry. In poetry, the voice, the experience, the rhythms, all seem to compel me to write in one particular way, so that as the poem is being made it's much more fully formed than when my prose arrives. The rewriting in prose is a way of discovering what I might mean. I revise in the poems, but it's a different type of revision. The whole shape of the poem will be there—the images, the music—everything will be in place so that what you're doing is just a little housecleaning, a little straightening up.

So that by the time you write the poem down you've figured out a lot of the order?

I don't know that I have. I still feel the adventure of writing the poem is essential, that I don't know and I'm finding out as I go, that the experience is coming to me simultaneously as I'm writing it down.

It's not coming as I write the story. I can write the story and have no idea what it's about or whether it's right, even. Then I let some time pass. I come back to it and begin to think, "This is what's important in this story." And I throw out an enormous clump of writing. I find the essence only later.

But the essence in poetry seems to arrive with some kind of simultaneity that belongs to the experience of trying to set down the next line. The impulse for the next thing I'm going to say somehow carries the direction.

Does it operate by association?

Almost any connections you make could be associational. I don't think that way of moving toward an experience belongs to poetry alone. But in poetry you're so much more involved with texture and tone and language than the kind of writing I happen to be doing in prose. One of the things that has been said about my book of stories is that it doesn't seem like a book of stories that a poet would be writing. I don't depend on images in it. I don't depend on metaphor. I don't depend on the texture of language to carry what's important in the stories.

So it's character that carries the stories?

Character, and what's happening and how people respond to one another. It's the complexity of the relationships.

And so you want the surface of the prose to be smooth?

Yes, I don't want it to impede, I don't want it to call attention to itself. I'm not a painter in my prose.

Is your prose quite different from your poetry?

As a fiction writer, the attention to details seems quite different from the use of images, say, when I'm writing a poem. Also, the poem is much more involved in the moment. It can be a moment which intersects with many other past moments and future moments, but it really finally has to happen in a shorter time than the story.

And if the story is realistic you've got to know things. Poets as a group tend not to know facts. Young poets especially tend to read other poetry, and I'm surprised to find they often don't read non-fiction books, many of them.

And often they don't read poetry further back than fifty years.

Right, so I find it very refreshing to be writing fiction because it requires me to have this attentiveness to people and practical things. I enjoyed writing a story where I had to recall all the ways I used to work on that newspaper job, and the whole vernacular of newspaper life and my experience in the darkroom developing photographs.

Do you think that writing fiction has changed your poetry?

Working with Ray on his fiction had already begun to turn me toward story. In *Willingly* you see those long narrative poems. Those weren't happening to that degree before I began writing and being interested in fiction.

The poems in Willingly *really seemed to open up. There was a kind of transparency about the writing that made its meaning very clear.*

Poetry is emotion. What you want in making the poem is to deliver a feeling, and usually it's a complex feeling, but you want to have an impact, you want that intake of breath from the reader when you're finished.

In short stories you also want people to feel. You want that pause, you want that stunned silence that one comes to when someone has received something. I think that poetry and short fiction are very closely related in that sense. Especially as I saw Ray writing stories, those stories seemed very closely related to poetry in some respects, and so I felt I could do it.

Does Ray Carver read your stories?

Yes, he does. We read each other's stories and poems and essays and even important letters we're sending out.

How does that work in regard to fiction?

It's very nourishing, it's very helpful. We're affected by the dialogue. For instance, Ray was recently working on a story entitled "Menudo." When it went out to a magazine and then came back I said, "Let's look at that story again." I spent a day with it, and just slashed away, cutting out things that we could agree weren't needed. The essential element was clogged up. You couldn't get at it because you couldn't see it clearly. It was twenty-eight pages and we cut it to twenty-two pages. We also changed the ending a slight bit but in a very important way.

It's a story that asks: if you don't believe you have a destiny, how do you make decisions in your life? When Ray was writing the story he didn't have this in mind in a conscious way, but as we began to discuss the story, this began to reveal itself. At the end of the story his character makes a decision to cross the street to his lover's house, leaving his wife. Ray at first wrote, "I had to do something. I crossed the street." And as we talked I said, "'I had to do *something*.' Maybe it's not as interesting, not as crucial, if you put it that way, because we all have to do something." So we began to try other possibilities, and discovered that there's more definition if you say, "I have to. I cross the street." I'm much more interested in that kind of a character, who's been compelled to cross that street by the force of circumstances which have accumulated.

That turns out to be the situation with this character; it's not that he just has to do something, anything, but that he has to cross *that* street. It's maybe the point at which choice is so eroded that it may as well be destiny. He doesn't have any choice. He can't go back. The situation with his wife is ruined, and he's ruined it. He's responsible for it. And he's forced to do the next thing.

Those are the kinds of decisions we help one another with. But we're each also very protective of our sense of rightness in what we do, so we don't worry about being over-influenced. We can take or ignore the advice. But more often than not we take it.

And he helps you with your writing?

Right. We both go over each other's work at different stages in the writing. It's a relief actually, to work in somebody else's garden a little, as Simone de Beauvoir put it. She had been criticized by American feminists for helping Sartre, and giving much of her energy to his work. She said, "It pleases me to work in the garden next to my garden. Why shouldn't I? I do it because it pleases me."

It pleases me to help Ray, and to be interested in his work, and also to have him reciprocate with interest in my work. I wouldn't have written this book of stories if it hadn't been for him. I got interested in the short story because of working with his stories. He began to rely on me as a reader. Here again, my expertise as that loving reader from my childhood, that person who could disappear into the work. That's become very important.

Do you think that his influence has rubbed off on you?

How could it not? I look at influence as gift. I'm influenced by where I've chosen to live. Some influences you can choose, others you don't. I know I would be a different writer if I had been living with Don Barthelme or Alexandre Dumas.

And Ray would have been a different writer if he hadn't lived with me. I have influenced him. It doesn't work in just one direction. He has the reputation as a fiction writer, and I don't have a reputation as a reader or an editor—two much underestimated talents. But I lend a sharp eye and consciousness to his work.

His work does seem to be changing.

Yes, it is. It's important that it change. He couldn't just stay there writing those same slice-of-life stories of *Will You Please Be Quiet, Please?* where people are left in their predicaments and who cares after a while. I love that book but I'm glad he's moved on. His characters in many of the late stories are more fully drawn.

Right, the people's lives in the early stories are often dead ends.

How do you see his work changing?

In Cathedral *the stories were longer and looser, and even when things didn't work out for the characters the tone was lighter.*

That's interesting. That probably has something to do with the circumstances of his life changing; he wasn't in that vise of the alcoholism any longer. When your life is terribly difficult, your writing tends to show that.

It's not that his life is completely removed of barriers even now, but it allows him some ease, I think, in how he sees what's possible. If there are more possibilities for him, there may be more possibilities for his characters.

I noticed that some of your poems were about religion. How does it find a way into your poetry?

Since I haven't adopted an organized approach to religion I'm saying to myself, "What are you operating out of? How do you know you're going in a moral direction?" At least if you have an orthodox religion it has some rules. It says, "You do this, this and this and you'll do all right. You'll be living well."

If you make this other decision I've made, not to follow any formalized religion, then you're borrowing all the time, and that tends to be what we do in the West, not just in the West of the United States, Western culture itself seems to be a borrowing culture. People are much more open to an amalgamation of different religious ideas, and of applying those in different, innovative ways.

In that poem "Linoleum" I look at the Jains, a religious sect in India which seems to be at a real extremity. If you look at that extremity, then maybe you can locate where you are. What you find in looking at a religion so excruciatingly exact—they can't step on a single insect or they will be trespassing, failing—is that this religious sect is much more complex than one sees at first. These people are money-lenders, something that we consider a venial activity, but that's all right for them. So it's all cultural. Religion is a cultural event.

Just by looking at the Jains I feel challenged, as if I'm not doing enough. I think it's good to find those ways you fail, even by somebody else's terms; even though you won't really adopt that strictness with yourself about it, something corrective will happen.

I have Gandhi's picture up in my study. If I'm having some mean or lost moments I go in and look at him and say, "What do you think, Gandhi?" I'm not a follower but he's an example that's very strenuous for me. He will bring something down to an essential way of thinking for me. Things I thought were important, if I bring them to my idea of Gandhi, they aren't so important; another perspective comes to me and the best is asked of me. It's important to find something or someone to ask the best of you; you want the people around you to be those who are going to ask for your highest effort, and who are going to let you know in a generous manner, one hopes, when you're veering off, maybe even show you gently by example how to grow.

I think the writing of poetry has to do with making of self and making of soul. It has to do with seeing the world, too.

Do you feel that it's possible through writing to make your experience meaningful to others?

It must be, because I've gotten a lot of response to even very private feelings that I thought might be only mine. You write in that fear that you won't interest anyone, that this is some peculiar neurosis of yours, some obsession. You just have to give it and hope that people can understand you. It's something of a miracle when they do.

Yesterday, I was at the lake enjoying the sunshine. My brother, my sister-in-law and her sister were there, and she picked up my book of short stories. She said she was going to read the first story because she had read the first line and liked it. She sat there and read the story. All of a sudden she turned to me and she said, "Is this what you wanted?"

I looked at her and she was just weeping. And I said, "Yes, I did put those tears in there. I'm glad you got them."

She really had felt that story. I wept writing it, tears weren't running down my face, but in my heart and my being I felt tears. That was part of the emotional release I had by the time I got to the end of writing that story. It delivered a cargo of tears. The experience that I worked from was my experience, but those tears went out to enter the reader.

So you've developed a way of translating your own experience to others?

Some others, anyway. I must have been able to write it fully enough so the emotion of the story communicated itself and acted physically on my friend so that she couldn't withhold tears. It isn't a sentimental story, either. Those weren't sentimental tears, those were tears of release from having entered the pain of the story.

It must be gratifying to be able to do that.

I just feel grateful. I finally feel that story was a kind of gift. Other people say this and you think, "Oh, well, come on, take credit for it lady, you did it." Yeah, you did it and you wrote a lot of other stories, too, but I guess you realize at some point that there are certain pieces of writing you're absolutely given to write. There's some sense of a divinity or of having a right to produce that piece of writing. You couldn't have written it badly, because it was too important. It was going to be given to you, and it was going to be given whole. With that story, I felt I was writing out beyond what I knew I could write.

Do you feel that about all the stories?

I don't feel it about all the stories. I feel it about very few stories and very few poems. I tend to feel that more consistently about poems, but then I've been working longer in poetry. Maybe I'll feel that more as I write more fiction. But my sense of fiction now is more of a pioneer experience, more of struggling, more of being lost, more of exploration.

I wondered if you've actually felt the need to physically bow before certain things, as you described in "The Kneeling One"?

It's a gesture which is almost missing in this culture. If you go to India, or Moslem countries, or Catholic countries, you'll see that posture more, that kneeling, that humbling of the entire body.

I had just watched a film on India when I wrote "The Kneeling One," and that gesture became interesting to me. I realized how we didn't see it so much and then I started to think of all the times that kneeling had been important to me. I wanted to explore the ritual element of kneeling, and so I developed this character who went back and paid homage. Because this is essentially a foreign gesture in this culture, it was interesting to try it on.

And it seemed appropriate?

I found ways of making it appropriate in the poem.

Do you try to find ways of doing this yourself?

Yes, I think it's very important to acknowledge the various sanctities. My writing is the way I do that most. That's my kneeling, my homage.

Your atonement?

Yes, it's my way of making right. If you kneel, you're on a different level, you allow something to be over you. To be on your knees is an attitude of worship and obedience and spiritual attention.

Do you feel that way when you're writing, for instance when that one story arrived?

That came like a blessing. I felt, "Well, I have done certain things to prepare myself for this, and I've always hoped this sort of story would be given me." But I wrote those stories for six years and that one story happened to me. I work for six years and I'm blessed for one day to write that story. That's a lot of work, a lot of waiting, a lot of patience. That's not to say that all the other stories are for nothing, and they're not even preparation, they're just what you had to do. It's a matter of skill, fortitude and blessings, wherever they come from, God or not. I have gods in me, invented or actual—sometimes I'm unsure—and they require things of me. I'm addressed by them, and I address them, and I'm inventing the form of our dialogue all the time.

What direction do you see your writing taking in the future?

I'm at work on poems for *Amplitude* right now and doing research for a novel. I'm thinking a lot about the novel. I have a contract from Harper and Row for the novel. A lot of my dream-time now is involved with the novel, and writing things down about that, and waiting to get these projects out of the way, so that my time is clear to work on that.

Have you been wanting to do that for a long time?

I've been wanting to, as a kind of ultimate writing experience. In a novel you know you can't have that quick enjoyment of the poem, you have to have a long eye to the future, you have to work over a very extended period of time. I've wondered whether I would have enough in me to sustain that. I'm curious to see what will develop. It's a bigger risk than any of the other things I've done so far, so if your reward has any relationship to the amount of risk volunteered. . . .

I do things like that to myself; I'm terrified of water and yet I make myself go down and swim in this pool. [Laughs] When I get really ready I'm going to be swimming out there in the ocean.

Do you feel ready to write a novel?

I have a way of working in prose, after having written all these stories and rewritten them. So I just have to gear up for this long haul, for the patience of that kind of adventure, staying with a group of characters for that long, staying with a voice for that long. I think that the novel is quite different. I'm leaving most of the familiar ground; it's like trying to swim the Pacific and pull yourself up onto the shore of China.

And then you did those screenplays?

Yes, I think that work helped develop the feeling that I might have the stamina for the novel. Working in that steady way to draft those screenplays makes me feel that once I get going, things will work, things will happen. I'll use that as my collateral.

Ernest K. Gann

*E*RNEST K. *Gann is a writer who is saturated in the subject of fly-*
ing. Having piloted a variety of aircraft, Gann has come to know
the business of aviation inside and out. He writes convincingly
about nearly every aspect of it, from the Spads and Nieuports of
early aviation to the most sophisticated military aircraft in oper-
ation today. His painstaking attention to detail has made him espe-
cially popular with pilots and professional flyers.

In his long and productive career, Gann has concerned him-
self mainly with aviation, but he is by no means limited to that sub-
ject. He has also written about commercial fishing, the courts of
law and many other subjects. His books include: Island in the Sky
(1944), Blaze of Noon *(1946),* Fiddler's Green *(1950),* The High
and the Mighty *(1952),* Soldier of Fortune *(1954),* Fate Is the
Hunter *(1961),* In the Company of Eagles *(1966),* The Antagonists
(1971), Band of Brothers *(1973),* A Hostage to Fortune *(1978),* The
Aviator *(1981) and* The Encounter *(1986). Gann is also the author*
of several screenplays based on his novels: The Raging Tide *(1951),*
Island in the Sky *(1953),* The High and the Mighty *(1952),* Soldier
of Fortune *(1955) and* Twilight of the Gods *(1957).*

Born in Lincoln, Nebraska, in 1910, Gann was educated at Yale University. He has been married twice and has three children. He served from 1942-46 in the U.S. Army Air Force Air Transport Command, where he became a captain and received a Distinguished Flying Award. He flew as a commercial pilot for many years and still regularly pilots his three private planes.

Gann lives in Anacortes, Washington, in a house with a huge bay window facing east toward the Cherry Point oil refinery and Mount Baker. The interview took place there in the spring of 1986. Gann is a short, compact man with sandy brown hair and a gravelly voice. He had set aside an hour for the interview, and, being very punctual in his work habits, once it was over he immediately went back to his writing desk where he resumed pecking away on an old manual typewriter.

Why did you start flying?

I made a short-subject movie called *Control Yourself* in 1935. I had to shoot it from an airplane. And I fell in love. From then on I was hooked. I never got over it. That was fifty-three years ago.

Were you the pilot?

Not to start with. I just was riding in the back of an open-cockpit airplane with a camera, shooting all kinds of acrobatics and stuff. I finally sold the movie. I think it broke even. And then I started taking flying lessons in between other jobs. And then I finally went barnstorming.

I'd sit under the wing of the airplane writing flying stories, because that was something that I could do with a minimum of investment—like paper and pencil—and maybe get myself out of this mess.

What mess?

Financial. I had a wife and one boy and no money and we were starving to death in aviation. I did very well when I was in my other jobs, but I wanted to fly; that's all I wanted to do. I didn't want to be near the theater, which was where I was working before. I just got fed up with it.

What kind of a theater?

All kinds. I went to the Yale School of Drama on a kind of a fluke. And when I got out of there—I only went two years—I went down to Broadway. I wanted to be a director. I got a job pretty soon, and I got a couple more jobs. Then finally I got a job directing movie tests. I did very well at it; a lot of people were hungry then. That's how I got going. When I left the theater I wasn't making any money and I wasn't selling any stories. So I eked out an existence flying.

What about flying appealed to you?

Danger; it was pretty dangerous then. Being different. Being what I thought was pretty close to being your own boss. The absence of money. Anyone in the business then had to be in love with it; they sure weren't paid anything. The beauty. The beauty really got to me. I've never gotten over it. I'm still flying. As a matter of fact I'd probably be flying right this minute if I weren't sitting here talking to you.

Why did you stick with flying?

I don't know. It's like a narcotic—you get hooked on it and you never get over it. I've never seen any real pilot get over it. There are some pilots that came along in later days who got into it for the money. And they are able to turn their backs and walk away. A lot of military pilots were able to turn their backs and walk away because their only experience in flying was horrible. But most of them didn't actually get shot at, most of them still have a great love of flying.

Do you feel the same exhilaration in flying a small private plane that you do in larger planes?

Well, it's better than nothing. Actually flying a big transport or a 747 is pretty dull going because it's doing most of the work anyway. I like to fly military planes, that's fun and exciting. I'm one of the few civilians who has flown so many different military planes, including the U-2, which is very rare. And the F-111. The F-111 is a very exciting airplane. I've flown everything from the Goodyear blimp to the Curtis Pusher.

Do you still fly military planes?

I flew the U-2 last September for the second time. I'd flown it about three or four years ago. I haven't flown any military planes since.

Why does the military allow you to fly planes like the U-2?

It's a trade-off. That's how I got to fly the B-52 and some of the others. I get invited to address the dining in or dining out. And I say, "I don't do it. It's bad for my digestion."

"Well," they say, "We'll fix your digestion. Come on, you be the speaker and guest of honor."

I say, "No. There's no way I can do that. It's bad for my digestion. It takes my time. My normal fee is $3,000 and all my expenses for a twenty-minute talk."

Usually that kills them—military, that is—other people get fooled every once in a while and take me up on it. The Port of Bellingham did once.

I say, "But there is a way we can do this. Why don't you fix me up to fly one of your airplanes."

"Ohhh. Well, we'll see what we can do."

And then they get on the horn to Washington. By the time it gets through the president and the chief of staff and God knows who else, a couple of weeks have gone by and I hope they've forgotten about it. Then they call up and say "Well, if you can be here and go to school on the 10th. . . . "

What was it like flying the U-2?

Oh, marvelous. Great experience.

How fast does it fly?

Not very fast, fast as an airliner—480 knots—but it's outer space.

Do they still use it on reconnaissance missions?

You bet they do. There's only one squadron. The 99th Squadron. And they're a marvelous bunch of guys. They're very unusual; they're not the ordinary Air Force pilot.

Is there only one pilot in that plane?

One pilot, except when I go. I have a pilot instructor. But I do all the flying. I do everything.

How high does the U-2 fly?

Well, the first time I got to 71,200 feet, but the second time I couldn't get to 70,000.

And where did you fly it?

The time before, I flew it up across the San Juan Islands and back down to Beal Air Force Base.

And you've also flown World World I aircraft?

Oh, yes. All of them—Spad, Nieuport, Sopwith—you name it. The ones I've flown in recent years are usually restorations, a couple are the original airplanes, and a few are built specially. I haven't flown any German World War I aircraft. I've flown a Messerschmitt 108, a little reconnaissance airplane. I was all scheduled to fly an ME-109, and the damn engine couldn't get going. That's a very touchy airplane.

Did flying change you in any way?

I don't know if it changed the personality or not. It did teach you then—because then you didn't have any help at all—to have a fierce sense of independence. That was one of the things I liked about it; you did everything yourself, including analyzing the weather and everything else. No computer told you anything; there wasn't any computer. It reinforced my sense of self-reliance and at the same time taught me to always have a back door open. Before you get yourself into trouble, have a place to go high. That's been very beneficial, I still use that all the time. Except in literature, in writing, sometimes you get yourself in a bind and it seems like there's no way out. Once in a while you crash. I've had twenty-some books and I've got some turkeys, but with that many books you're bound to. There isn't anybody that doesn't have them, that includes William Shakespeare.

I can read you off a list of them: *Island in the Sky* was successful. *Blaze of Noon* successful. *Benjamin Lawless* was a disaster. *Fiddler's Green* was successful. *The High and the Mighty* was successful. *Soldier of Fortune* was very successful. *The Trouble with Lazy Ethel* was a bomb. *Fate Is the Hunter* was extremely successful. *Of Good and Evil* was a bomb. *In the Company of Eagles* did so-so. *Song of the Sirens* did so-so. *The Antagonist* was tremendously successful. *Band of Brothers* was so-so. *Flying Circus* was so-so. *A Hostage to Fortune* was so-so. *Brain 2000* was a bomb. *The Aviator* was tremendously successful. *The Magistrate* was so-so. *Gentlemen of Adventure* was a little better than so-so. Well, it's pretty obvious that I can usually hit.

What do you mean by successful?

That it sells copies. And gets good reviews. Anybody that says, "Oh, poohey. It's a bestseller, so therefore it must be a bad book," is out of their gourd. That's crazy. That's like saying *My Fair Lady* is a bad show because it ran for twenty years. That's ridiculous. The whole purpose of any art is to inspire and entertain. And the more people who are inspired and entertained, and still keep some taste, the better. I'm not advocating that everybody film *Rambo*, for example. There are some damn good films that have done very well, and damn good books that are bestsellers. The public will tell you whether your book's successful or not.

Do you also listen to what pilots say about your books?

I don't have to listen to them—I was one of them.

But do they tell you whether they like your books?

All the time. I even get it when I'm flying my own airplane. The controllers call me on the radio. They say, "Is this Ernie?" I say, "Yeah." They say, "I enjoyed your books." I say, "How nice of you to say so." This is in the middle of traffic over Portland or somewhere.

Sure, that happens a lot. I'm very proud of it. It kind of humbles me, frankly, that these guys would come through on that sort of thing. But I also get letters from little old ladies. One of them lives on Gingerbread Lane. She's eighty-nine or something like that—writes me regularly.

A lot of my books don't have anything to do with aviation. I don't think I'm going to write any more flying books. I've exhausted it. I've said everything about it there was for me to say.

Are you considered the premier contemporary aviation writer?

That's a matter of opinion. Some people have been kind enough to say so. I haven't heard any complaints. One of the nicest things that ever happened to me was when I wrote a book called *In the Company of Eagles*. It was a so-so success. It was about World War I flying. And I got about four letters from guys who'd been in World War I who wanted to know what outfit I was with. I thought that was very touching. I had to write them and tell them that I was seven years old at the time.

What qualities are essential to airmen?

A calm nature is sort of taken for granted. You can't be excitable and do a good job flying. But I think self-reliance is the number one thing: don't go calling for momma when you're in trouble. You've got to handle it or nobody else is gonna. I think that's the number one thing. I'm not speaking about combat pilots, who are a whole other bag of weeds—then you get some wild-ass guy who may be pretty good—but that's a different matter. I'm talking commercial aviation and just plain surviving in the aviation world, test pilot and so forth, all the various ways except actual combat. Actual combat I can't tell you about because I've never flown in actual combat. I've been mixed up in it, but nobody ever aimed eight machine guns at me.

Were you ever involved in a crash?

Yes. I flew through some high-tension wires. I'm one of the three guys I know of who've done that and survived. I never got a scratch.

You must be lucky.

I'm very lucky. I've broken just about every bone in my body, except my neck, but I'm still alive talking to you. I'm seventy-five and I'm still playing tennis.

Are these qualities that you described as necessary today?

No, but they're still necessary. It's funny, some people think if you've got a control tower you can talk to, that solves all the problems. But the control tower can't do a damn thing when you're in trouble up there. Just the other day I had a little trouble getting my landing gear down. I had to fly past the flight service station in Bellingham to make sure all three wheels were down. That was helpful, but anybody could look up there and see if there were three wheels or two wheels.

Will there come a time when pilots are obsolete?

No, because you can't depend on the machinery 100 percent, any more than you can depend on a human being. And there'll always be crashes.

But some of these new planes have guidance systems and other devices.

That's right. Blind landing system, the whole works. It makes it much easier, but somebody has to monitor it, because it doesn't always work. A human being has to sit there and say hey, just like there's a human being driving a train, which is on a track. You should be able to do all that automatically. You can do it. There's no operator on short-line trains like at the Seattle-Tacoma Airport from one terminal to another. Those are all done automatically.

They've got automatic switches; you can turn them off if anything goes wrong. And it's not a big problem. But when something is up in the air you've got to have a human being up there when the machinery fails.

Is flying still a place for people who are adventurous?

Yes, because as earth-based aviation fades, things will expand in space. In another twenty years or more there will be tremendous adventure in space. And there's no limit to that—that can go on and on and on for thousands of years.

And pilots will be needed for things like that?

Oh, yes. Things go wrong.

Why did you start writing about flying?

It was the only thing I knew.

Did you want to write before you knew much about flying?

Not wanted to write. I never had that inspiration so many people get, to be writers. It never occurred to me to be a writer. I wanted to be a director. I'd still like to be a director. But I can't stop writing long enough to even try for it. And now it's too late. I'd still like to be a director, but I've made my bed and I have to lie in it.

How did you get started writing?

I wrote flying stories for magazines like *Flying Aces* and *High Flyer* or whatever, and never sold any of them. Then I wrote a couple of articles on the radio beam for *Popular Mechanics*. I got twenty dollars or something like that. I did several articles like that, and then I drew, and wrote, a book. It was never published because it would have cost a jillion dollars to publish; it was all in color and everything. But the agent that I took it to called me one day and said, "Do you think you could write a book about airplanes that fly now?"

I said, "Sure," because I was making about $190 a month as a copilot on American Airlines. I wrote a book called *Skyroads*. I got pictures from the publicity department at American Airlines and I drew some pictures and put a little script in, and I made $15,000 on it. I said, "Wow, how long has this been going on?"

They wanted another book, and I wrote them another book called *Getting Them Into the Blue*. These books were for teenagers. And I wrote a book called *All American Aircraft*; I picked a team, like a football team, the best airplanes. Then the war came on; I didn't write anything for a while till I got mixed up in a rescue and wrote *Island in the Sky* and it was a tremendous success. And from then on I was in trouble.

Why were you in trouble?

Because I'd had a taste of some money, though not a lot. I kept on flying, and then wrote a book called *Blaze of Noon* about the early airmail. And that was a big success. It was bought by the movies. Ingrid Bergman gave me the check. I decided to take a leave of absence from the airlines. I said, "This is great. I'll just write another one." That's when I did *Benjamin Lawless*. It sold about 3,000 copies. I fell on my face good and hard. Fortunately it was just a leave of absence, so I went back to flying and licked my wounds.

What makes aviation good material for fiction?

It's becoming less and less good material. Because it's impossible, absolutely impossible, to personalize computerization, unless you kid it as they did in *2001: A Space Odyssey* with a computer named HAL. You can't make it romantic. You can't make the thing live. You can't make it interesting to the average person. There's no love, there's no challenge, there's no nothing, unless you're a computer expert. Then it's a different matter, but computer experts don't read much fiction.

What about books like The Right Stuff?

The Right Stuff is not about computers; it's about people. He left all the computer stuff twenty miles behind.

But it's still possible to make modern aviation interesting.

It's possible but it's very, very difficult. That's one of the reasons I gave up. How am I going to lay a story in a modern cockpit, for example, where the guys read a list to each other, where they're almost personality-less themselves, so poured out of a mold? Their chief subject of conversation is their seniority, the stock market, and how they can get the most for the least. They rarely talk about flying; that's all they used to talk about.

Is it different in the military?

The military is a different matter, but it's even hard to make military flying interesting.

How about the fighter planes?

The fighter planes are worst of all. Because the guy doesn't come up and have a look at the enemy and circle around and all this stuff. It doesn't work that way. He's got a little screen up here. He's directed from the ship or the ground to the target. I've done it, quite a few times now. He's directed to the target until he gets fairly close, a couple of miles. You can't see it, things are going by too fast; it's just an infinitely little speck. But it'll show up on your little screen. There's a little diamond and a little circle, and you move the two of them together and you press the button and boom that missile goes off and even if you miss him it's going to hit him. It's going to follow right up his tail.

This is not very interesting. That's why I've abandoned it. That's why when I write aviation, or have recently, I write about the old times, not because I like to look back, but because then it was glamorous and colorful. There's damn little color left.

Have you lived the lives of most of your characters?

Yes. Almost all of them, because it gets pretty hard to write about anything else but what you know. If you haven't done it, I don't think you can write about it. There are some exceptions to that. I'm now doing a book on narcotics, and the only narcotic I ever had was a marijuana cigarette forty years ago. And so I don't know anything about taking it, but I spent months in research and learning about what's going on with it. I'm determined to do my little bit to ease the situation, which is very serious.

So it's difficult to write about people whose lives are different from your own?

Very difficult.

When you try it, how do you do it?

Well, I do a year or so of research first. I talk to people, I spend a lot of time in libraries.

What kind of books did you read as a kid?

The usual, I guess. *Treasure Island*, Mark Twain, Zane Grey, Booth Tarkington, Sinclair Lewis. About the usual for the kids that read. I think more kids read then than do now because we didn't have television or radio.

What did you read as you got older?

I liked Hemingway, Dos Passos, Steinbeck, Thornton Wilder. Pretty much the usual thing again.

How about St. Exupery?

Oh, yes. I read St. Exupery—everything—in French as well as in English.

Did you try to model your stories on his stories?

No, however I think it's the same as it is in music. Every musician listens to music, and every musician subconsciously takes on some of his favorites, and then after it goes through the sifter, it finally comes out and you'll notice a little Sibelius here, a little Bernstein over here, and whatever. That's inevitable, and that's not bad, that's good. It is the way that art grows. Every painter studies the masters, and in his painting out comes a little bit of the masters' stuff.

And the stuff that you like best will most likely . . .

Influence you. Of course. You don't copy, but subconsciously it comes out. It's got your own mix in there so it's a little different.

Why do you write adventure stories?

Because I'm incapable of writing about a love story in a kitchen. I'm not interested in a love story in a kitchen. I'm not interested in soap opera situations where the husband is in love with a somebody, and somebody else is in love with a somebody. I'm just not capable of doing it.

Are adventure stories more appropriate to writing about flying?

It's hard to write a love story except with the airplane in the background.

You've lived in a lot of places. Why did you settle here?

I just kind of fell in love with this house. But I'm going to move out. I can't stand this climate any more. It's cold. This winter really did it to me. A real bitch titty. Never again.

Has the Northwest played a large part in the history of aviation?

Oh yes. It's played a tremendous part, mostly in Seattle and

Boeing Field. Starting with the Boeings and Old Pacific Air Transport and the early United Airlines and old Varney Airlines. For any single place, with the possible exception of Los Angeles, I would say Seattle was the heart of early flying. There's no place back East to compare with it. I can't think of any other place in the United States.

What kind of changes has air travel brought to the world?

I'll give you a frank answer. For me personally it's screwed up the world. What it has done for civilization I don't know. I'm not qualified to say. To me it's a shame that there are no countries left that are any different from any other country. You have to pick up the newspaper to know what country you're in when you're at the airport. They're so much alike. That's a shame.

There ought to be a law that says if they're going to be in Brazil, the airport should have a Brazilian structure, if it's in Japan it ought to have arches that go this way [makes shape of Japanese arch with hands], instead of all being one big copy of concrete fruitcake. It's a shame. We're losing so much color. Everybody dresses like you do. Everybody—young Japanese, young Germans, young Frenchmen—same thing you got on today. No difference. I think that's a shame.

And you think that the airplane has had a lot to do with that?

When the big airplanes, the big boys, the big mothers with 600 passengers at a crack, start coming in there's no place left in the world that's safe. Because the people come off in a horde like a bunch of cattle and they change the whole place. I've seen it happen so many times; it's heart-rending. And every place that I seem to go to where nobody comes, two years later in comes a jumbo jet, and then comes another, and then comes another: there goes that little piece of the world.

Norman Maclean

NORMAN Maclean's novella, "A River Runs Through It," tries to come to terms with the tragedy of his family's inability to help his brother Paul—a gambler, a street fighter, a genius with a fly rod—who, one day in 1938, was found in an alley, beaten to death with a gun butt. The novella makes sense of his senseless death in the only way it can: it makes beautiful through art and love that which will always surpass understanding.

"A River Runs Through It" is the title story of a collection published in 1976 by the University of Chicago Press. The other stories, "Logging and Pimping and 'Your Pal, Jim'" and "USFS 1919: The Ranger, The Cook, and a Hole in the Sky," bring together Maclean's practical knowledge of logging, fire fighting and woodsmanship with his deep sensitivity to language and prose rhythms.

Born on December 23, 1902 in Clarinda, Iowa, Maclean spent much of his youth in and around Missoula, Montana. He graduated from Dartmouth College in 1924 with an A.B. and received a Ph.D. from the University of Chicago in 1940, where he began teaching in 1930. Three times the institution awarded him its prize *for excellence in undergraduate teaching. When he retired from the university in 1973, he was the William Harper Rainey Professor of English.*

The author of many articles and stories, scholarly and otherwise, Maclean also helped to edit Critics and Criticism: Ancient and Modern, *published in 1952 by the University of Chicago Press.*

On September 24, 1931 he married Jessie Burns, who died in 1968. He is the father of two children. Most of the year Maclean makes his home in Chicago, but in the summer he returns to his cabin on Seeley Lake, Montana. The interview took place there in September of 1985. The log cabin sits on the west shore of the lake in a magnificent grove of larch trees that form an immense canopy over the cabin. The sun filtering through the branches produces a light as meditative and otherworldly as that of the great Gothic cathedrals.

Maclean is a short, stout man with a face creased with wrinkles. In talking about his work, he often salted his speech with profanity; sometimes he colored it with anecdotes and local legends; and always he spoke with the rhythm and music of poetry just underneath his prose.

When did you start fly-fishing?
I was about six when we came to Montana, and almost immediately we started going on these vacations and my father started teaching me to fly-fish. My father was a Presbyterian minister and always had at least a month off in the summer. We would camp out for a month on some big river, the Bitterroot or the Blackfoot.

Do you still fly-fish?
No, I don't. I hope that's a temporary answer. A couple of years ago I hurt my hip and I haven't been able to work very well since then. I quit fishing but I'm getting better. I hope I'll still be able to fish a little before I quit for good. It's hard though. I don't think I'll ever be very good at it again. I've lost my sense of balance, and I can't stand up on those big rocks and I can't fish that big hard water. And that's the only fishing I like to do, fishing the big rivers. If you want big fish, you fish big water.

I miss it a lot. I suppose I get some second-hand pleasure by writing about it.

What has fly-fishing taught you about the nature of grace?

It's taught me many, many things about grace. I think it's one of the most graceful things an individual can do out in the woods. It's very difficult art to master. My father thought it had the grace of eternal salvation in it.

In "A River Runs Through It," you wrote, "Good things come by grace, grace comes by art and art does not come easy." Is that true of writing?

Oh, yes. It's conceivable that someone could find it smirky and pleasurable on some kind of level, but I think it's a highly disciplined art. It's costly. You have to give up a lot of yourself to do it well. It's like anything you do that's rather beautiful. Of course some people can do it seemingly by genes and birth, but I don't think nearly as often as one would think. I think it always entails terrific self-discipline.

Why did you start writing fiction so late in life?

I can't answer that, but I'll make a couple of stabs. There will be a certain amount of truth to them, but no one ever knows why he tries something big in life.

One stab is that in the literary profession, which was my life profession, it was always said that no one began serious writing late in life. That was kind of a challenge. I thought, "As soon as I retire, I've got some serious things I'd like to write, and I think I know enough about writing to do them well. We'll see how they come out."

Just the fact that you would ask me such a question is part of the reason why I started. I wanted to answer it. But it must have been deeper than just showing off.

When you teach literature, you're so close to it, and yet in some ways so far. If you don't have a lot of extra energy, you don't have time to do what a lot of teachers claim they always want to do but seldom do, and that is both write and teach. I suppose I said it too, but being Scotch I was thick-headed and so I tried it.

It's very costly to start writing when you're so old as I am. You don't have any of the daily discipline built up. Some writers get up every morning and it's like shaving to them. They can do it without thinking.

In "A River Runs Through It," you talked about God's rhythms. I wondered what you meant by that.

One of my fascinations about my own life is that every now and then I see a thing that unravels as if an artist had made it. It has a beautiful design and shape and rhythm. I don't go so far as some of my friends, who think that their whole life has been one great design. When I look back on my life I don't see it as a design to an end. What I do see is that in my life there have been a fair number of moments which appear almost as if an artist had made them. Wordsworth, who affected me a great deal, had this theory about what he calls "spots of time" that seem almost divinely shaped. When I look back on my own life, it is a series of very disconnected spots of time. My stories are those spots of time.

Did you feel a real need to write about these spots of time?

I've given up everything to write them. I'm now getting so old I don't know whether I can write much more. I knew when I started, of course, that starting so late I wouldn't get much done, but I hoped to get a few things done very well. It's been very costly, though, and I don't know whether I would recommend it. I've sacrificed friends. I've lived alone. I work on a seven-day-a-week schedule. I get up at six or six-thirty every morning. I don't even go fishing up here any more.

When you're this old, you can't rely on genius pure and undefiled. You've got to introduce the advantages of being old and knowing how to be self-disciplined. You can do a lot of things because you can do what the young can't do, you can make yourself do it. And not only today or tomorrow, but for as long as it takes to do it. So it's a substitute, alas maybe not a very good one, for youth and genius and pure gift. And it can do a lot of things, but it's very, very costly. Sometimes I wish that when I retired I'd just gone off to Alaska or Scotland and played croquet on the lawn.

Do you want to write many other things?

I'm too realistic to entertain such thoughts. Even when I began, which was right after I retired, I knew I could never become a great writer, if for no other reason than I didn't have time. When I started, I agreed to myself that I would consider I'd accomplished my mission if I wrote several substantial things well. And I haven't lost that sense of reality; in fact it deepens as I grow older and see I was right.

I am now trying to finish a second long story based upon a tragic forest fire. I've been on that for some years, and I hope within the next six or seven months to have it completed. But I have been hoping that for some years now. I'm being enticed into making a movie of "A River Runs Through It." If I do those two fairly big things, then I won't try anything very big again.

Do you write every morning?

I don't write every morning, but I keep my writing schedule. I'm the only one who keeps me alive now. I don't have a family living with me any more. I have two homes, here and Chicago. I have a lot of accounting and just plain housework to keep both those places going.

And even when you just make a small success, there are many people who want to see you. So I spend more time than I should seeing people and writing letters. I still go on four to six talking tours each year.

Your book has only three stories in it, but because they're so well written, it's made you more renowned than writers with four or five novels.

Yes, I would grant that, but there are probably a variety of reasons for that. To some at least, the book is a kind of model of how to begin a story and how to end a story, and it is taught as such. When people are good enough, they try to teach it as an example of prose rhythms. It has a special appeal to teachers of writing, and of course it has a great appeal to fly-fishermen, for many of the same reasons: it seems expert at what it is doing. I've had biologists write me and tell me it's the best manual on fly-fishing ever written.

Did you enjoy writing it?

I don't know how to answer that. Writing is painfully difficult at times, and other times I feel like I have a mastery over what I'm trying to do, and of course there's no greater pleasure than that. But when you feel that words still stand between you and what you want to say, then it's a very unhappy business.

Where did you learn to tell stories?

When I was young in the West, most of us thought we were storytellers. And of course we all worshipped Charlie Russell, partly for his painting, but also because he was a wonderful storyteller. I feel I learned as much about storytelling from him as I did from Mark Twain or Wordsworth or any professional writer. The tradition behind that of course was the old cowbody tradition —coming into town with a paycheck, putting up in a hotel, and sitting around with a half a dozen other guys trying to out-tell each other in stories. Whoever was voted as telling the best story had all his expenses paid for the weekend.

The storytellers' tradition is a very, very deep one in the West. It probably doesn't exist very much any more, but then you don't have the great sources of stories. You don't have bunkhouses for loggers and cowpunchers any more. They live in town with families. They don't sit around at night and tell lies to each other. So part of it has been lost.

I learned as much, even technically, about storytelling from Charlie Russell's stories as I did, say, from Hemingway. He [Russell] was still alive and kicking until I was in my twenties. He was an idol of Montana, much more so than now. He's an idol now of course, too, but then we worshipped him, and with good cause. His stories are only two to ten pages long, but if you want to learn how to handle action economically and just have every sentence jumping with stuff, take a look at him. Marvelous storyteller.

A volume of his called *Trails Plowed Under* is just a miraculous piece of narration. Good title, isn't it? That title pervades not only his paintings, but all of his stories. All the time he was writing and painting he had this feeling that "the West that I knew is gone." There's always a nostalgia hanging over his paintings and stories.

When you were writing your stories, how did they change as you turned them into fiction?

They changed long before I started writing them. I'm not sure that after a few years I could tell what happened from what I say happened, which is fortunate if you want to be a storyteller. I had a drenching of storytelling in all the years when I was in the Forest Service and logging camps, and so it's easier for me to tell a story about what happened than telling it exactly as it happened. They became stories long before I told them.

Did you have to make them longer when you wrote them down?

No. From the time my father gave me my first lessons in writing to the end of my training in writing, I always had teachers whose chief criterion was literary economy—use of the fewest words possible.

When you were writing your stories, did you write them down all at once, or bit by bit?

I know pretty well ahead of time what I'm going to do in the whole story, and often I come home after going for a walk in the afternoon and take a bath before dinner; in the bathtub I sit in the hot water till it gets cool, trying to figure out what I'm going write the next day. The next day I'm concerned with saying it. That's probably highly individual. A lot of guys when they sit down don't know where they're going. They even use the act of writing to make them find out what they're going to write about.

Do you work over the stuff that you've written a number of times?

Yes, three or four times.

Sentence by sentence, paragraph by paragraph?

I suppose so, but that would vary. I'm a great believer in the power of the paragraph. I can't say that I always write by paragraphs, but I often do. I think that paragraphs should have a little plot, should lead you into something strange and different, tie the knot in the middle, and at the end do a little surprise and then also prepare you for the next paragraph.

Why did you choose to write those particular stories?

The title story, "A River Runs Through It," was the big tragedy of our family, my brother's character and his death. He had a very loving family, but independent and fighters. We were guys who, since the world was hostile to us, depended heavily upon the support and the love of our family. That tends often to be the case with guys that live a hostile life outside.

There was our family which meant so much to us, and there was my brother who was a street fighter, a tough guy who lived outside the mores of a preacher's family. We all loved him and stood by him, but we couldn't help him. We tried but we couldn't. There were times when we didn't know whether he needed help. That was all and he was killed. I slowly came to feel that it would never end for me unless I wrote it.

The others? Well, they're all spots of time. Spots of time become my stories. You get that very openly in the Forest Service story. That's the plot. They go out and it's spring, and the things that they do and their order are determined by the job. There's no human preference indicated. The first thing you did was clear out the trails from the winter, dead trees and all that fallen-down stuff. Then you made some new trails, then pretty soon fire season came and you fought fires. It was determined by the seasons and the nature of the job.

The plot starts that way and then things begin to happen in such a way that human decisions are determining and changing this natural order of things. It's the change in the causes that order the events which is the story.

I'd had a good training when I was young in the woods. My father didn't allow me to go to school, kept me home for many years until the juvenile officers got me, and as a result I had to work in the morning, but the afternoons were mine. All the guys my age were in school, so I went out in the woods alone. I became very good in the woods when I was very young. I trained myself, both in the logging camps and in the sawmills. I was going to know the wood business from the woods to board feet.

When World War I came along they were looking for young guys or old men to take the place of the foresters who were getting grabbed up as soldiers. So I was in the Forest Service when I was fourteen. And it became a very important part of my life. I almost went into it; I thought until I was almost thirty that I was going to go into the Forest Service as a life profession.

All these things are important to me: my family, the years I spent in the logging camps, the years I spent in the Forest Service.

Why are these stories about your life in Montana, rather than about teaching in Chicago?

I've written many things about Chicago and teaching, some of my best things in articles, stories, talks, discussions about teaching. I wrote a story about Albert Michelson, who measured the speed of light and was the first American scientist to win the Nobel Prize. Strangely, when I was quite young I came to know him intimately. I was just a kid from Montana, a half-assed graduate student and teacher in English, and I was knocking around with this guy who was regarded as one of our two greatest scientists (Einstein being the other). Now I suppose Nobel Prize winners are a dime a dozen, but in those days we had only two in the whole country; he was one of them, and Theodore Roosevelt was the other. I was very touched, as a young boy from Montana, to be trusted with the acquaintanceship of such an outstanding, strange and gifted man. I think my story about him is one of the best things I ever wrote.

Did anyone help you in editing the stories in A River Runs Through It?

I'm a loner in respect to writing. First I should go back to my origins. My schooling was lonely. My father taught me himself, and the prime thing he taught me was writing. I studied by myself and reported to my father three times every morning. I was brought up as a lonely kid and that's continued. Now that everybody has gone off to town after Labor Day and there's nobody on this side of the lake, I'm just coming into my own here. That's the way I am, and it's pervaded my writing.

Having said that, though, I always try to turn, somewhere short of publication, to four or five friends to read over the manuscript. Two or three are from the University of Chicago, and then the first woman full professor at Yale in the English Department, who was a student of mine in her day. She's a great critic. Then three or four from the woods.

I have this three-fold cadre of critics. I give it to them before it becomes a manuscript to be submitted. I listen a great deal to what they say. They're tender with me, but they know me from a long, long time back and I suppose they know what to say and what's useless to say.

What did your father have you read when he was teaching you?

I think the most important thing was what he read out loud to us. He was a minister, and every morning after breakfast we had what was called family worship. And family worship consisted of his reading to us. We'd all sit with our breakfast chairs pulled back from the table and he would read to us from the Bible or from some religious poet. He was a very good reader, and if he had any faults as a reader it was that he was kind of excessive, as preachers often are. But that was very good for me because in doing that, he would bring out the rhythms of the Bible. That reading instilled in me this great love of rhythm in language.

Now when I teach poetry or prose I can teach it quite analytically. When I was at Stanford, I had a long session analyzing prose rhythms with their advanced creative writing class. That's not easy to do, partly because the rule of prose rhythms is that you better not have them show very much. And most of the time you better not have them show at all. Any time you or I or anybody else who has any taste at all suspects that the writer's trying to write pretty, then he's dead. That guy is just as dead as a dead snake.

If you are a writer whose prose falls into rhythm you have to be very, very careful. Most of the time you just approach rhythms and then drift away from them, and then drift back towards them, not really going into any rhythmical passages except as the tension mounts, as the passion increases.

If you look at the last page of "A River Runs Through It," you can scan it as if it were written in accentual rhythm. But when you're on the sand bar with the whore and that goddamn brother-in-law of mine, you don't hear any rhythms although they're there. They're very faint. They come close to rhythm and then drift out. My ordinary style is better than ordinary speech, but not so much you would notice it.

In that story, were you more conscious of the differences in rhythms?

It depends upon the kind of emotional level you're operating on. "A River Runs Through It" is my notion of high, modern tragedy. It's tragedy and deep feeling, and I tried to write about how men and women do things with great skill and loving kindness, with their hands and their hearts, both at the same time. Fishing is such an example. But rhythm is there even when I stop and tell you how you put hobnails in a shoe and why you put them where you put them, and how you pack a horse. I like to tell you about things that men and women can do with their hands that are wonderful. I write about them very carefully. All the time I'm on a level above ordinary speech because what I'm trying to tell you is above ordinary speech. I'm trying to tell you how you do things expertly. When I do that, the language goes up a little bit.

And certainly when you come to the great tragic moments, when you're just pouring out your heart, you don't have to worry about your rhythms; they'll be there if you're at all a rhythmic person.

So the ear has a great deal to do with your writing?

Yes. It goes along with the art. The great fly-tier from Livingston, Dan Bailey, said, "The bookshelves are full of books on how to fish, but only Maclean tells you how it *feels* to fish."

Could these stories have been set anyplace other than Montana?

Montana is very dear to me. You talk about a man without a country, but I'm a man with two countries. Montana's always been one, no matter where the other one is.

So you wrote the stories because the area was important to you?

It's my homeland. I love it, I've always loved it and I always will. When I tell my doctor I'm getting old, that I better close up that place in Montana, that it's getting too tough for me to run, he says, "If you do, Norman, you'll die." So here I am.

Why was it important that you get every detail of those stories correct?

Again, I could answer "because my father told me so." But I'll jump to the other extreme. If you are interested at all, as I told you I was, in whether there are designs and shapes in the passage of events, then design is very important to you. It's very important whether the design or shape or form of a series of events is really in the thing or whether it's something that you, the artist, have manufactured. It's important to me that there is a design and shape to quite a few things that we do in our life. So I'm very, very careful. I don't want to be cheating; I want to get the design as exactly as I can, in itself, not from me.

So you see it as something outside of yourself?

I want to. I'm not always able to. I have to admit that I'm not always sure there is a design and shape to things. Sometimes I think I must be the cause of the designs of things, but I don't really think that is always true. I think that there have been designs and shapes in my life, and I've been almost apart from them. I was a character of them, but I wasn't the author of them.

So in what sense are your stories true? Do you tell them exactly the way they happened?

No, I always allow myself a literary latitude. Often things don't happen fast enough in life. Literature can condense them. I wrote the story on the Forest Service as if it happened all in one summer. But it happened in two or three summers. I didn't consider that a violation at all.

Everything in the story happened to me in the Bitterroots. In the story I have a big fight. The fight was actually in a Chinese restaurant, but in the story I had it in the Oxford, a restaurant and gambling joint in Missoula. It's been there for sixty or seventy years and a lot of us Missoula guys were brought up in there. And they said, "God, how could you put the Oxford up there in Hamilton?" I don't think it made much difference in terms of the story. I felt at home in the Oxford, and I didn't feel at home in Chinese restaurants. Little things like that, mostly for the sake of hastening the story on, of sharpening it.

But you're still true to the spirit of the stories?

I hope so. As I told you, I'm engaged now with several others in trying to make a script out of "A River Runs Through It." They're always saying, "You make it too tragic. A movie audience, unlike a literary audience, won't accept that much tragedy." It's just too bad if they won't. I didn't ask to write this script. It wasn't my idea. I'm unbending about this, just totally unbending. I'm not going to compromise.

How was your education in Montana different from the one you got back East?

It wasn't a very good education. In 1920 when I was going to go to college neither my father nor I had a very high opinion of the University of Montana. The state was still dominated by the Anaconda Copper Mine Company [ACM]. You had to watch what you said about them and about politics. They owned the whole state and they'd just crush you out of existence if they didn't like you.

At the time I worshipped the chairman of the English Department at the University of Montana. His name was H.G. Merriam. The ACM was out to get him night and day, but never did. He came to be recognized as a kind of martyr, sacred to the history of Montana.

I wanted no part of being a sycophant for rich companies, and the education was not very good at the time. Now I think both state universities in Montana are fine schools.

What sorts of things did you learn in the woods as compared to the things you learned in school?

I learned what little math and science I know, in surveying. The only branch of mathematics I remember anything at all about is trigonometry, the thing that we needed in surveying. In respect to biology, I learned a good deal of what I know in a very wonderful kind of way—through direct observation. I suppose fishing, as much as anything, helped me, the close observation about what fly should be used. In a backwoods kind of homey way we were good naturalists. Although home-spun observation has big gaping holes in it, it also has rich parts that you hardly get anymore. If you didn't know a caddis fly when you saw one, and you didn't know whether they spawned in shallow water or deep, you just weren't going to get any fish on certain days. And you developed from that a sense of their beauty. It's odd, but insects are an important part of life to me.

Did you have a hard time getting adjusted to the East Coast?

I suppose so. I don't know if I ever did get really adjusted. But they were very kind to me. I think the East is very different from what most Westerners think it is, at least the Westerners of my time. They thought of the Easterners as socialized jerks, snooty, kind of removed from life.

I didn't find that at all. They were very kind to me. They were very interested in me, much more so then than now probably, because I was one of the early guys from the West going back East. So I was supposedly kind of an oddity from the high brush. But they were better than I ever thought they would be.

Why did you come back to Montana?

Because I didn't want ever to leave, and never left. Very, very early I formed this rough outline in my mind of this life I have led. I love Montana with almost a passion, but I saw I couldn't live here really if I was going to be a teacher; I'd have to be degraded and submit to views that I couldn't accept. I felt that this was imposed upon us from the outside—that wasn't our true nature. I tried to figure out a way to continue this two-world thing that I had begun by going East.

And that's probably the chief reason that I quit teaching and then went back to it. I figured teaching probably was the only way I could live in the two worlds. I could teach in the East, and that would give me a chance to come back a fair number of summers and retain a permanent footing in a homeland that I knew so well. I thought that out as I was doing it. I just didn't stumble on the life I have lived.

Did you come to like Chicago?

I love Chicago. My wife was very wonderful in helping me come to feel that. I was very provincial in a lot of ways. She was gay and loved life wherever she lived. She really worked me over in our early years in Chicago. I was insolent and provincial about that city. She made me see how beautiful it was, made me see the geometric and industrial and architectural beauty.

You can't look for Montana everywhere. There are all kinds of things that you should be looking for. There's no architectural beauty in any big city that equals the modern architectural beauty or the industrial beauty of Chicago. You see this great big crane, a giant in the sky, picking up things as gracefully as a woman picks up a child. So that's the way our early married life went. She tried to get me to see many kinds of beauties.

In a lot of ways I think that helped me immensely in writing about Montana. I think many Montana stories are limited by being too provincial. They're about roundups and cattle rustlers and whatnot. That isn't even up-to-date.

I was concerned when I wrote about Montana to write with great accuracy about how it really was, but at the same time to show fundamental concerns with universal problems of existence: here is a member of a family who doesn't always abide by the rules and regulations of his society, and he's living something of an underground life and he's getting desperate about it and he needs help. Can't we do something to help him? And you can't find anything that will help him.

I received over 100 letters about that story, saying, "I have a brother just like that, and I can't find anything to do that will help him." From New York City, Jewish girls in New York City.

Seeing the kinds of problems that run through the hearts of sensitive and intelligent people, no matter where they are, will give an enrichment and enlargement to those problems present in any region.

Chicago is very much a home to me, too. I probably couldn't do without either home; my life depends on both of them. I don't feel that because I love both places I'm living the life of a schizophrenic. I feel that they work for each other. I can see more about each one, because of the other.

Why do you like living in the mountains so much?

There's something about mountains that does strange things to us mountain people. We were brought up in the mountains and always looked at people from the plains as deformed. We took mountains to be the natural state of affairs. I still do. I look at plains and I think, "Christ Almighty, once there were mountains here and then something came along and knocked them over. How could something like this be a natural product of the universe?"

I remember the first time I got disabused of that. When I was up here one summer at Seeley Lake, an old farmer from the Dakotas came out here to visit. He'd never seen the mountains before. This poor old bastard had been living out on the flat plains all his life, hadn't really seen any good country. He lasted about two or three days here before he hurried back home. He was terrified of the mountains. He was afraid they were going to fall on top of him and kill him. As he hurriedly left, we were stumped. We thought we were doing him a favor showing him this country.

Did the stories in A River Runs Through It *help connect your life in Montana with your life in Chicago?*

Often the way things that seem disparate and different are unified is by art and beauty. When you see it and are moved by it, you are about as close as you can get to putting the whole shebang together. Somewhere it says all things merge into one and a river runs through it.

Is there a prejudice among East Coast publishers against Western stories?

Not until recently have the Western writers ever gotten a good break from the publishers in New York. I feel that deeply. If I heard that one of the New York publishers was coming across Grizzly Basin I'd be out there and shoot him on sight. They are a filthy bunch.

I had the good fortune of a dream coming true. I'm sure every rejected writer must dream of a time when he's written something that was rejected which turns out to be quite successful, so that all the publishers who rejected him are now coming around and kissing his ass at high noon, and he can tell them where to go.

Alfred A. Knopf, probably the most celebrated of all publishing companies in this country, rejected *A River Runs Through It*. Two or three years after it was rejected, I got a letter from an editor at Alfred A. Knopf asking me if Alfred A. Knopf couldn't have the privilege of getting first crack at my next novel.

Well, well, well. I don't know how this ever happened, but this fell right into my hands. So I wrote a letter. It's probably one of the best things I ever wrote. I understand it's on the wall of several newspapers in the country. I can remember the last paragraph:

"If it should ever happen that the world comes to a place when Alfred A. Knopf is the only publishing company left and I am the only author, then that will be the end of the world of books."

I really told those bastards off. What a pleasure! What a pleasure! Right into my hands! Probably the only dream I ever had in life that came completely true.

Have your stories done anything to change the prejudices against Western stories?

I hope so, but a change like that has to be very broad. You talk about New York publishers, and in a way there is no such thing; there's this bastard and that bastard. It takes a lot of things to affect a good many of them. It may be that the most important thing is not that they're accepting more Western writing, but that Western writers are getting broader-based themselves, more generally interesting and more generally concerned about problems of mankind instead of just cattle rustling.

It's a much healthier situation now. Not very much happened for many years, but now things are happening. You have a guy like Ivan Doig writing. I don't care how much of a New Yorker you are, you better realize you're reading a helluva good writer when you read Ivan Doig.

What was the reaction to A River Runs Through It *back East?*

There were four or five New York publishers who turned it down. On the other hand, New York reviewers, from the very beginning, have thought very highly of it. *Publishers Weekly* was very warm-hearted about it. There were probably 600 reviews of it, and I think I read only one poor review. Reviewers consistently have been very warm-hearted, irrespective of the reason. So I have no kick about reviewers.

Who were some of the writers that you've learned from?

The Bible. Wordsworth. Very early, through my father, Wordsworth became a favorite poet of mine. He's influenced my life a great deal. When I was in the woods I always carried a copy of his selected poems with me. I think poets have influenced me more than prose writers. Gerard Manley Hopkins has influenced my poetical side, and I think some of it comes out in my prose. I like his passion. I think Browning is the best English poet after Shakespeare. I learned a tremendous amount from him about how to handle dramatic dialogue, dramatic speech and character.

Same way about Frost, who had a lot of influence on me. He was an occasional teacher at Dartmouth when I was there, so I had the privilege of being in classes that he taught. I liked him even before I went to Dartmouth. He talked straight to you, and often poetry was there, or something close to it.

What did Frost teach?

Creative writing. We had evening classes in a great big basement room with a wonderful fireplace in it. He'd just walk in front of the fireplace in circles. As a teacher he was like a poet: he composed nothing but monologues. Nobody ever stopped him.

How about Hemingway?

Hemingway was an idol of mine for a while, as he was for

practically all of us of that generation. He and I were about the
same age. Unlike a lot of people who thought a lot of Hemingway,
I still think a great deal of him. Now Hemingway is in disrepute as
a kind of fake macho guy. I realized that he did put on kind of a
show, but on the other hand I don't see how you could be a real
American writer unless you knew Hemingway well, and had
learned a great deal from him. He was a master of dialogue of a
certain kind, that very tight crisp kind. He was a master in handling action, too. He was almost as good as Charlie Russell. In a
page or even a paragraph he could tell you the most complicated
action. So I don't fall into the school of so-called modern critics
who dislike Hemingway.

According to The Westminster Shorter Catechism, *which you
mention in "A River Runs Through It," man's chief end is to glorify
God and enjoy him forever. Did writing the stories help you to do
that?*

I don't know whether I can answer that. I suppose that in any
conventional sense I'm a religious agnostic. There are things that
make me feel a lot better. I don't particularly find them in a
church. I find them in the woods, and in wonderful people. I suppose they're my religion.

I feel I have company about me when I'm alone in the woods.
I feel they're beautiful. They're a kind of religion to me. My
dearest friends are also beautiful. My wife was an infinitely beautiful thing. I certainly feel that there are men and women whom I
have known and still know who are really above what one could
think was humanly possible. They and the mountains are for me
"what passeth human understanding."

Jean M. Auel

JEAN M. *Auel is the author of some of the most popular books in the world today. Her titles* The Clan of the Cave Bear *(1980),* The Valley of Horses *(1982) and* The Mammoth Hunters *(1985) have set publishing records and won acclaim from critics for their accurate and imaginative portrayals of the lives of prehistoric peoples. Despite her phenomenal success, Auel did not begin writing with the intention of becoming a best-selling author. She first sat down at the typewriter because she had a story to tell, a story that she felt the world needed to hear.*

The story concerned a young woman living in prehistoric times with people who were different from her. Auel wasn't sure who these other people might be, but subsequent research revealed that during the last Ice Age the earth was populated with two different kinds of human beings, Cro-Magnons, who were the first modern humans, and Neanderthals, who were also Homo sapiens and quite advanced, but different from Cro-Magnons. In Auel's story, Ayla, the young woman, a Cro-Magnon, was growing up among Neanderthals and was caught between the two cultures and two ways of thinking.

*Extensive research enriched and enlarged the story; the origi-
nal novel entitled* Earth's Children *became an outline for a series of
six books. The first book in the series,* The Clan of the Cave Bear,
was followed by The Valley of Horses *and* The Mammoth Hunters. *Auel plans to continue the saga of Ayla in three forthcoming
volumes.*

*Auel is a longtime resident of Oregon, a firmly rooted trans-
plant from Chicago, where she was born in 1936. She attended
Portland State University, and received an M.B.A. from the University of Portland in 1976. She is married to Ray Auel, and they
have five children and nine grandchildren.*

*The interview with Auel, a bright and engaging woman, took
place over the telephone in the spring of 1986.*

When you started writing the Earth's Children *series, did you
have any idea how popular it would become?*

No. I hoped what every writer hopes: that the first book
would find a market and an audience, and maybe the second one
would do a little better. That certainly has happened; it just started
at a much higher level. The first printing of *The Clan of the Cave
Bear* was 75,000 books. And the first printing in hardcover for *The
Mammoth Hunters* was a million books. It broke the record. Somebody figured out that that would be a stack of books twenty-nine
miles high.

Did you have any model in mind when you wrote these books?

No. I was just trying to write these stories. I'm still writing for
myself. I'm writing the story I always wanted to read. As it turns
out a whole lot of others want to read it, too. I'm not writing for
critics, or to please a teacher or to please the public, or anyone
else; I'm writing stories to please myself.

The first rough draft has become an outline for the *Earth's
Children* series. That's why I know I'm going to have six books.
People think, "She wrote *The Clan of the Cave Bear* and since it
was successful, she decided to do a sequel."

But this series is not like *Clan II,* and *Rocky III* and *Jaws IV.*
It is a continuation, not a repetition. I won't be telling the same

story over and over again. I really did know, before I finished *The Clan of the Cave Bear*, that I had six books in the series.

Do the other books go further into Ayla's life?

All of the books feature Ayla. They are the story of her life. It's not a generational saga, one of those things where you start with the first generation and you end up with the great-grandchildren. I'm trying to show the diversity, complexity and sophistication of the various cultures during the Pleistocene. Ayla's story is the thread that ties them together.

Did you base the cave dwelling described in The Clan of the Cave Bear *on a particular archeological site?*

Not expressly. It's more like a typical site. It was based in many ways on the cave at Shanidar in Iraq on the southern side of the Black Sea, but the setting is in the Crimea on the northern shore of the Black Sea, because there were Neanderthal caves all through that area. It typifies a Neanderthal setting.

How did you become interested in prehistoric people?

[Laughs] I wish I had a wonderful answer for that. Everyone asks, and I don't have an answer. I started out with an idea for a story. I thought it would be a short story. That was in January, 1977. I had quit my job as a credit manager. I had received an M.B.A. in 1976, so I wasn't going to school, and my kids were almost grown. I was in between, not sure what I wanted to do, in a floating state, which I hadn't been in before. I had had a very busy life.

It was eleven o'clock at night. My husband said, "C'mon, let's go to bed." I said, "Wait a minute. I want to see if I can do something."

An idea had been buzzing through my head of a girl or young woman who was living with people who were different. I was thinking prehistory, but I don't know why. I was thinking, "These people were different, but they think she's different." They were viewing her with suspicion, but she was taking care of an old man with a crippled arm, so they let her stay. This was the beginning. That night I started to write the story. I had never written fiction before. It got to be the wee hours of the morning, I was about ten or twelve pages into it and I decided, "This is kind of fun." Characters, theme and story were starting.

But I was also frustrated because I didn't know what I was writing about. I'd want to describe something and I wouldn't know how or where they lived or what they looked like, what they wore, or what they ate, or if they had fire. I didn't have any sense of the place or the setting. So I thought, "I'll do a little research."

I started out with the Encyclopedia Britannica, and that led to books at the library. I came home with two armloads, and started reading them. I learned that the people we call Cro-Magnon were modern humans. The stereotype of Neanderthal is of a knuckle-dragging ape, but they were Homo sapiens also, quite advanced human beings.

I felt as though I'd made a discovery. "Why don't we know this? Why aren't people writing about our ancestors the way these books are depicting them?" That became the story I wanted to tell: the scientifically valid, updated version.

So you wanted to clear up this misunderstanding?

Also tell a story. It's always been the story first. I discovered that I love being a storyteller. I wanted to write a good story, but also to characterize these people in a way that is much more acceptable currently by the anthropological and archeological community.

Was it difficult to turn this archeological material into a story?

Well, any kind of writing is difficult. Basically, as I was reading those first fifty books, I began to take notes of what might be useful to the story. Then I put together a page, or page-and-a-half outline for a novel. I sat down at my typewriter, and started to tell the story to myself.

Now, if I were to compile a bibliography of my reading for the series, it would approach a thousand entries. I've also traveled to Europe, and taken classes in wilderness survival and native life ways. In terms of the research, I probably read about ten or 100 times more than I needed, until I got so comfortable with the material that I could move my characters around in the story with ease.

I wasn't thinking of getting it published. I was just thinking of the story. As I started to write it, the story started to grow and develop, and the ideas I had picked up in the research were finding their way into it.

How long did it take you to write the rough draft?

It didn't take any more than six or seven months, from the time of the first idea to the time I finished a huge six-part manuscript that became the outline for the series. I had free time then. I didn't have any other demands on my time, except just to live and say hello and goodbye to my husband once in a while. He was really quite supportive. I became totally obsessed and involved and excited. I found myself putting in every waking moment. I'd get up and I'd almost resent taking a shower before sitting down at the typewriter. I was putting in twelve, fourteen, sixteen hours a day, seven days a week.

What happened to the rough draft?

I went back and started to read it, and it was awful. I was telling the story to myself but it wasn't coming through on the page. I thought, "My feeling and my passion are not there." So then I went back to the library to get books on how to write fiction.

After doing a lot of self-study, I started to rewrite this big mass of words. I thought I was going to cut it down. About halfway through the first of these six parts I discovered I had 100,000 words. In adding scene and dialogue and description and everything necessary to write a novel, the thing was growing. I thought, "I'm doing something wrong. At this rate I'm going to end up with a million-and-a-half words." Talk about a writer's block.

I went back and really looked at the six different parts, and realized that I had too much to cram into one novel. What I had was six different books. I can still remember telling my husband, "I've got six books." He said, "You've never written a short story, and now you're going to write six books?"

Earth's Children became the series title, and the first book became *The Clan of the Cave Bear*.

The series seems to have a very modern sensibility. Is it as much about people today as it is about prehistoric people?

It's about the struggles of human society. My characters are fully human; they have as much facility with their language as we do, which is why I started to write it in perfectly normal English, even though it would have pleased some critics if I had invented some kind of a phony construct of a language.

I think it's more accurate to show them speaking with ease. So I said, "I'm going to write this as though I am translating it from whatever language they spoke into our language." And good translators don't translate word for word, they translate idiom. There were some words I was careful with. For example, you can say, "Just a moment," but you can't say, "Just a minute."

What made these people's lives different from our own?

The world they lived in. There are a lot of things that we take for granted that hadn't been invented yet. But when Ayla in *The Clan of the Cave Bear* is five years old, she could have been anyone's five-year-old daughter today.

Because we're talking about people like ourselves, it allows me to look at ourselves from a different perspective, through a long-distance lens. I try to see what makes us human. What is basic to being human?

For example, if you plunk somebody down in a hunting-and-gathering society rather than a society where you go into your supermarket and get your meat out of a nice clean plastic package, what will be different and what will be the same? And is one society more or less violent? In most hunting-gathering societies, people feel a great deal of reverence for the animals they hunt. And we who get our packaged, sterilized meat that doesn't even bleed any more really have very little sensitivity to animals.

So there are some definite changes. But there certainly had to be some things that we suffer from, that they also suffered from.

Did you find that you admired these people?

Well, I felt that they were as human as we are, and I admired them, the same way I admire us. Unlike some people, I don't think the world is necessarily going to hell in a handbasket. I think that the human race is a very young race, and I am hoping that we will have the sense to keep ourselves from the destruction that we are potentially capable of dealing to ourselves. For all the stereotype about the brutal savagery of our ancestors, you find almost no evidence of it in the research, not among the Neanderthals and not among the Cro-Magnon.

One of the skeletons found at that Shanidar cave was of an old man. If you read about an old man with one arm amputated at the elbow and one eye that was blind, then you'd have to start asking, "How did he live to be an old man?" Paleopathologists believe that he had probably been paralyzed from an early age, because there was extensive bone atrophy and he was lame on that side. The paralysis may have been the reason his arm was amputated. So he was probably a paralyzed boy and at some time in his life became blind in one eye.

How does that fit in with survival of the fittest? These were Neanderthals taking care of a crippled boy and a blind and crippled old man. Evidence indicates he died in a rock fall as an old man. When I read about him I said, "Oh, my God, there's my old man with the crippled arm. There's the character in my story." That made me feel I was heading in the right direction. He became Creb.

And as you researched this book, did you find that your story grew in a lot of ways?

Exactly. And it was so much more interesting and fun to write within the modern scientific interpretation. I thought, "There's so much to write about, and I'm going to be the one to write it."

Did you do research in fields other than archeology?

Oh, yes. Many others. I would wonder, "How did they carry water? What kinds of things will carry water?" And by reading the reports of field anthropologists into more modern societies—the aborigines, the Bushmen, or the American Indians—you find out that watertight baskets will carry water, or carved wooden bowls, or water-tight stomachs.

I drew from all over the world. If it was appropriate and came together, then that's what I would use. I tried to give the sensitivity, the feeling of the hunting-gathering society.

For example, the idea of ancestor worship: when I was reading about the Australian aborigines, I learned that at one time they didn't really have a full understanding of procreation, particularly the male role in procreation. They knew a woman gave birth, but they weren't sure how she got pregnant. That led to speculation for my story. I thought, "What if this was a time so long ago, that the male role wasn't understood by most people. What would be the result?" Well, the only parent they would know for certain would be their mother, and her mother before that, and the mother before that, and maybe somebody would think, "Who was the first mother?"

You could see how a whole mythology based on the miracle of birth could evolve. Then I remembered about all these little figurines dating back to the early Cro-Magnon period, these round, motherly women carvings. I thought, "I wonder if they aren't meant to represent a great mother sense." That's how I derived some of the culture ideas.

When you were telling a story, did you have to pick and choose among the evidence to decide what pieces to use?

Of course. For instance, did Neanderthals talk? There are two schools of thought on that. Professor Lieberman at Brown University is the proponent of the idea that there probably was some limitation in Neanderthals' ability to communicate, to talk, verbalize, and Lewis Binford finds little in the archeological record to show that they were able to make the necessary abstractions for full speech. But their cranial capacity, the size of their brains, was, on the average, larger than ours. And other scientists say that the evidence of their culture suggests that they were able to understand some abstractions. They were the first people to bury their dead with ritual and purpose. Somebody must have been thinking, "Where are we coming from and where are we going?" That gives us a clue that the way they thought might not be so different from the way we think, or at least feel. Emotions such as compassion, love and caring come through most strongly.

So they must have had, if not language, at least. . . .

At least a very strong ability to communicate, which is why I came up with the sign language idea. I said, "Okay, I'll take both of these ideas and combine them. I will say, 'Yes, there was a limitation in their language, but not in their ability to communicate.'" Sign languages are very complex. I did some research into that.

So if there's a gap between pieces of evidence, you can bridge the gap with your imagination?

Yes. And sometimes I can push things out. I can go a little farther than a scientist can go, because I am writing a novel. I might stretch the barrier, but I don't want to break through it. I don't want to write anything that would do a disservice to the latest findings of science. I want the background to be as accurate as I can make it. If the basis is factual, then I have something for my imagination to build on.

The character of Jondalar is based on an actual skeleton found at the site called Cro-Magnon, the site that gives the name to the early race. They found five skeletons at this particular site. One of them was of a man who was 6 feet, 5¾ inches tall. As soon as I read that, I said, "That's got to be Ayla's man."

Does this attention to detail make the story more believable?

People say, "You're writing fiction. What do you do research for? Why don't you just make it up?" Well, in a work of fiction, even if it's a modern novel set in Washington, D.C., if you're going to mention the address of the White House, you'd better have that address right. Because if all the basic facts that you put down are as accurate as you can get them, it aids readers in suspending their sense of disbelief. As a novelist you want to have readers believe, at least while they're reading the story, that all this could be true.

Where did the information about the herbs and medicines that the people used come from?

I have a research library now of books I've purchased, and I got some of the information from public libraries. We know that they were hunting-gathering people and we know that modern hunter-gatherers are very, very familiar with their environment. Some groups can name 350 plants, know all of their stages and all of their uses. While we don't know precisely what plants Neanderthals or Cro-Magnons used, from pollen analysis and from the way we're able to tell climate, we know what plants were probably growing there because the same plants are around today. Except domestic plants were in their wild form.

Did it give the people any advantage to be closely tied to the natural world?

It would give them the advantage of being able to live in their world. They needed it to survive. That is survival in the natural world. There's also survival in New York City. If you were to take an aborigine, or a Cro-Magnon moved up in time and set him in the middle of the modern world, and if he were an adult, how would he make a living? He wouldn't have grown up in our society, or gone to school. He might have all kinds of knowledge and background but it would not be useful to him any more, and would not have the same value.

That happened in this country to native cultures when the white Europeans invaded and began to settle. For example, the Northwest Coast Indian society was a very rich culture and they built houses out of cedar planks. It is very difficult to split a log and make it into planks by hand with wedges and mauls; it takes knowledge, skill and effort, so each one of those planks had a high value.

Now, if a white settler puts in a sawmill, and suddenly they're whipping out planks at many many times the number per day than a person can do by hand, the plank no longer has the same value; it has lost its meaning within Indian society. Culturally and economically the Native American people were deprived. And that's part of the problem today, the displacement that many of them feel.

What our early ancestors knew enabled them to live and survive in their world. We wouldn't know how to follow the tracks of an animal or when they migrate, but we have to know airline schedules and how to cross a street without getting hit by a car.

Do you use elements of the Northwest landscape in your work?

Oh, absolutely. It was really kind of fun when I discovered, particularly in *The Clan of the Cave Bear*, that there's a little mountain range at the south end of the Crimea, which is a peninsula in the Black Sea, and a strip of coastland which is Russia's Riviera today. During the Ice Age that was a temperate climate. There were cold steppes to the north, but the mountain range protected the southern end. This small coastal area was a well-watered, temperate, mountainous region subject to maritime influences, not so different from the Northwest. I even discovered that azaleas grow wild there, as they do here.

Did setting the story in that particular kind of landscape create certain constraints?

Well, you can't have a story, you can't have anything, if you don't have limits, boundaries. You can't have one setting that is arctic and equatorial all at the same time. So yes, it puts limits, constraints, but those are usually fairly welcome limits. It gives you a frame to write within.

Was there an abundance of food during that period?

Most scientists and most researchers think that the last Ice Age period was probably richer than it was later during more temperate times. The glaciers caused a certain kind of environment that made for open steppes, or grasslands. Those vast grasslands fed grazing animals in hundreds of thousands of millions. It was also rich in terms of the produce that was available, so there were both animal and vegetable resources.

As the glaciers retreated, the forest started to move in, and forests aren't as rich. They don't support great herds of animals. Instead, animals stay either in small family groups or alone. The deer that run through the forest don't congregate in huge herds like the bison on the plains, and they're also harder to hunt because the animals can find trees and brush to hide among. It's much easier to hunt an animal on an open plain than when it's hidden in the woods.

In forests, there's more tree-growth, but not necessarily as much variety of plant-growth. So when the glacier melted, it reduced the abundance and variety of plant species. In the late Pleistocene, after the Ice Age, evidence of much more use of fishing and shell food was found. Such climatic changes may have caused pressures toward agriculture. The great variety and abundance was gone. Some way had to be found to feed the population.

Do you get a lot of mail back from your readers?

I do get a lot of letters from readers, and I'm very grateful for them. People become quite ardent; there are readers who feel very, very strongly about these books. It's a surprise to me. I'm delighted, but I'm a little overwhelmed. I don't really know what I'm doing right.

I get letters from men and women of all ages, twelve to ninety-two, and all walks of life—engineers, scientists, marines, lawyers, teachers, and people who barely can put together a grammatical sentence.

I even get letters from prisoners in jail. The one that I didn't know quite know how to handle was a letter from a man who said he was on death row, and would I hurry up and finish *The Mammoth Hunters* so he could read it before he died? I didn't know what to say.

What do you plan to write in the future?

I intend to write all six books in the series. That's an internal pressure. I have to finish telling Ayla's story. She won't let me alone.

And after that?

I may do anything. I may write about other prehistoric people. I may change to a different part of the world. I may write about later prehistoric periods. I may write something historical. I may write something modern. I might write science fiction. I might write a horror story, or a mystery. Who knows? I've got many things that I'd like to try. What I do know now is that I want to keep on writing, but I was forty before I knew what I wanted to do when I grew up.

Why was that?

I don't know. I suspect part of it is that I couldn't have done it any earlier. There are many young people who are fine writers, but I could not have been one. I needed to live some life and gain some experiences. I couldn't have written what I did without having gone through having a family, raising children, accepting responsibility, being out there in the world, working, coming across many different kinds of people and learning how to live with them.

Marilynne Robinson

*F*EW *first novels have received such lavish praise as Marilynne Robinson's* Housekeeping. *The novelist John Hawkes called it "...a quiet, humorous, beautiful book filled with what I can only call the ecstasy of wisdom.... I think that there are few first novels published since mid-century to compare with* Housekeeping *for sheer perfections of language and for conveying what it means to be human. It is a work of pure grace."* Housekeeping *was awarded the Ernest Hemingway Foundation Award for best first novel, and a Richard and Hinda Rosenthal Award.*

Housekeeping *is the story of a family living on a large lake in northern Idaho, a family which has endured two deaths by drowning and many defections, but which continues as a family, though not in any conventional way. It is a story of the ties that bind some people to a house, a yard, a community, and the restlessness that keeps others continually moving, from job to job and place to place. It is a novel written for the ear, delicious in its sensitivity to the sound and the rhythm of words. Few readers of the book have come away from it unmoved, and many, years later, can still recall the melancholy dream it evokes through the most beautiful and haunting of language.*

In addition to Housekeeping, *Marilynne Robinson has written articles for* The New York Times *and other publications, including an exposé on the Sellafield nuclear plant in England (*Harper's, *February, 1985).*

The author was born in Sandpoint, Idaho, in 1943. Her father worked in the lumber industry and his career took the family to various places around the area. Robinson is a graduate of Brown University and received a Ph.D. in English from the University of Washington. She lives in Northampton, Massachusetts, with her husband and two sons.

The interview took place in the summer of 1985 in room 248 of the Mechanical Engineering Building on the University of Washington campus. Robinson was in Seattle as an instructor at the Spectrum Writers Conference. Proud of bearing, she has an extensive, almost Shakespearean vocabulary with which she can fix with great precision any idea, emotion or thought she is attempting to describe.

As a first novel, was it difficult to get Housekeeping *published?*

Not at all. I had no problem. A friend of mine who's a novelist sent it to his agent. She accepted it, she sent it to Farrar, Straus. They accepted it and that was that.

Were you surprised at the reception the book got once it was in print?

Yes, I was. I thought when I was writing it that it was probably not a book that would be published, and I took a sort of churlish satisfaction in the idea that it wouldn't be. Everything that has happened subsequently has surprised me, but also pleased me enormously.

What prompted you to write the book?

I just wanted to write a book. Since I was a little kid I always thought of myself as a writer; never a doubt in my mind that I would write a book sometime. What prompts people to write books normally is that they want to write a book—with very few exceptions, where people are very cause-oriented. The book was its own reason.

When did you get started on it?

When I was a graduate student I would write little bits of metaphor and imagery just to try my hand because I wasn't doing fiction writing. I saved it all up and it wasn't much but it had a significance for me. It would make up ten to fifteen pages in *Housekeeping*. That was over years of time while I was a graduate student. After that I wrote the book very quickly; it took me about fourteen months to write the book, once I began writing full-time.

How many revisions did the book go through?

I don't revise. It didn't go through any.

Did you learn to write fiction in the process of writing Housekeeping?

Well, I did take writing courses at Brown and I think they were a lot of help; that was my major preparation. I don't know what learning to write fiction means; I have the feeling I learned not to distract myself. My first creative-writing teacher was John Hawkes and he was a marvelously good editor/critic. He was very good and very businesslike about making me sensitive to real and unreal language: what worked and what didn't work. He's enormously good at seeing what you do well and enhancing your sensitivity to the things you do well, which I think is the best thing a creative-writing teacher can do.

Are there things about the book that you would change now that it's out?

No. It's not because I consider it perfect as it stands but because I consider it to have its own life. I don't think about it anymore from that point of view—it's a finished thing. Sure, anything could always be done over. When I read it sometimes I come across a passage and I think, "I don't like this at all," and the next time I read it I think that it was a good part. It changes for me like that. Even if I could tinker with it I wouldn't, because I don't think my judgment in the second instance would be any better than my judgment in the first instance.

Is the success of Housekeeping *in any way an impediment to your writing a second novel?*

No. I've had the problem that I didn't want to do the same thing twice. One of the things that makes the second novel difficult for anybody is that the temptation to repeat the same solutions is very, very strong. I found myself doing that. It seems to me that the problems I have writing are problems that I have really with language as an issue. It's not just anxiety about whether the second book will be as well received as the first, but simply, what do I want to do and how do I want to do it? That's a problem that's been very difficult for me to solve. But if I had had the same things on my mind when I wrote the first novel as I have now, the first novel would have been difficult in the way the second is now. It's not a sort of sibling conflict that's going on between them.

Are you at work on another novel now?

Yes. In a certain sense I started the second novel before I finished *Housekeeping*. I was already thinking about it and even had done some work on it. But it's been difficult for me; it is not an easy child.

I've been doing a lot of things, writing and not writing. I'm pretty well adjusted to the fact that I'm not a prolific writer. We non-prolific writers have our place too; life is long and I'll put in my share.

How do you work?

I'm not systematic about it as you can probably tell by what I've just said. When I can work constantly, I work a few hours in the afternoon every day.

Do you consider writing as a career or vocation?

A vocation, I suppose, a calling, although that sounds kind of silly. I don't think of myself as a professional in the sense that I consider writing to be primarily how I make my living. I consider it something that I arrange my life in order to be able to do.

Could you describe how the process of composition differs between a novel and an essay?

One of them attempts to deal with reality and the other attempts to simulate reality. In one case you're attempting to organize what you take to be true in a meaningful way, and in the other you are inventing something that will have the appearance of truthfulness. They're completely different uses of one's brain.

And something like your Ph.D. dissertation would be yet another way of organizing things?

Yes, it's different from either journalism or novel. Critical writing, if it's good, is closer to fiction writing. And if it's bad, it's a totally illegitimate form and should be expunged. [Laughs]

How did you go about doing that piece on the Sellafield nuclear plant?

When I was living in Britain I found out that the thing was there. I was perfectly amazed because nothing had ever hinted to me that such a thing was going on. I thought it was extremely important. So I found out everything I could find out about it — within the parameters I had set for myself—and came home and wrote the article.

I thought that there should not be silence about this. I think that the silence that has covered this whole thing is absolutely creepy. For example, Greenpeace is very, very aware of the problem in England and somehow feels that our tender ears cannot be shocked with this information. Which means that Americans go to Britain, eat radioactive fish and swim in radioactive water. It makes you feel a little ill when you see a "Save the Seals" button. There's a lot more at stake in the world than seals, and they're perfectly aware of it.

There was no reason why I shouldn't say something. I knew enough about the sort of things that were involved that I felt confident I could venture some interpretation. Since I was a writer I had a good opportunity of having what I said heard. I couldn't have lived with myself if I hadn't made some effort to make this information available. If the things that people say about plutonium are true, then this is a very serious disaster, an ongoing and even accelerating disaster. How could I not say anything? I don't understand the mentality of all the other people who have not said anything.

What was the reaction to the article?

It was split down the middle. The British government was of course mad, called me a hack journalist and so on. There were a lot of people who felt that I had attacked Britain. This is very strange to me. If the American government were allowing Americans to be exposed to hazards of this kind and anybody—Libya or Iran—objected, we would be in their debt for attempting to do something in our interest. It seems to me that a crime is being committed against the British population by the people that are involved in this, and I think that I'm a better friend to the British people than their own government in this instance.

It makes me mad because people say that this is anti-British, and obviously I think something is profoundly wrong that would allow this to happen, but it's not anti-American to be opposed to the things *we* do wrong. I think the same thing about Britain. The best friends they could have would be people who would try to get them out of this wretched mess.

Have you always been aware of ecological issues?

I'm interested in biology and botany and all that. The greatest source of metaphor in the world is the natural world; the orders that spontaneously seem to appear in natural things are utterly beautiful. I read about them because I find them marvelous, marvelously suggestive. And I have a certain admiration for the biosphere; I like to imagine that it could go on without end. The old "world without end" formula is one of great appeal. I hate the idea that the well is being poisoned, which it is.

It seems that in Housekeeping *you were able to use the natural world to express things that would have been hard to express in other ways.*

I wouldn't make that distinction, because the natural world is very much the subject of *Housekeeping*. I was more interested in looking at it than I was in using it to create other things.

How did studying Shakespeare as a graduate student prepare you for something like writing Housekeeping?

I'm not sure it did. I really enjoyed Shakespeare. The reason that I wrote the thesis on him is simply that he is pretty good [laughs]; he doesn't wear out on the second reading. I really enjoyed writing that thesis. It was more a piece of historiography than literary criticism, or at least fifty-fifty. That was good for me. That was the first attempt I had made in that area, and it turns out to be something that consistently interests me.

In your thesis, you talked about how Shakespeare should be

judged in relation to his contemporaries —
   You have read my thesis? [Incredulously]
   I read the introduction, and some of the rest.
   Good grief, that reaffirms my faith in humanity.

   I remember you said in the thesis that Shakespeare should be judged in relation to the other writers of his period. And I wondered how you saw your own work in relation to the other writing that's going on now.
   Well, literature tends to have two phases. There are periods when people are looking for a solution—periods of anxiety—and then there will tend to be an outburst of production with some solution, like Romanticism after the eighteenth century, or history drama at the end of the Middle Ages—a style of articulation or some invention that solves the problem and releases a flood of energy which spends itself; and then the problem is again to find the solution that will again release what people need to say.
   It's very hard to know, yourself, whether you're in a period of groping or in a period where the groping is rewarded by a creative outburst. I think that we can't know because it's hard to get a perspective on it. But I would speculate, from talking to writers, that this is an experimental period where people are enormously engaged by problems of art.
   This is a very respectable state of mind. The people in this phase are the ones that do all the heavy intellectual work for the latecomers who will prosper on their solutions. So both of these phases are interesting, but I would say that we are in the phase of understanding the difficulty of art, and not bringing together for ourselves at the moment satisfactory conventions, or modes or forms or whatever, to do what we want to do. And so there's a lot of experimentation, a lot of hesitation.
   And I see myself simply as another laborer in this vineyard: you should think of something and try it out. The context that we have as a group of writers now is something that will be visible later but is not really visible now. I couldn't really place myself aside from that.
   It seemed that you achieved some kind of synthesis which allowed you to write Housekeeping.
   For me, yes. In *Housekeeping* I found my way around prob-

lems that I have never succeeded in finding my way through, which is a perfectly respectable thing to do. But the problems remain interesting, and I would like, if not to solve the problems, at least to evade them in a new way. [Laughs]

What kind of problems are you talking about?

Problems of language, how language is used now, what terms of reference are available, what kind of allusive weight and suggestion words carry on them. In a certain way language is free of you, in the sense that if you use certain kinds of vocabulary you are implying a certain kind of story. Contemporary experience has so much literary weight lying around on it, from *Babbitt* to *Death of a Salesman*, or *The Waste Land*, and on and on and on.

There's been a profound consensus through that whole period of literature, giving one version of the world and completely appropriating the vocabulary of ordinary life to its purposes. And if you find that a little bit old-mannish and you don't want to mess around with it anymore, you still have the problem of how to pry language loose from this enormous concrete statue these writers have made to themselves.

And so it will be difficult in your next book to find a way around these problems in language and literature?

Yes. It's something that I've always felt was difficult even when I was a student writer. There is a certain mentality that has grafted itself onto the language of contemporary experience that I don't consider terribly smart or terribly interesting—as a matter of fact I think it's a great bore—but the capture of the language by this mentality has been so absolute that it's very hard to say a word like "suburb" or "supermarket" or "highway" without having people say, "I know what she means," and supplying a whole world around it, which is perhaps not a world that you attach any meaning or value to at all; you're really not telling *Babbitt* again.

So it's a problem of association?

Yes.

Is there something else that you want to say about these subjects?

There's something else that I want to *know* about them. Part of the problem is that the things are encased in the assumptions that you have about them, and they remain unknowable to you.

One of the things that fascinates me about this thing that I did, and am doing, about Britain is that I'm sure that one of the reasons I was the first person to say anything about this is because Americans are not intellectually capable of understanding that Britain would do anything that crazy.

I knew people who were there who read the newspapers that I read, and it was as if this did not pass before their eyes. Preconceptions block out reality all the time, probably block out more than they let in. Most basic perceptions that you have about the world are conditioned by other people's conceptions. I find that trying, and I wish that there was some way to get a purchase on it, to make one's experience more one's own.

To what extent does Housekeeping *depend on your own experience?*

Books always depend on people's experience, but it's like when you have a dream, very often dreams are extremely strange and you wonder with perfect reasonableness, "Where in the world did I get that?"

Writing fiction is very much the same. Nothing comes out but what goes in, in some sense. It's simplistic to say that something is or is not based on experience because obviously everything has to be based on experience, but in no simple sense.

So an experience might take on a new form in fiction that it did not have in real life?

Just like dreaming. Things transmogrify. There's no point really in thinking about experience as if it would translate straightforwardly into artistic behavior, because it simply never does.

What part did religion play in your upbringing?

I grew up in a setting where the sort of religious atmospheres that were characteristic of this country persisted. The language was around, the conception was around. The Bible was still read in schools then—I don't think it should be—don't misunderstand me —but nevertheless in various settings I read King James English, which is very, very beautiful.

So you were brought up Protestant?

Yes.

Did you find that religion was useful in interpreting things?

I think it is. It's always one of the oldest and most ambitious and most elaborated systems of understanding in any culture. Among us, the same religion can be thought of as going on for 4,000 years. It was people's major way of understanding for 3,800 years. Yes, it's a very important system of understanding.

Did your ancestors come from the Midwest?

My mother's ancestors did, my father's came from the South.

What drew people to the mountains?

I've always wondered, I've always wondered. It's literally true that my grandfather came there because he had grown up in the Middle West and wanted to see mountains. Others of them I really don't know. I can understand it as an aesthetic choice, but I don't know if that was their motive.

In the novel, the old man moved west because mountains were his idea of paradise. Was it something like that for your grandfather?

Probably not.

Could the story of Housekeeping *have taken place on the East Coast?*

I have no idea, because I don't know the East Coast that well. If you live there as an adult you don't know really what people's attitudes are at that most basic level. I don't see the story as plausible or implausible in those terms. It's an invented tale, and I don't think that there's any hint that it's not. It's like a foundling story. The eastness or westness of it...I don't think of it as particularly more or less likely to occur anywhere. People from Finland have told me that they knew precisely similar circumstances.

Do you feel a strong sense of connectedness between yourself and the land?

Less than I wish I did, but that's often the way it is. You imagine what it would be like if you felt the way you wished you did feel, and that becomes a sort of feeling in itself.

Do you think the feeling of being close to the land is more peculiar to the West or something common to other areas of the country?

Very common, very common. Lots of urban writers write

about the city with exactly the same feeling as rural writers write
about a potato field. It's your significant place; it's not any particular terrain.

*Do you think that the landscape is outsized for the characters,
such as in the town of Fingerbone?*

In certain moods I have felt that to be true, yes. I do sometimes feel here that the landscape seems to be tolerating little en-
croachments, and at some point the whole human civilization
could just be shrugged off like crumbs fly off a tablecloth. [Laughs]

*So the landscape tends to diminish human constructions like
cities and towns?*

In a sense yes, in a sense no. They become much more strik-
ing because they look out of place on the landscape, and it seems to
inspire giganticism. Like this university. It's like somebody took a
university and blew it up with a tire pump—pfft, pfft, pfft. It's just
enormous. Everything is enormous. This university is out of scale
with everything except this landscape.

*What do you think that does to people's perception of the
land? Are they frightened of it?*

Probably in part. They ought to be if they're smart. It's not a
stroll in the park. It's a real landscape, that's the charm of it. It's
got real woods with real creatures in it.

*Do you think the Western landscape encourages a sort of
transience?*

It's hard to know. People that have come here are relatively
recently arrived here, compared to people that are elsewhere, and
they feel more mobile because they have a more recent history of
mobility in their families. For all Westerners it's true that the option of getting up and going away to another place you like better
has been an option that has been exercised in their families often
repeatedly. That does make them feel more free. Transient, I
don't know. That has other connotations.

William Stafford

IN HIS *gentle, idiosyncratic, often personal poetry, William Staf-ford doesn't try to advance any particular social program or polit-cal agenda, but instead chooses words which chime together to produce a magical effect, an effect which reveals the workings of his remarkable consciousness.*

Although he is known primarily as a poet, Stafford also writes short stories, essays, sermons and non-fiction books. His first book, Down in My Heart *(1947), describes his experiences as a conscientious objector during World War II. His other books of prose have dealt primarily with the art and craft of writing, includ-ing* The Voices of Prose *(1966), and* Writing the Australian Crawl: Views on the Writer's Vocation *(1978). His work began to com-mand national attention after his book* Traveling Through the Dark *(1962) received the National Book Award for poetry. Sub-sequent volumes of poetry such as* The Rescued Year *(1966),* Al-legiances *(1970),* Someday, Maybe *(1973),* Stories That Could Be True: New and Collected Poems *(1977) and* A Glass Face in the Rain *(1982) have enhanced and widened that reputation. But de-spite all the admiration for his work, Stafford remains committed to writing to please himself, and seems remarkably unmoved by the commotion around him.*

Born in Hutchinson, Kansas in 1914, Stafford married Dorothy Hope Frantz in 1944. They have four children. He received a B.A. from the University of Kansas in 1937, an M.A. in 1945, and earned a Ph.D. from the University of Iowa in 1955. Stafford worked in sugar beet fields, oil refineries, construction projects, the U.S. Forest Service and the Church World Service before becoming a professor of English at Lewis and Clark College in Portland, Oregon. He taught at the school for over thirty years before retiring several years ago. The interview took place in an empty classroom there in the spring of 1986. Stafford is a modest, self-effacing man with clear brown eyes and a light, musical voice which still holds a hint of a Midwestern twang.

Why were you a conscientious objector in World War II?

I was pretty well-established in this point of view before World War II came along. When I was in high school and college in the '30s, many students were anti-war. People saw it coming. They said, "It's coming, it's coming." Then it came. Well, other people changed. I didn't change. That's it. Roosevelt got elected by saying, "I will not send our youth to war." Then he changed. Then they changed.

Did you have strong religious objections to the war?

It's hard to say what religion is. In fact, in World War II the law said that conscientious objectors were "those who by reason of religious training or belief are conscientiously opposed to war." But nobody wanted to define religion, least of all the Army. So if you said you were a conscientious objector, if you were opposed to war, that in itself was considered a kind of religion. So the law became a tautology really. Those who are opposed to war are religious, is one way of saying it.

Did being a conscientous objector change you in any way?

That interval made a big difference in my life. I went to camp, concentration camp or whatever it was, for four years, doing so-called "work of national importance" under civilian direction, rather than military. It delayed a lot of things but it also hurried up a lot of things. Didn't slow down my writing; it may have enhanced my writing. Because in camp I had a little bunk and I had writing materials, so I wrote a lot.

I liked the poem that you wrote about the fire lookout. Was that written about this time in your life?

That was when I was a C.O. in northern California on Peg Leg lookout near Mount Lassen. That's a souvenir of those times. It's a kind of meditative poem about eating animal crackers and reading all of those big books.

When did you start writing poetry?

In grade school. All kids write in grade school. I kept right on. When I was in high school I began to be sort of ambitious about my writing. I can remember one of my high-school English teachers reading my paper to the class. That was my first publication and maybe my best. It was quite invigorating to feel that it was possible to write things that would interest at least me. And it has stayed that way for me. Most of the things I write, people don't see, nobody sees, except me. But now and then there's something. . . . It's not the same as writing to sell or even publish somewhere, because I don't want to be inhibited by editors' wants. So I get onto something that interests me and I follow it, like whittling.

So you write for yourself?

Yes, I've found the best way for me to go is to be without purpose, without publishing aim. It continues to be amazing to me how many things that I write just for me turn out to be for somebody else.

I just have a lot of things around my house. It's like running a big warehouse. Some editor gets in touch with me, "You have a poem about the Bible?" "Ooh, I'm sure I have here somewhere."

Do you work on things besides poetry?

When I write, it can be anything. I mean today, for instance, I was writing a homily. The host at a college got in touch with me and said, "Would you present a kind of a poetic homily for a church service on Sunday morning?" I'll be there Sunday and Monday. So I said, "Sure."

Who were the poets that you read when you were growing up?

Many, many poets. My parents were eager about reading and I got an appetite for it early. So I read, and they read to me. They kept on reading to me, and we'd read to each other. It proved to be something that I liked to do. I'm an effortless reader. I can read without effort at any speed. We read many poets—Whittier and Longfellow, and the English poets Tennyson and Hardy; all kinds of people. Kipling was a favorite.

When did you decide to commit yourself to writing poetry?

I don't feel that I've ever made that commitment, it's just crept up on me. It turned out that I could manage poems, in the spare time I had while I was teaching, better than I could bigger pieces. I like big pieces. I like prose. I'm addicted to novels, and other kinds of writing too: how-to, science and biography. But it just turned out that those things that got taken most often were the poems. In my warehouse, the poetry section is the hot section.

Have you written novels?

I haven't written novels. I've written short stories and articles and prose books. In fact I have a prose book that I'm all done working on. It is about writing. It's for the University of Michigan series. I have an earlier book in that series called *Writing the Australian Crawl*.

Why did you become a teacher?

I knew that I had to make a living somehow. I worked at many things: construction, oil refinery, Forest Service, Soil Conservation Service, in the sugar beet fields, all sorts of things. But teaching is a natural thing for a person who reads and writes, so I fell into it.

When did you move to the Northwest?

Once World War II was over and people were let out, my wife and I moved to southern California. I took some courses at Berkeley and got myself registered there for teaching positions and was hired. I taught in southern California in a high school, and then got a job up here in 1948.

What was your impression of the Northwest?

I liked it. C.O.'s I had known who were up here said, "Oh, Bill, you'll like Oregon and you'll like the Portland area." My wife and I both liked it when we came up and scouted the place, and we've liked it ever since.

Were you writing at this time?

Yes, I was writing, even before I came up here. I had things published in *Poetry* magazine and a few other places before I moved to Oregon.

Did it take you a while to start writing about the Northwest?

I can't really tell that I started writing about this place, or that I now write about this place, in a certain sense; I'm going to try to explain this. Many writers in a place that is as definite a region as the Northwest feel that it is very much a part of their writing. I'm not too sure of that about me. I wrote about Kansas, I wrote about Arkansas, I wrote about Illinois, I wrote about Indiana; wherever I was. And if I moved tomorrow I'd write about where I showed up, no matter where it was.

And so my attitude is this: where you live is not crucial, but how you *feel* about where you live is crucial. Since I live in the Northwest, yes, I do write about the Northwest in the sense that place names get in my poems, but as for anything mystical, it hasn't registered on me.

In some ways, let me say, the most minimal scenery is my kind of scenery. This is too busy a place. I stand it very well. It doesn't make me nervous. It's just that it's superfluous. Any Kansan knows that Oregon is a little too lavish.

When you tried to write about this place did you find that you had to change some things in your writing?

No. I didn't feel any change at all. I'm interested in this. I'd be interested in other people's reactions, and I would like to be corrected if possible, but I don't get a glimpse, even a glimmer, of being corrected about it, because I can say without any problem that the language is what I live in when I write. I don't want to say I'm not impressed by scenery; it registers. I know some writers who apparently live on it; they need a lot of scenery. It's kind of a distraction to me.

So your poems didn't change much after you moved to the Northwest?

I don't think that they changed because of the region. As a matter of fact, I have felt that the unity in Northwest writing that's ascribed to scenery and a mystique, you can account for more by the kind of company the writers keep. If Theodore Roethke hadn't moved to Seattle, the scene would be the same, but the literary scene wouldn't be the same. I think he had a great effect on that. But I hit all that too late for it to do anything to me. I was already an Osage orange, hedgewood Kansan.

So it was Roethke's personality and style of writing that gave Northwest writing a particular style?

I think so. It's a pleasant thought, but the idea that the style is rooted to the landscape just sounds sort of quaint to me.

In a couple of your poems, you talked about the stories that the Northwest had to tell. Could you explain what you meant by that?

If I said that in a poem, I was probably ready for any story, actually, but there are people elsewhere and a lot of people in the Northwest who think that there are certain stories that are Northwest stories. I can enjoy that delusion. [Laughs] I don't want to shut it out. Maybe there are Northwest stories. But I'm not ready to swear there are. If I were in another region, I would say Alaska stories.

So there aren't stories that are particular to this place?

I can't persuade myself that they are particular to this place.

In one of your poems, you talked about how it was necessary to find your place out here.

Yes. Dick Hugo wrote me a letter. He said, "What does the earth say, O sage?" He liked to say things like that to his friends. And so I wrote this poem back to him, "What the Earth Says," something like that. I had the earth say things that came to me when I put myself in the frame of mind to let the earth say something. But what the earth is really saying, I don't know. The poem isn't accurate about what the earth says, it's that it says a succession of things that chime together to become a poem. If I had the earth saying something, then the next thing I had the earth say might as well be something that reinforces that first thing. It may reinforce it by contradicting it, I hasten to say; it's quite complex. Nevertheless, it relates to that first thing. If it's not related, it's not a poem.

It's another poem maybe, but it's not this poem. Whatever I start the earth to saying, I let it speak through me consistently or at least poetically, jumping over a number of problems in the way. So you see what I'm getting at? It's not a matter of accuracy, it's a matter of resonance in what it says to a human being.

So maybe Hugo gets this poem back and he says, "Exactly. You know, Stafford, you got it." He never said that but he might have. I wouldn't have been persuaded by his concurrence that it's any more true, I would just have thought, "That's the way poetry is, Dick. That's the way it works."

So you wouldn't be any more persuaded that the earth said something like that?

No, no. It's a fantastic idea anyway, but since he used the phrasing, I used it back and then proceeded to make a poem out of it. I'm afraid, for all of us, that when we find our way toward what we call truth, we are really finding our way toward effective poems. The concurrence and resonance of juxtaposed experiences is what influences us. We say it's beautiful or it's true. Actually, maybe it's chance. I don't know.

But it usually doesn't end up being a statement?

Unless a human being is involved in this art-sensitive way, it doesn't become an incremental, mutually-reinforcing experience that a work of art is. So I think you lend yourself to what you start to do, then it begins to have unity and reinforcement, human reinforcement. Whether human reinforcement equals cosmic accuracy, that is another story.

I noticed in reading your poems that the natural world seems animate. Is that something you believe or is it a kind of strategy?

I begin to shift even when talking about this because I don't quite know how to respond. I don't feel anything spooky and ghostly about the world around us, but any time something is outside our control and beyond our ready mechanical explanation, one of the big metaphors it can slide into is animate. I'm not above using that. It's comfortable. For instance, I have this poem in which the engine is purring and it sounds like a cat. People say, "Oh yeah, it's animate." But it's similar; that's all.

Is it helpful for a poet to be able to personify things?

I think it's helpful for a poet to be able to side-slip into alternative ways of saying or perceiving things or accommodating things, so the acceptance of an engine as being alive may do you some good in some circumstances, and if so I would have no hesitation in assuming it, but if someone were to ask me, "Is the engine alive?" I'd say, "Of course not. I'm like you. I know what it is."

But when you see in those terms, it seems that you don't see just rocks, plants and trees anymore.

I like that idea. I'm not sure it's mine, but I like it. I would like to see in every way there is to see, and hear in every way there is to hear. Parallels, similarities are welcome; that's the way we live; I certainly would not try to exclude them from my poetry.

Do you ever consciously imitate other poets when you write?

I have imitated other poets for kicks. I'm sure everything influences my language, the people around me, the way they talk; but writers themselves as individuals are a very small part of the influence on me. It's the ocean of language around me. I'm that kind of oyster. I'm getting the nutrients out of the big ocean. And these channels, no matter how powerful, are trivial compared to the ocean.

When you write, do you pay attention to what's under the surface of things?

It's even smaller than that. It's the influence of syllables, it's the cadences. I'm trying to make this be both the sound of syllables and something about the lumbering sentence, that goes along, rising and falling, putting little things in the middle and stringing out little things on the end. It's those things that are registering for me when I write. I haven't really thought of this before, but maybe one thing that might distinguish people who have a sustained interest in writing from other people is that those with a sustained interest retain some excitement about what emerges from language in the process of language. It is sound, but it's other things; it's more than sound. It's even things that are left out. Sometimes those are delicious.

Now what do you mean by that?

It would seem to most people that if you're trying to use language, you're trying to communicate, right? Well...yeah. But the language itself becomes interesting while you're doing it. And the things you don't say to someone are fascinating.

I was just reading a review about a magazine by Jim Hall, a person I knew at Iowa and still know. When he identified that magazine he always put in Inc. at the end. Why did he do that? He didn't need to do that. Lots of magazines are incorporated. But he just sort of torpedoed the magazine by putting Inc. in. See what I mean? It was delicious to me. He made it so commercial, so stodgy. But it's accurate.

It sounds as if your poems come more from your appreciation and attention to language than out of observation of the world.

You can say language, and I did say that. I want to add something, though. The language itself as an entity is fascinating but it also relates to what's out there or in here, to experiences, emotions, thought; those fascinate me, too. And language may be just the channel for getting at those interesting things, those not-very-easily perceived but crucially important things in a scene or in an event or in a person. Language relates to that, not exactly, because it has its own quirks, but it does relate to that. So I don't want to leave out the world, experience; those also fascinate me. But I get at it in my writing through language.

What sort of things do you take from this "whole ocean of words" and put in your poems?

The things that are available are incipient stories or almost subliminal hints. For instance, I was just writing something about trying to go along Main Street without being hurt, but then I see someone at one of these tripods ringing a bell over a bucket with chickenwire over it. Well, I can't help thinking about that. So the next stanza is something else that comes along that makes me aware, when maybe I'd just as soon not be aware. So there are these little boobytraps around us all the time. "Boobytraps" implies harm, but they may not be harmful; happy boobytraps. Little implied events in things. You identify the things, you let the reader have the events.

What kind of events?

I'm thinking about experiences a person may have that will be private. It's as if you're identifying it so as to put it on a shelf in your warehouse. But other people's shelves in their warehouses are a lot like your shelves in your warehouse. So when I talk about someone old with a tripod and ringing a bell, that's the way it comes to me, but it also comes to someone else. My assumption is that the emotional or experiential overtones will be something like mine.

How do you match the sound to those experiences?

The sound comes by itself, in the first instance. It's not as if I'm taking sounds off a keyboard or something. For instance, on this thing I was talking about, "Main Street," I say you encounter Cassandra ringing a bell by a tripod. Well, Cassandra has got hundreds of years of echoes in it, as identification as a person, and woe that's going to come. I'm trying to damp down the drama of walking Main Street, and what do I run into? Cassandra. It's also a nice rolling name, Cassandra. Well, that just comes to me. I don't stop and think, "Now, I must think of a classical name that will bring in the idea of drama." That just comes to me. I don't know how.

Is it maybe from all the reading that you've done?

Reading and listening and talking. Some syllables are fun to say, and the writers who have used them before got them from another writer. Someplace you're going to come to a jumping-off place and say, "Where did they get them before any writer used them?" They got them the same way I got them: they come. They present themselves.

So you don't have to consciously start selecting?

I'm flooded with options, as we all are, even when we're talking. And even here I said "flooded" with options. Aha, figure of speech! Well, I was just trying to get from here to here, and that's what occurred to me to say. Without planning. Maybe I should have planned and said something more original. Irradiated? No.

Do you find that the way you feel about something is often the way other people would feel in a similar situation?

I think almost always. It's true we can pick it apart, find differences—Republicans, Democrats, Tweedledum, Tweedledee. But essentially human beings are embarked—whether they like it or not—as one vast harmonious bunch of beings. Inhale, exhale. There's no one in the room who isn't in this business. They may talk a lot about whether they're black or white or man or woman but they're all breathing. And you shoot off a gun and they all jump. They've all got these things in common.

Does that makes your work as a poet easier?

It's easy. It's quite easy. It is not at all inventing something to outwit nature. It is ganging up with nature.

In what sense do you write for other people?

If you use language, it's social. It's available to other people. So in that sense, it's certainly true that you're doing a human and communicative thing. But earlier when we were talking about what guides you, I intruded the idea that I just do these things and supply my warehouse with what occurs to me. But because I'm human and share a lot of characteristics with others, what occurs to me is at many points congruent with other people's experiences. So in that sense it's for other people. But it's not guided by my anticipation of their delights, it's guided by my appetite for my own delights.

And then after you've written it...?

After you've written it you look at it in a different way. I do. I feel that you shift gears. Now something's written. Something has come to me and I've toyed with it and juggled it around, so satisfying for me. I get to looking at it and I might think, "Does this have characteristics that would interest other people?" If I think so, I'll send it out. And from here go many trails. What people? The kind of people who read *People* magazine? The kind of people who read the *American Scholar*? But that comes after.

It's first what you like.

Yeah.

Does it bother you that people nowadays don't pay much attention to poets?

No. It doesn't bother me. People have other interests. How do I know what inner problems or inner delights they're contending with? And so if someone would be apologetic, as they often are—"I'm sorry. I've never read your poetry,"—I never let my face change, but what I'm really feeling is, "What are you sorry about? I don't understand. Why be sorry? I haven't read yours either. People have different things to do."

It is true that I have determined estimates of the relative value of some kinds of activity, and reading I think is a good thing —but not for everybody, and not poetry for everybody, and not my poetry for all the people who are interested in poetry. They've got to sniff it and decide.

So it just works out that poetry in a time like our own doesn't get much attention?

I'd like to make a distinction here. I think there's poetry everywhere in our lives. Poems are a special kind of thing, but the life of poetry, the excitement of discovery, the human reverberation about related events, that belongs to many, many people. I've said it this way before. Someone meets me outside of church and says, "Isn't it too bad, Stafford, nobody's interested in poetry these days?" They've just been in church chanting, reading. They're overwhelmed by the Bible, which is poetry. They're all caught up in it, but it doesn't fit this little category people use when they say, "Nobody pays attention to poetry now."

When President Reagan gets himself positioned under the right lights with the camera on him and recites one of his poems to the nation, they jump through hoops for it. They don't even know it's poetry; they think it's truth.

Do you think that your own poems have any effect on this larger world of poetry?

It has a small, very small effect, in the sense that everybody's language has an effect on everybody else's language. And it may be that persons who write and get published have a little more leverage on other people than those who don't write and get published. So in that sense, yes. But of course it doesn't always have the effect that would be the nicest for me; they may feel disgust, and I can't do anything about that.

Does reading contemporary poetry help understand at all what's going on in the world today?

That's a wonderful question. That's one that I'll go away from this encounter thinking about. In most senses, I think it doesn't help. And in many cases I believe it hurts. Poems have an especially large element of fakery in them, and they are especially prone to be misleading. Why do I read them then? Well, I'm like a filter, I get the good and leave the bad. "Hold fast all which is good, prove all things"—Saint Paul, I think. At any rate, I do prove all things, but I don't hold fast to much of it. Of course I'm including my own poetry in this. I think that there's something hazardous about poetry. It induces you to indulge in great wild loops of feeling and excitement, and it's all too likely to enable a person to indulge in some kind of a hobby or distortion that they customarily put upon the world. You may read a poet who is suicidal, and thinks everyone ought to be suicidal, naturally, because that's the way the world looks to them. I read them, I prove them, I don't approve them.

In your own poetry, is there some kind of a standard you aim toward?

I don't try when I'm writing to be positive or negative for other people; I just try to maximize the experience that I'm having when I'm writing. So I wouldn't say that my poems are guides to conduct. They are just little flares which illuminate something, but it may not be illuminating a place you want to stay, just a place that you happen to be.

So if a hundred years from now someone read poetry written today, it might not be that reflective of the time?

It would be a mistake to assume that poetry is an accurate picture of a time. It's of course what people use because they don't have much. And certainly the historians are not reliable either. So what are you going to do? You keep on being befuddled, the way we've always been. So I can understand using it, but it's wildly unreliable.

Do you feel much responsibility to the rest of the world as a poet?

I just said that those who write and get published do have a little more leverage, so I suppose you should feel a little extra qualm about what you're doing, but in my own writing and my life I feel a harmony between my beliefs and those things that come naturally to me to write. I don't feel that my writing is a violation of my beliefs, even though I'm not trying to harness my beliefs to my writing. I don't feel a discrepancy, a dangerous discrepancy, so I don't worry about it.

Do you feel that by paying attention to what goes on in your own life, you can understand what goes on in other people's lives?

I like that question too, and I'll naively charge into it by saying it does help. By paying attention to what goes on in your own life, you enhance your chances of knowing what goes on in other lives and in the world. Especially as we become more and more aware of the fallibility of our senses, and the inherent weaknesses of our ways of operating, it behooves us to realize the gross distortions we put on what might be out there for us. And I feel a great hunger to know what is out there, to understand, to get right with things. I do have that hunger. And I do believe that paying attention to the lens will help you understand the image.

Is writing poetry paying attention to the lens?

I feel that it is. I feel that poetry is enlightening for the poet, and let the reader beware.

Do you find that your inspiration waxes and wanes?

Until recently, I would have said it's a little spring, a steady little spring, but I feel recently a number of influences that make me not quite so sure of that. For instance, I feel some flagging of motivation to pursue these things as they come along. I jot them down, but it gets easier for me to leave the jottings. It used to be that I just couldn't rest until I'd put a lot of pressure on this and turned it into a poem. Now I have a lot of loose journal entries and things that I call poems that I'm not sure are poems. So you see I've kind of side-slipped this; for one thing it's scary when you say inspiration. I would say that there are times or moods when more coercive poems come to me than at other times.

Is it hard for you to judge your own poetry?

I don't know whether it's hard, because I don't judge it in a certain sense. I feel that I accept it all. But I do assess it. I assess it as being more or less negotiable for other people. I'm not too confident about being able to do that assessing myself. On the other hand, I never ask anybody else to do it, except an editor. I don't show it to other people. I don't worry everything I write until I think that it's worthy of what I should be writing; not by any means. The only people who see it, almost entirely, would be editors. That's their business, to decide what could be published or should be published in their publication.

But for you yourself...?

I accept it. It's true that I've been more excited about some things than others. I remember a wonderful story about Roethke. He got on his knees and wept, he was so happy about something he had written; he was so grateful. And I have stood up and walked around when I thought I really had something.

Is it a lot of work to write poetry?

It doesn't feel like work. It's like saying to a skier, "Isn't it a lot of work to do downhill skiing?" He'd have to stop and say, "Well, you do use up a lot of energy. And it's work in the physical sense. But it's not done like work. It's done for appetite." That's the way I feel about writing.

Do you feel that you get better at poetry as you get older?

I don't think so. There are certain things that become more sure, but there's a lot that you give up when things become sure. You give up that recklessness that kept you from being sure. And that's more precious than being sure. So there are trade-offs. Things change, but I don't want them to change. I just want to be reckless, inept if that will bring me more experiences in my writing. That's fine with me.

Do you write on a typewriter?

No, no. I usually write with pen, paper first. The poems are hand-written.

Do you write the poem after you've thought of it?

No, I don't. I write it almost before I think of that. There's no waiting to be sure that I'm only putting down those things that are worthy or thought-out. No, it's more like putting down things *before* they're thought out, so it'll be easier to think them out.

And after that happens, is there then a lot of revision?

After that happens, there is quite a bit of juggling around usually. Because you drift through it again and you get different impressions and all sorts of things happen. My pages have arrows, things scratched out, and then there are parts that I don't even bother to scratch out but they're scratched out in my mind.

Do you read your poems aloud as you're writing them?

Sometimes. There's a certain kind of restlessness that comes over me sometimes when I'm writing something that I've found my way toward in terms of thought and feeling but there's something wrong. Sometimes I read it aloud. There's another way to do it: how it sounds in your mind. If I'm desperate enough, I may talk it to myself and see why I feel there are extra syllables or the cadences are wrong.

But it's that internal voice that decides?

It's pretty largely that. That's how it comes for me. If I can slide into the beginning of the cadence of a poem with some phrases that seem to be coming all right, those phrases will help me keep it coming all right. But if I just go slogging into some material, it's hard to make it begin to be like a poem. For example, I began to write one day, "Tell me you years I had for my life, tell me a day..." I liked that. For several reasons. It had that repetition. Also it side-stepped the issue of that awkward thing of stopping someone and telling them something. It says, tell me. So the reader sort of overhears it. And that just made me feel good. And then something about the cadence of it seemed all right.

Do you scan your poems?

The short usual answer would be no, because I think the questioner would be asking me whether I try to put it into a certain kind of beat. I don't consciously do that, but I can't be sure that my habits of reading don't make it automatic. And so maybe the conscious part would be unscanning it; keep it from scanning too simply. That I can very well understand. I have to watch out about that. It's not a problem of getting it into a form, the problem is what form, and should it be just a rocking chair kind of form? You've got to watch out about that.

There's another way though that I do scan. Lines begin to come to me with a certain number of stresses. Maybe four-stress lines. I'm conscious of working to pack something else in or take something out, if it goes under or over. I'm conscious of that.

Did you go through this process in composing "Traveling Through the Dark"?

I'm aware that that poem is pretty much formed. "Traveling through the dark I found a deer/ dead on the edge of the Wilson River road." Five stresses, it goes like that.

But it wasn't so regular that...

No. That's true. Maybe I unscanned it a little bit.

But there is a definite pattern there.

Yes, there is. I think more than usual in my poems. And you

have a kind of a rhyme pattern too. Not heavy—I probably un-rhymed it a bit—but it's there.

Does the process of writing continue to surprise you?

Yes, it does. I suppose that's the most significant thing I could say. The witness I could give to young writers is, it never quits surprising. Early, it came to me that I could start to write some morning without anything at all to say and just be overwhelmed with splendid things. It's a surprise, again and again and again.

Is that why you keep doing it?

I think so. It's like being given something again and again, something you don't deserve, something you may have worked on, but the work doesn't do it. It's a gift. It just comes somehow.

So if you decide to stop, it won't really be your choice.

Well, I wouldn't feel worried in my life if I tried to stop, tried to taper off. There are a lot of things that interest me, and I have had twinges sometimes that maybe writing is blocking some things out of my life. It might make you a kind of observer of your friends, rather than a gung-ho, forget-it-all friend. I've felt it as a photographer. If I take my camera to a party it's different than if I don't. I'm not quite in that party if I'm taking pictures. I'm skulking around the edge. I'm double-thinking the scenes. And maybe my whole life has turned into being adept at wringing out of life poems and stories and articles. As Keats said, "There are things more important than poetry."

Charles Johnson

CHARLES Johnson's novels, short stories and television scripts explore classical problems and metaphysical questions against the background of black American life. His approach to writing is phenomenological, in the style of philosopher Edmund Husserl, but he also draws inspiration from the entire continuum of Asian thought, from the Vedas to Zen Buddhism. His work brings together Eastern and Western philosophical traditions, with the hope that some new perception of experience, especially black experience, will emerge.

Johnson was born in Evanston, Illinois, in 1948. He demonstrated an early talent for drawing, and began a career as a cartoonist at seventeen. After graduating in journalism from Southern Illinois University at Carbondale in 1971, Johnson went on to write and co-produce the PBS series "Charlie's Pad." He received his M.A. in philosophy from Southern Illinois University in 1973, and while there met novelist John Gardner, who guided him in the writing of the novel Faith and the Good Thing (1974). Johnson did graduate work in phenomenology and literary aesthetics in the Ph.D. program at SUNY-Stony Brook before becoming a professor of English at the University of Washington in 1976.

He is the author of the novel Oxherding Tale, *a collection of short stories entitled* The Sorcerer's Apprentice *(1986), two collections of cartoons, and television scripts for the PBS series "Booker" (1973) and "Charlie Smith and the Fritter Tree" (1978). He is currently at work on the novel* Rutherford's Travels, *and has recently completed* Being and Race: Black Writing Since 1970, *a book-length essay which will be published by Indiana University Press. He is the fiction editor of the* Seattle Review, *and received a Guggenheim Fellowship in Fiction in 1987.*

In 1970, Johnson married Joan New, an elementary-school teacher. They and their two children live in Seattle.

The interview took place in the spring of 1985 in Johnson's office on the campus of the University of Washington. Surrounded by the works of Hegel, Kant, Marx and Heidegger, and equipped with several packs of cigarettes, Johnson talked long into the night about his approaches to fiction and philosophy.

You've been a cartoonist, a student of philosophy, a television producer and a photojournalist. Why did you choose to write fiction rather than continuing in one of these other fields?

I still do all of those things. It's not like one got left behind and another was picked up, but when you're talking about language, you have the possibility of multiple levels of meaning. If I shifted at all from the image to the word it's because the word is polymorphous and you can create a work of fiction that has more dimensions than a drawing or even a film. Film of course is wonderful, but I can't think of a single film, even the ones that I love, that are as rich and complex, and have the same vision and depth, as the greatest novels.

Do you think that you will keep writing fiction, or will you use it up and go on to something else?

Right now, fiction is at the center of my work: telling stories in many different forms. I just do the film because it's fun, and because I like to work with producers and creative people who extend my own imagination, and because I want to make some money. But fiction is the basic thing. When you write a story, you have to do everything that the entire film crew listed in the movie credits does, which is work as a scriptwriter, producer, prop person, costume designer—the whole thing. You have far greater freedom as a writer of fiction, and you're challenged to force your imagination into all these different roles.

So fiction is a more aristocratic art form, whereas film is more democratic?

More aristocratic, yes. Every film is a celebration of the crew. Every book, no matter what the writer might have drawn upon, is ultimately the product of a single consciousness.

Did writing come easily for you?

Writing came easily, yes. I enjoyed writing. I enjoyed writing papers in college, because I enjoyed expressing myself in language. So when I started writing novels it seemed to me to be an extension of what I was already doing.

Why did you start with a longer form of fiction like the novel?

Because the novel, of all the fictional forms we have, is the most expansive. It has the greatest room for exploring experience, for character development, and creating a coherent, consistent, complete world.

What did drawing do for your writing?

My concern with commercial objectives got exhausted early through drawing. When I was in high school I did six drawings for a magic-magazine company in Chicago; I thought my life had changed. I still have that first dollar framed. I was obsessed with publication. I think I published a thousand drawings.

By the time I got to fiction I was more patient. I didn't have the hunger to publish that I did when I was a cartoonist. That was good because it taught me to let the story develop as long as it needed to. I care about the process of fiction now more than the egotistical joy of seeing my name in print.

How did you develop your writing style?

The first six books I wrote were heavily influenced by three writers—Richard Wright, James Baldwin and John A. Williams—all of whom I admired a great deal. The books were very naturalistic. They were about racial politics for the most part. They were dark, grim, murder-filled novels. I couldn't read any of them after I was finished.

I started feeling that a change was necessary after the sixth book. There were levels of meaning that I wanted to achieve, philosophical questions that I wanted to raise, and naturalism as an approach prevented that. It was at that time that I met John Gardner, who changed my life and literary approach. He had twenty-five years of experience as a writer behind him. I looked at his work very carefully, even to the extent of reconstructing scenes to see if they could be done differently. And he taught me two things that I couldn't get a handle on as a young writer: voice and prose rhythm. He was very helpful with that because he was a very gifted stylist. Also he was a polymathic writer: he could write in several different forms. He had a strong philosophical background. He was passionate about fiction, not just his own, but good writing by other people.

So my writing changed under the influence of Gardner. I found the outlets I needed for philosophically interesting fiction in respect to the black experience. I still write some stories that are naturalistic, but only if the meaning of the story demands that approach.

And so naturalism is just one of many approaches?

Naturalism is one approach to interpreting reality. It came into its own a hundred years ago with certain writers who wanted to achieve the illusion of objectivity, but it leaves out any number of experiences people claim they have had in this world, experiences that don't fit within the narrow confines of the naturalistic method. So instead of being the only approach a writer has at his disposal, it's one of many. Every novel that I do has a strong realistic element, a naturalistic element, but not only that. There are other aspects of experience, of conscious life, that come in and create a more rounded picture of reality.

You see, naturalism is very Greek in its structure. The Greeks have gods manipulating the destinies of man. Naturalism hasn't a god any more, but it has a modern equivalent—social forces. The social forces operating within a naturalistic story are pretty much the equivalent of the old Greek gods.

It's a strange form of literature. It's social determinism, which I don't particularly like. I think people are free and in control of their destinies, if they really want to be. Naturalism is a literature of victims, as far as I can see. Most of the characters are moved by internal forces or by social conditions or by the age, and are not free to choose how they're going to act. And that's one of the reasons I had to move away from naturalism because I just don't believe that's true of people. I don't think we're puppets. I don't think we're marionettes, whether you're talking about Greek gods, or the economic state of the United States at the moment. Even people who are radically poor and down and out still manage, if they wish, to be self-sacrificing, to care for others, to love and be compassionate, to rise to all the great virtues that we consider to be most human. They are not victims.

Does naturalism rob them of their dignity?

Yes, it does. It gives them no dignity. I don't like that. It's one of the problems I have with a lot of black literature. I'm not knocking naturalism. Everything I've written for television has been naturalistic. It's a very good discipline to make you think about ideas in a particular way and people in a particular way. But you can only get to certain aspects of experience through that. If you look at the life of the spirit naturalistically, you would have to conclude that there is no life of the spirit, there's only a psychological life. If you had to write a story about some of the great saints, Thomas à Kempis, Thomas Aquinas, you would have to think about them not in terms of what they said about themselves, but in terms of modern theories of psychology, Freud down through Maslow. As much as I like Maslow and Jung, I don't think they give a full account of the subjective life. And yet within the framework of naturalism, psychology is all we have in terms of talking about the life of the spirit. It psychologizes it. It makes it mechanical, just a series of causes and effects.

So it's too limited an approach for you?

The great fight in life and in literature always is to prevent some form of idea or situation from enslaving you. It's to keep your mind open and your eyes open and your life open, to find ways of not being limited. Fiction should open us up to new possibilities. It should clarify for us. It should change our perception.

Why has black literature for the most part been written in a naturalistic style?

One reason is because Richard Wright, who had the first best-seller as a black writer in 1940, selected this as his mode of expression. Wright set the style for the literary approach of a generation of black writing.

Now there are exceptions. There were writers in the past who tried other approaches, for example, Jean Toomer in the '20s. There's a little bit of Eastern thought that creeps into his writing. His work is extraordinarily surrealistic and hallucinatory, very different from the naturalistic tradition. But he didn't set the style for other imitators. His work is just unique.

And then we have Ellison's *Invisible Man*, another unique work which is, by God, more surrealistic, larger-than-life, allegorical and metaphoric than probably anything in black American fiction. But he did not create a body of imitators either.

Naturalism remains the primary style, up to this very day. The main reason for this is that most black writers are interested in social realism, addressing social questions, and naturalism gives you access to that maybe better than other approaches. Wright is rightly understood as the father of modern black fiction, but his approach is a cramped approach; it leaves out a lot.

Are you trying to extend the range of black fiction in your own work?

I'm not going to limit myself to a particular form. As a story suggests itself to me, I look for two things: I look for the fictional form to express it that's most appropriate, I look for the voice that's most appropriate, and then I let the story bring in as many aspects or prismatic sides of reality as it needs to.

When I was a philosophy student reading fiction, I would look at black American literature and be impressed by what I didn't find there. I didn't find a philosophically systematic body of black fiction—black fiction addressing some of the perennial problems of Western man, taking up questions of value, ethics, meaning, the good, the true, the beautiful, the self, epistemology—right on down the line. There was none of that.

My work basically addresses those philosophical questions. For example, if you're going to talk about the assault on black identity in a culture that is primarily white, primarily Christian, then you must talk about the higher question of identity in an intelligent way. You must take up the question and follow it through as methodically and systematically as you can.

In a work of fiction it means dramatizing that question against the backdrop of black American life. Say you start out walking around today, and you're black and you're thinking about how somebody just denied you a job and you feel that there was bigotry involved, or you go to the counter and give the woman your money and instead of putting the change in your hand, she puts it down so that you have to scrape it off the counter. You wonder, "Why did she act like that? 'Cause I'm black? What does that mean?" Your feelings are murky.

Most people only get to the first level of describing that. They don't take the issue further and begin to explore the question of what it means to be a self. Suppose this person made the decision, "Well, all right, they're bigots and I'm black, and my identity is black." You wind up like George Hawkins. That's exactly the decision he makes in *Oxherding Tale*. He's hurt by this incident and he becomes a cultural nationalist. He's trying to find some way to make himself feel good, and does it by denying everything that the white world represents, and by elevating everything he feels the black world represents. And even that's a joke, because he says, for example, it means "emotion and not reason, passion and not thought."

But, if you think about it, and you go back and look at other things that other men and women have said about identity, and the great sweat they put into trying to figure out the question, then you have something you can use as fuel for your own investigation. It's like somebody else did a report on it, and now you can use their report. You don't have to agree with it. You don't have to buy their conclusions, but at least they covered some of the territory that you yourself are murkily involved in. And you can come up with something maybe that nobody has ever said, but yet includes what they said. At the heart there will be a philosophical question applicable to all people, but as it takes on the particular form of black American life, we understand something new about it because the universal has to be realized or embodied in the particular.

Are you a practicing Buddhist?

I would call myself a practicing Buddhist, but not a very good practicing Buddhist. I was raised in an Episcopal church in Evanston, then later fell away in college from a belief in institutional religion. But the study of Eastern religion gave me a deep appreciation for the mystical core at the heart of Christianity—the similarity between Meister Eckhart and twelfth-century Zen Buddhists, the parallel statements from Christ and the Buddha— so that I still have my roots in Christianity, but have a deep involvement in all forms of Asian thought and meditation. I meditate and I read the literature, and I do other related disciplines because it feels right for me. For a long time it has. From the time I was nineteen and first in the martial arts, the teacher I had said, "You don't have to study Buddhism to make progress in this martial art, but it will help." So I did. Since I was in philosophy already it was easy to do. But I didn't really get serious about meditating until 1979 or '80. Now it's a large part of my life. I do it every day, twice a day sometimes. It's clarifying. It helps to clear my head, get rid of a whole bunch of ideas and just experience things, sometimes with a great deal of immediacy. Right after meditation, language is not operating, I'm just looking at things. It's later that language comes into it and I start making judgments. I say, "What's in front of me is a flower vase." Well, just after meditation it's only this object. I'm just looking at it. It may appear as a particular kind of image that I've never seen before. It's after language, and after you get into the course of the day, that you begin making easy judgments, and don't see things clearly any more.

What influence has Buddhism had on your fiction?

It amazes me that some people have never pointed out one very simple thing about storytelling, and that is the nature of desire whenever we talk about a conflict for a character. Handbooks on writing, even John Gardner's, say, "To have a story, the character must have a conflict." There must be conflict, because if there's no conflict there's nothing a character can act upon; there's no plot. And the conflict is either something in the characters' world that they don't want and they have to get rid of it, or it's something not in their world that they desire to bring in. Well, all fiction which operates on that basis defines part of human nature as involved in desire. It's implicit. It's saying, "This is universal for all men. Desire is fundamental to all of our experience."

Now I wonder if that's true. I'm not entirely convinced of that. I know that there are people on the planet who do not live that way. Buddhists, for example, do not live that way. The first two noble truths of Buddhism are: "Suffering is universal," and "The cause of suffering is desire." The Buddha was an incredible empirical psychologist, because I do think those ideas are universal. As I look at the world, I see suffering. Being alive is suffering in a certain sense, even for insects. And for human beings, the cause of suffering is desire.

Oxherding Tale brings this forward in a way that has not been brought forward in any other book that I've seen, certainly not in black American literature or within American literature. Reb is the Zen Buddhist in the novel, and a lot of reviewers don't realize that. They don't know enough about other cultures to recognize him as such. He doesn't operate out of desire, he operates out of duty. It's duty that is the foundation for all of his behavior.

But isn't there something else behind this sense of duty, such as a god or deity that helps him to decide what his duty is?

The novel never says that. I never mention God. I never even mention Buddhism, as a matter of fact, and that was the hard thing about that novel, because I knew that as soon as I did, people would have a knee-jerk reaction, they would shut down on it. So there's a line that says, "Something acted upon him. A push, a shove, a finger on the spine, only then did he move." You could say it's instinct if you wanted to. But I don't pin it down with God and the universe because modern readers just wouldn't be able to deal with that.

But there's another line, "Reward he did not expect, nor pleasure, desire was painful, duty was everything." That's almost strictly the description of a true Brahman out of the *Bhagavad-Gita*. It's duty, not desire, that makes Reb do what he does.

If there's an objective situation in the world that is not being fulfilled, you can fulfill it, not because of any egotistical reason, not because you think you're going to get anything out of it, not because you want to edify yourself, but because it needs to be done. You will perhaps alleviate suffering in some way, or maybe you will suppress the evil that exists, and make the good come forward a little bit more clearly. But you do it because it needs to be done.

And that's what motivates Reb. Man does not have to operate out of the basis of desire, so that when people describe it as fundamental to conflict and character, there's a presupposition operating that they haven't really thought about. They haven't thought that they're presenting a view of man metaphysically, and that they are also not thinking about other alternative ways of existence.

Do you agree with John Gardner's thesis that fiction should be moral?

I agree with that absolutely, but in a slightly different way than John. I think that he's right, but I don't believe you can ever successfully argue for moral fiction. It's a faith in man that Gardner had. It goes all the way back to his first book *The Forms of Fiction* where he says that man is one step lower than the angels. He sees a nobility and dignity in the species, but you will never be able to argue that philosophically and convince all the modern readers who have suffered through the tragedies and disasters of the twentieth century.

What did Gardner mean by moral fiction?

Moral fiction has nothing to do with pre-existing moral precepts that the writer brings to the page. That leads to *Pilgrim's Progress*, which no one is going to be convinced by in 1980. When Gardner says moral, he means that the writer is responsible for the kind of fictional world that he puts onto the page. A lot of writers try to cop out by saying, "I'm just trying to tell it the way it is." But whenever you have a fictional work, you have an interpretation of reality that immediately refers back to the consciousness of the writer. If the writer sees only gloom, despair, entropy, then we have to ask that writer, "Why is this all that you see, when there are other people out there whose experience is somewhat different, who can argue this is not a complete portrait of reality?"

The second thing is characterization, which Gardner was very concerned about. You must approach characters with the same empathy, identification and effort at understanding that you do with people you care about in the world. To slight characters, to set somebody up as a tool, a device for a story, is to perform in a fundamentally immoral way.

Gardner once raised the question of whether you had to be a good person to be a good writer. And in a sense you do. You have to care about how other people see the world, in order to create a rich, complex fiction that has the feel of the real world where other people's interpretations are in conflict with your own. In the final analysis, the conflict of interpretations may be what fiction is all about, because this is one intersubjective world, a world of multiple interpretations.

Do you strive to write moral fiction?

Yes, I strive for truth and accuracy of character. If you look at a story, what you have is the writer presenting an interpretation of experience that should clarify your experiences for you. We read fiction not just for entertainment, but for clarification, for greater knowledge of who we are and why we behave the way we do. The plot of the story is in effect the writer's equivalent of the philosopher's argument. You say this kind of person is in this situation, and this happens because of that. You're saying in effect: this is the way life works, given these conditions and premises. So plot is extremely important. And if a writer is to abandon plot, it means he's abandoning the responsiblity to make sense out of the world and his own experience. Plot is crucial, and intimately related to character.

Do you think that a novel should be as tightly constructed as a philosophical argument?

A novel or story should be as tightly constructed as a logical proof. There shouldn't be anything superfluous in it. There should be no narrative slop. There should be no excesses that get in the way of exploring the characters, the issues; and at the same time entertaining the reader. Readers want three things: they want to laugh, cry and learn something. If you forget any one of those, your fiction is a bit slim.

Are you consciously aware of the theory behind everything in your fiction?

I may be different from other writers in this respect. I have to understand the story philosophically before I can write it. Coming out of philosophy is helpful because I understand 2,000 years of philosophical arguments and positions on different issues in the West and East. So it allows me to get to the major aspects of the problem quickly, but it may still take a while to get to an aspect that is new or original. The process of writing the story helps to do that. It uncovers things. It is a laboratory. You go into the story not knowing the answer, but you know a lot of other theories about the experiment that you're going to do. You've seen other attempts to resolve it. By the end of the story you may be startled by the conclusion that you come to.

So language is the laboratory where the fiction writer works to discover truth?

Language is something that we find ourselves in the midst of. Before my kids were able to speak they found themselves surrounded by all these words and babbles and sounds, till one day magically they made sense and the kids were able to imitate and repeat the sounds, and live within language. It was at that point that the child's very consciousness was structured by the structure of language.

Language has a capacity to rigidify and calcify our seeing; we think only in terms of certain words and certain experiences, and don't break through to anything else. The writer of fiction has to break through that. As Heidegger says, it's language that covers over our perception. And it's language in the hands of an artist that uncovers our perception. It's the same phenomenon that conceals and reveals. This is why I think fiction is exciting. When I'm writing, things happen and I don't quite know where they came from. I'd like to attribute them to the language itself, to its unpredictable possibilities. It's like a trap door, the language drops you down to this whole other level of seeing.

And by rearranging the language you create new perceptions?

It can only happen through words. Heidegger's famous phrase for this is, "Saying is showing." To say is to show, which is why the language of newspapers, television, and the media basically covers over our experience. We get used to talking in shorthand terms; people become incapable of seeing.

It's really hard in writing to free yourself from clichés, ideas minted in the media or other people's minds, so you can see the issue clearly, not thinking in terms of social formulas, social clichés, but really trying to look at the subject with radically unsealed vision.

How does this phenomenological approach apply to writing?

It's very easy. It's something that writers and painters use all the time. If you go to an art class, you see people drawing a figure. The people who are not truly seeing will look at the figure on the stage, and something will happen between the time they look back at the page and draw because they won't draw what they see, they will draw what they think a figure looks like—it will have nothing to do with the real person on the stage.

Phenomenology is basically forgetting what you think the human figure looks like, and looking at the human figure in front of you. Every artist does that. You have to divest yourself of the prejudices, the comfortable preconceptions about what you're dealing with. That's hard to do. It makes the process of writing exhilarating but at the same time exhausting.

How does the final result of this process, a work of art, convince us?

A lot of people seem to think that a work of art boils down to being only a matter of taste, subjective difference, and finally fashion or whatever the hell it might be. That's stupid. That's dumb. If somebody is trying to describe a particular character, they can achieve greater and greater accuracy, so that they can come up with a description that nobody will be able to deny.

Art can be looked upon in very objective ways. One of the reasons that art in this country, and particulary in writing programs, is so sloppy is that writing people think art is not serious, that it doesn't have the rigor, the rules of science. But if we're talking about truth and accuracy, then art does have objective standards. We can say, "This story is replaying stuff that the writer has seen in other stories, and is not advancing the form of the novel or the short story." Or we can say, "This writer has written about things that have never been written about before, or has written about things in a way that's deeper than any other writer."

You can say many things about how art objectively can advance. But you must know cultural and intellectual history and the history of literature to make these judgments. Most writers write totally off the top of their head. They don't know how their work fits within the tradition of literature, they don't know really what their objectives are. But art, like science, has rules, objectives. It's only on the basis of having a sense of tradition that you can say that something fits within the continuum and advances it.

Do you enjoy the process of writing?

I love the process of writing. I am at my fullest when I'm writing. I can think of no activity that brings so much of everything that I am—everything I've learned, everything I feel, all the techniques at my disposal—into one suspended moment that is the work of art. So it's very exhausting when it's working exactly right.

Do you think there will come a time when you will not need or want to write any more?

Every writer should leave that possibility open. There was a time before I was a writer when I did other things. There may be a time after which I don't write but do other things. Art is part of life, it's not the whole of life. It's not the reason for existence. It takes a writer of courage to admit that he has said all that the universe has given for him to say, and after which he would only repeat himself, fall into formulas, imitate other writers, or just basically destroy what he has built if he continues. I don't think a writer should just babble on and on. If you have something to say, you should say it as effectively as you can, then you should shut up.

In his essay, "Poetry and Ambition," Donald Hall says he sees no reason to spend your life writing poetry unless your goal is to write great poems. Do you agree with this approach to writing?

When it comes to the crunch, the only two worthy goals are to serve this discipline you have entered into by contributing something great and to make a place for yourself in the literature of the age. The ambition of the writer should be to be one of the American writers. That's the highest ambition, to leave behind a work that will be meaningful to people many years after you're dead.

Who do you measure yourself against?

Most of the writers I read on my own time are pre-twentieth century—Dickens and Hawthorne, Poe, Chaucer, Shakespeare, particularly Homer. That's about it. Those writers and also the philosophers—I read a lot of philosophers—who have stood the test of a millenium or 500 years. Those are the ones I think most about, whose works I return to most often. I won't go into all the problems I have with contemporary literature but I have a lot of problems with it. I don't think that most writers write out of the deepest sense of seriousness that Donald Hall talks about. We have an apparatus in America that will give awards and grants and fellowships and a little money to writers. And you can work that game for a lifetime, and never do anything important. You can also find publication, because there are literally hundreds of literary quarterlies, so getting published is nothing really to crow about. And I think that apparatus, which had a good intention, mainly to support the arts, can become a way of degenerating into supporting second-rate writers with very limited ambitions.

I think a real writer simply has to think in other terms. Not, "Will I get in this magazine? Will I get this NEA next year?" but whether or not this work is something he would do if a gun was held to his head and somebody was going pull the trigger as soon as the last word of the last sentence of the last paragraph of the last page was finished. Now if you can write out of the sense that you're going to die as soon as this work is done, then you will write with urgency, honesty, courage and without flinching at all, as if this were the last testament in language, the last utterance, you could ever make to anybody. If a work is written like that, then I want to read it. If somebody's writing out of that sense, then I'll say, "This is serious. This person's not fooling around. The work is not a means to some other end, the work is not just intended for some silly superficial goal, this work is the writer saying something because he or she feels that if it isn't said, it will be never be said."

Those are the writers I want to read. And there are not many twentieth-century writers like that. Writing is a "career" in the twentieth century. It's a "profession." And I use those words pejoratively. I think writing is a passion. I don't think you choose writing, I think writing and art choose you. I think you write because you have no other choice, not because it's a celebrity thing.

I got a letter many years ago from a woman. She told me that she read *Faith and the Good Thing* on the verge of committing suicide and after reading it decided to live. You're left with the feeling that you can do some good in this world through what you do, as if art in the old religious sense were good works, or in the Indian sense, karma yoga. You do it because someone's going to benefit from it: that's why you do it.

Tom Robbins

*I*N HIS *novels* Another Roadside Attraction *(1971)*, Even Cowgirls Get the Blues *(1976)*, Still Life with Woodpecker *(1980)* and Jitterbug Perfume *(1984)*, Tom Robbins takes a deliberately subversive attitude toward Western civilization. While the bright surface of his prose enchants and enraptures, the philosophical underpinnings of his books call all kinds of attitudes and institutions into question. But whether he's castigating the Roman Catholic Church, poking fun at Ralph Nader worshippers or satirizing dead-serious feminists, Robbins remains a critic in a clown costume, a modern-day court jester, a writer as much interested in entertaining and amusing his readers as in making a point.*

Born in Blowing Rock, North Carolina, in 1936, Robbins was raised in small towns in Virginia. He studied journalism at Washington and Lee University, where he was expelled from a fraternity for tossing biscuits at the house mother. After spending some time in the Far East as an Air Force meteorologist, he enrolled at the Richmond Professional Institute, a school of art, drama and music from which he graduated in 1961. He worked as a copy editor at the Richmond Times-Dispatch *before moving to Seattle, Washing-*

*ton, to attend graduate school in Far Eastern philosophy at the
University of Washington. While in graduate school he began
working as a feature editor and art critic at the* Seattle Times. *He
left to work part-time for the* Seattle Post-Intelligencer, *and while
there, began writing* Another Roadside Attraction, *the publication
of which got his career as a novelist off the ground.*

*Robbins has been married twice, and has a teenage son, Fleet-
wood Star Robbins. He lives in La Conner, Washington, in a modest house on a quiet street. The interview took place there in the fall
of 1986. Robbins is a low-key fellow with a soft Southern accent
and modishly-styled graying brown hair. Contrary to his public
persona as an outrageous character with a roguish grin, Robbins in
private is a quiet, introspective man who seems quite serious about
his life and his work.*

*There are several stories about how you got your first novel
published. How did it actually happen?*

Well, the true story involves the Order of the Golden Envelope, of which I'm a knight. You see, the post office is my favorite
institution. With some people it's the church, with some it's the
university, with me it's the post office. The mails have a lot of potential as an art form, correspondence artists can attest to that, plus
there's a certain amount of wonderment in the whole postal process. Paper mail is doomed by computers, so let's enjoy it while we
can. At any rate, ever since I was knee-high to a mail slot, I had believed that someday a letter would be delivered to my box that
would change my life. Alter it forever. And in my fantasy, that letter had a light, a golden aura around it.

In 1966, while I was living over a machine shop in Ballard
[neighborhood of Seattle], I went downstairs to the mailbox one
day and pulled out a letter. I opened it and was nearly blinded by
the golden light. It was from Luther Nichols, West Coast editor of
Doubleday, saying that he was coming to Seattle and wanted to
talk to me about writing a book. I thought, "This is it, the life-
changing golden letter has arrived." I'd had books on my brain
since I was a tot.

I met Luther in a coffee shop in the Benjamin Franklin Hotel, which now has been replaced by the Westin. It turned out that he wanted me to write an art book, a book about West Coast art. He'd been reading my art reviews.

I was disappointed. I told him I was really interested in writing a novel. Then he was disappointed. But I covered my disappointment and he covered his, and we continued to converse. He said, "Well, what's this novel about?"

And I said, "It's about the discovery of the mummified body of Christ in the catacombs under the Vatican and its subsequent theft and reappearance in America in a roadside zoo."

His interest picked up. He said, "Tell me more." Well, I didn't know any more. That was an idea that had been kicking around in my head for a few years, but I'd never done anything with it. But when he said, "Tell me more," I started improvising on that idea, plotting on the spot.

He said, "When can I have a look at the manuscript?"

I said, "Well, it's in pretty rough shape." I hadn't written a word, but I didn't want him to know that, so I said, "I'll try to clean it up and send it to you." I went home that day and told the girl I was living with, "I've got to write a novel."

I tried for a year to get something done on it, but I was so enmeshed in the Seattle art world that I couldn't find time to write.

Eventually I cut my ties and moved down to South Bend, Washington, into a storefront that was rented for eight dollars a month, not eighty dollars, but eight. That's where I began *Another Roadside Attraction*. I actually wrote all of it in South Bend, though not all of it in the storefront; we moved to a more legitimate house later on.

I worked weekends at the *P-I*, drove up from South Bend. The girl I was living with was a waitress in Raymond, and she brought home left-over shrimp and scallops and oysters from diners' plates; that's how we survived. Slops de la mer.

That was for a year?
Two years.

Did you have anybody read it over as you were working on it?
I wrote thirty pages and sent it to Luther Nichols. He liked it and he sent it on to Doubleday in New York. They said, "This is

unusual. Can we see some more?" So I wrote seventy more pages.

The younger editors liked it, but the senior editors weren't too sure. Even the younger editors said, "Well, this is really interesting, really different, but we can't tell where it's going."

I thought, "I can understand that perfectly. I don't know where it's going either. If I knew where it was going, I probably wouldn't be writing it."

By this time, though, I was determined to finish it. It had become central to my life. I was going to finish that sucker, whether they bought it or not.

I was hoping to get an advance. After neither of the initial readings would they give me a dime, but by then I was committed to the book. I finished it in my own way and at my own pace, eating left-over shellfish, and I thought I'd try Doubleday one more time and if they weren't interested, the hell with them, I'd send it to somebody else.

This time, as I understand, there was a real battle over it between the senior editors and the younger editors. Doubleday began as a Roman Catholic publishing house, I wasn't aware of that, and some of the senior editors were of that persuasion. They battled about it and finally the younger editors won out. I got a $2,500 advance and went out immediately and bought a ticket to Japan. Converted it to yen and sin. The rest, as they say, is geology.

Was the book autobiographical at all?

Any work of art is to a certain extent a self-portrait. It wasn't what you would call an autobiographical novel per se, too much of it came strictly out of my imagination. Some of it came out of psychedelic drug experiences. A lot of it came out of what was going on in America in the late '60s.

Were you attempting to make sense of the '60s?

I was trying to recreate and evoke the true mood of the '60s. I didn't want to write a traditional novel. I didn't want to report. I didn't want to write *about* the '60s, I wanted to make the '60s happen on the page. I could see all around me people writing about the '60s, and even those who didn't miss the point completely, as many of them did, were never quite able to explain the '60s to someone who didn't participate in them, particularly someone who hadn't had what we called "The Experience"—the ingestion of lysergic acid diethylamide 25.

So I based the book on a psychedelic model to recreate through style, as much as content, the mood of the '60s. *Rolling Stone* called *Another Roadside Attraction* the quintessential novel of the '60s. I think that's because it looked at the '60s from the inside out; instead of trying to describe the era, it evoked it, in style as much as content.

The narrator in that book is funny. He's always trying to sum up what's going on, just as an objective reporter would, but...

Yeah, it keeps blowing up in his face, which was the whole point. He wanted to relate to it in traditional ways. If you're operating from a base camp of logic and rationality and good old-fashioned literary values, you just end up with the '50s in '60s drag. When in Oz, you have to use Oz-mosis.

When you were working on the book, did you try to write it straight first?

No. I was trying to get over being straight. Actually, the straight and narrow path has never interested me very much. In fact, I've become convinced that if you find yourself on the straight and narrow path, you know that you're headed in the wrong direction.

Is it harder to find another path?

Certainly. That's why the traditional paths are so crowded. The wild and crooked paths, the left-handed paths, so-called, are not for the lazy and the faint of heart. You have to be willing to jettison a lot of intellectual and emotional baggage that has been piled on your luggage rack by people and institutions that, their claims to the contrary, do not have your best interests in mind. You have to have the nerve to cut free of ninety percent of what you've been taught by your family, your schools, your news media and, especially, your government and your religion. The paths of ignorance and superstition seem smooth and easy. The path of truth and liberty looks impossibly difficult. But it can be very exhilarating. So much so that the path itself becomes the destination. You can't be overly concerned with where it's leading. Who knows where it's leading?

How did you find that path?

Deep desire. Then hit and miss. Once you're on it for a while, even if it's but for a few steps, your toes start to tingle in such a delightful way that you're willing to take all sorts of risks to get back on. And even now I stray off the path frequently. No one stays on the path all the time unless they're enlightened, and even then I think there are times they wander off into the brambles. I'm in the brambles right now or I wouldn't be talking like this.

Are there certain books and traditions that help you stay on the path?

Oh, yeah. It's a crazy old road, but there are plenty of signposts, if you know how to interpret them. They are usually in a language you can't understand. An early signpost for me was a book called *Generation of Vipers* by Philip Wylie, which I read when I was eighteen. It was the first thing I'd ever encountered that really questioned all of the values I had been taught to hold dear. It went over those values, not with a magnifying glass or a comb, but with a chainsaw. It was a milestone in my life.

When you were younger, were you at all rebellious?

From birth. And I became more rebellious when the hot hormones of adolescence began to spin off of my artery walls. I have always been in a rebellious state. My goal is to be eternally subversive. But I think I'm falling short.

Is writing an acceptable adult way to be rebellious?

Sure. All art is in a sense an act of rebellion, a protest, at any rate. The Venus de Milo is a protest against every flat-chested woman in the world. And the Belvedere Apollo is a protest against every pot-bellied man. Art creates the world as it ought to be, and therefore is a protest against the world as it is, although I find plenty in the world as it is to celebrate.

What were you like as a young man?

When, last year?

No, more like a teenager.

I was sensitive and shy, but covered it up by becoming the class clown. I was such a mischief-maker that nobody noticed I was a bit of a loner. I was a closet bookworm, a regular little intellectual, but I kept that side of me well hidden. I'd even fail tests on purpose, writing bizarre, surreal answers to questions that I could easily have answered. I gave myself a completely secret education. In the redneck, rural South, this deception was necessary.

At fifteen, I went out for basketball and played well. Wore a varsity letter, chased cheerleaders, had dates and rowdy friends. But I also maintained a secret life. I still do. Except the secrets have changed.

Did you like growing up in the South?

I liked it just fine. I didn't think much about it one way or another; it was like a bird being born in a particular forest. It wasn't until I was about eighteen and began to experience directly the non-Southern world that various aspects of the South began to oppress and offend me.

To the extent that you wanted to move?

First, I wanted to change the South. I tried that for a few years, involved in civil rights and all, and then bloody but unbowed, I decided I could make better use of my time simply to transport myself to a more liberated part of the world. St. Augustine said, "Repair it by flight."

I don't want to be in a position of denying my Southern heritage, though, because it has had a great deal to do with who I am, particularly as a writer. Many writers have come out of the South, and I think there are some good reasons for that. So it's probably quite fortunate for me that I was born there, although I've often felt that I was a bit like a Tibetan Jew born into an Anglo-Saxon Southern Baptist family.

Why is the South such a fertile ground for writers?

For one thing, the art of conversation is not dead there; people still converse with dignity and imagination. Cantankerous old men sit around in rocking chairs on front porches and gabble for hours. With style and grace and eccentricity. The eccentric is vital to art.

There remains in the South a trace of the only true aristocracy America ever knew, even among people who never were actually aristocratic. It left a splendid residue, so that even in the midst of all that redneckery and racism and insecurity about manhood and all the other things that make the South so frustrating, there is a regard for language and for stories and for eccentricity and for honor. I think there's a lot of honor-seeking in writing. A lot of writing is concerned with avenging injustices, or is a conscious effort to perform some large, honorable act.

There's a sense of honor in the South, despite the Ku Klux Klan and that whole underbelly, that doesn't exist anywhere else in North America. And there's also an elitist attitude there, and I think all great art, great thinking, comes out of an elitist situation. There's no such thing as great egalitarian art; democracy does not produce great literature. Barbara Rose said that when elitism began to become a dirty word in America, it sounded the death knell for any possibility of the development of a high culture here. She may be right. Of course, we may not need a high culture. Our low culture is pretty wonderful.

Did the South retain a certain elitism?

Yeah, and a lot of it is ugly and stupid but, nevertheless, good for fostering literature. The regard for the eccentric that is retained is even more important, however.

Did you feel it was an honorable thing to be a writer?

Well, I decided to become a writer at such an early age that the word "honorable" probably wasn't in my vocabulary. I was five years old when I made that choice. I didn't care if it was honorable or dishonorable. I did know that there was a certain magical quality about books. I liked the way books looked, I liked the way they felt, I liked the way they smelled, I liked their weight in my hands, and the quality of the paper. So in a sense I was in love with the book as an object.

And for better or for worse, the fairy that tapped me with a wand in my cradle gave me a strong, active imagination. Around the age of five or six, I began to see where the book-as-object could be a vehicle or vessel fueled by that imagination. There was some kind of intermingling of the book-as-object and my active imagination. Somewhere in that molecular bonding between the book and the imagination, I was programmed to be a writer.

Did it take you a while to develop the writing style first seen in Another Roadside Attraction?

I think I wrote that book when I was in my early thirties. I was just over thirty. One reason I never really tried to write fiction before was because I knew that I hadn't evolved my own voice, and I didn't want to sound like anyone else. I didn't feel particularly pressured about it. I wasn't in any hurry. I looked at the field of literature and realized that there are no child prodigies, with the possible exception of Rimbaud. Most writers develop late.

Sometime in my early thirties, I recognized that in my nonfiction writing I was acquiring a voice that was decidedly my own. It happened to have been influenced by, and to coincide with, the psychedelic revolution in the '60s. So the time was ripe to inflict it on the world.

Did working for the newspapers help to refine your writing?

Yes and no. It's possible to hone your skills while writing for a newspaper, but only if, one, you're willing to stand up to editors, and two, if you're disciplined enough to push yourself toward excellence. I saw a lot of fine talent wither and shrink in Seattle's newsrooms. Newspapers are fairly timid and they don't much cotton to adventurous writing, writing that's likely to offend their advertisers or stretch the minds of their subscribers. Also, newspaper editors don't demand very much of you in terms of high intellectual or stylistic standards. Accuracy, clarity and good old meat-and-potatoes mediocrity are enough for them. I only grew as a writer because I wasn't afraid to rock the boat, and because I was too committed to personal growth to allow myself to snuggle into a nice, safe, comfortable journalistic niche. You know, when I was at the *Times* and *P-I*, there wasn't an editor on either paper who'd so much as thumbed through McLuhan's *Understanding Media*. I found that appalling. Perhaps today the brass is a bit more in touch. But generally speaking, newspapermen and women are the salt of the earth: they don't come any better. Seattle is really lucky to have two pretty good dailies. Our sportswriters, in particular, are outstanding.

When you decided to leave the South, why did you choose to move to Seattle?

Intuition, probably. I operate a lot on intuition and don't know why I do half the things I do. Seattle has changed so much since I landed here, in some ways for the better, in a lot of ways for the worse. I'm thinking of gentrification, French flu, tour buses in the Public Market, that sort of stuff. It was a good choice, though. I was right out of art school and bursting with ideas. I was able to manifest many of them in Seattle. It would have been impossible in Richmond. In my early years here, I staged happenings and things that I never could have gotten away with in Virginia.

What kind of happenings did you stage?

They were art events, although they usually took place on a stage. Today they would be called performance art. I staged one in Kirkland that was called *Low-calorie Human Sacrifice to the Goddess Minnie Mouse.* It created somewhat of a scandal. I was arrested at the end of it, although not booked. That was fun.

I also did one down in Pioneer Square [Seattle] in an art gallery. That was called *Stronger Than Dirt.* It had a scandalous effect, too. Lloyd Cooney [television station president] did an outraged editorial about it on KIRO.

After living in Virginia, did you find it hard to get used to the Seattle climate?

The rain appealed to me, and still does. It's one of the reasons why I live here.

Why do you find the rain appealing?

It allows for prolonged periods of intimacy. It's cozy and reduces temptation. It keeps you inside where you can turn inward, rather than scattering yourself about the beach and the boulevards. And it makes the little mushrooms grow.

I think that there was a lot of rain in my heart before I moved here, so in a sense it was simply finding an external environment that ran parallel to my internal weather. And when I say it was raining in my heart, I don't mean that I was depressed, because I don't find rain the least bit depressing. It's romantic, basically, and I am essentially a romantic being.

Why did you move to the Skagit Valley?

It's unusual to find a small town—particularly a small rural community, a farming, fishing community—where you can be yourself to the fullest extent of yourself; normally you'd have to go to a large city to do that. But there was a kind of sophistication in La Conner, and a tolerance of eccentric dress and behavior that made this place especially appealing, in conjunction with its natural beauty, the peace and privacy it offered. And that was largely the work of Morris Graves. When he moved here in 1937, he was treated very badly, because he was different, because he was an artist, because he walked around with a rope holding his pants up, and had a beard. But Morris is a very powerful person, and a singularly charming man, and he was able to break the ice, to clear a path for everyone else. He got through to the people and made it easier on the rest of us.

Why did you set Another Roadside Attraction *in the Skagit Valley?*

It was an area that appealed to me, visually and psychologically. It was an area that had not been written about very much and it had an enormous amount of natural charm and was unique— certainly unusual—in certain respects. It was a rich poetic vein to mine. And I knew it fairly well. I didn't write the book in the Skagit Valley, though. I wrote it down in South Bend, so I was far enough removed from it to write about it with a slightly different perspective than I would have had, had I been here in the middle of it. It actually allowed me to write about it in a fresher way.

When you started writing about it, did the landscape impose its form on the writing?

No. I suppose any poetic image, if it's good, will have been imposed upon to a certain extent by the object or place that's being described, but it wasn't the kind of book it was because of the Skagit Valley, it was the kind of book it was because of the landscape of my mind, which for several years had been tended by small green gardeners in Day-Glo robes.

Did taking LSD change your way of looking at things?

Definitely. It reinforced some things and threw others overboard. It gave me a lot more ease in moving between different levels of reality. It was a liberating experience.

Is it something you can remember and draw from?

I don't draw from a specific experience. The psychedelic experience was much like being handed a new kind of telescope or microscope through which I could look at the world for a few hours in a totally different way, seeing it for the first time without the filtered glasses on, the blinders of education and social conditioning. Maybe seeing it accurately for the first time, in all of its manifestations. And then somebody takes the instrument away. But even though you can't duplicate through your own eye what you saw through that micro-telescope, you can remember that there are other ways of seeing, other levels to see.

If you're looking at a daisy in a field, having observed a daisy through the magic acid lens, even though you're not seeing it now as you saw it then, you're still aware that the daisy possesses other dimensions and an identity as strong as your own. In a sense, it's the Zen concept of is-ness, daisy-ness, as well as an "erotics" of perception, to borrow a Susan Sontag phrase. There's the sensation that there are hidden energy forms beyond time and space which shape our time-space world. I can't talk about it without sounding demented or sophomoric or both. That's why I say it can't be reported, it can only be evoked, and even then inadequately.

So taking LSD made a big difference to you and your writing?

It was a watershed experience. I think psychedelic drugs, particularly natural plant drugs like mushrooms, are the most efficient way of expediting the evolution of consciousness. There's no other way that even comes close. And I think it's an enormous human tragedy that scientists and philosophers and artists haven't been allowed to make real use of those drugs, that the government finds them such a threat. The government has finally, twenty years after the '60s, succeeded in creating a climate of absolute anti-drug hysteria, which is sheer idiocy.

It's so stupid, so hypocritical, so wrong, so shameful. A million people a year, according to estimates from the United Nations, die around the world as a result of tobacco. Less than three hundred die from cocaine, yet the country's in an absolute hysterical frenzy over cocaine. Cocaine's not even a drop in the bucket. In my opinion, it's a bad drug not because it's dangerous physically, but because it makes people stupid, whereas psychedelics actually can enhance intelligence.

There's some real lunacy there, some real hypocrisy and muddled thinking. You'd have to be an idiot to get worked up about the evils of cocaine when there's so much death resulting from alcohol and tobacco. But on the other hand, it really isn't idiocy, because the totalitarians recognize unconsciously that drugs are agents of change, agents of decontrol, and the government doesn't want us to change, and it certainly doesn't want us to be decontrolled. It is in their interest to control us. Nice safe, Christian, family values are a wonderful way to sedate the population. Keep us docile, easy to manipulate.

The evolution of consciousness is not something the government favors, because ultimately it would transform the politico-economic system and cut into the profits of the people who are really behind the government, who really run this country and the other countries of the world.

So there is a solid, legitimate reason for this drug hysteria that probably really isn't known consciously to most of the people who are creating it. I think it's the most frightening thing to happen on this planet in a long, long time. It scares me more than the bomb.

It isn't even the drugs per se. I could go on at great length about the value that there is in psychedelic drugs, although not for everybody. As Hermann Hesse said in *Steppenwolf*, "The magic theater is not for everyone."

But say it's not drugs, say it's blue cheese; the fact that the government can get people so easily worked up over blue cheese, the fact that people will buy this propaganda, swallow it hook, line and sinker, and get in a panic over something they know nothing about, is extremely frightening. It's the Hitler technique.

Do you try to respond to issues like this in your writing?

A lot of my life has been spent fighting the tyranny of the dull mind. Obviously, I try to do it in my work. I'm not going to go out and lead a pro-drug crusade. What I can do is to try to set an example. And to offer people the tools they might use to liberate themselves from totalitarian, anti-life control.

You wouldn't want to go joining a political movement?

Absolutely not. Political movements are trivial in my estimation, except in a very secondary way. If we want to change things, then *we* have to change. To change the world, you change yourself. It's as simple as that, and as difficult as that. Politics is not going to make anything any better. There are no practical solutions. Sooner or later, we have to have the guts to do the impractical things that are required to save the planet.

And your job as a writer is to make an individual reader aware of the implications of some of these things?

And entertain them at the same time. My job is to awaken in the reader his or her own sense of wonder. An entertaining wake-up call from the front desk.

And this wake-up call should be funny?

There's no wisdom without humor, I'll say that flatly. Wisdom does not exist without humor. Humor is both a form of wisdom and a means of survival. A lot of evolution, which seems to be the primary force in the organic universe, is a matter of game-playing. A lot of things are done in evolution just for the hell of it. If evolution were only concerned with survival of the fittest, we wouldn't even be around. The world would be exclusively populated with cockroaches and ants; they're much better at survival than we are.

Evolution is constantly playing games, experimenting, inventing, innovating, trying new things, seeing if they work—"Let's put horns on this jackrabbit, see what happens. Well, it didn't work but it made a cute postcard." So to be playful is not to be frivolous; it is, ultimately, to be realistic, to be in tune with the universe, to be an agent of evolution.

One of the problems with playfulness for a writer is that there's a thin line between playfulness and cuteness. But that's a risk I have to take. Any artist who isn't taking risks is a mediocre artist. The best artists are willing to risk something, and that is part of my risk; I risk being cute. But I think I stay on the playful side of the line enough, so that it's a risk worth taking.

And to be playful at a highly conscious level is a very desirable thing. I'm not particularly interested in the tradition of Western literature. I'm interested in the tradition of word as celebration, metaphor as magic, language as an agent of liberation, and narrative as cosmic connection. That tradition is much older than Western literature. That's the old storyteller-as-enchanter, as spellbinder and counselor, around the campfire.

Is that one of the reasons you chose to tell a fractured fairy tale in Still Life with Woodpecker?

Fairytales are the most profound literature that we have ever developed. Many of them are thousands of years old, and they were honed and refined over tens of thousands of tellings until they speak directly to the psyche. They resonate there, if they're told in their pure form. The Walt Disney version or the nice safe liberal versions where nobody really gets hurt totally pervert them; you lose everything, you lose all that's valuable in them. But a true fairy tale is a remarkable piece of verbal science.

By using a fairy tale in the Woodpecker *book you seemed to be getting at what people want out of romantic relationships: a kind of love which is like a fairy tale.*

No. A fairy tale is not a pretty, idealistic deception. In the original fairy tales you got a strong dose of reality. On a psychological level, at any rate. There was Prince Charming, there was also the witch, and both of these were aspects of your own personality. When they said there was a witch, they didn't mean that there was some evil old woman who lived in a cabin in the woods; that witch was part of you, or part of your mother, or sister.

So the original versions of the fairy tales were quite instructive?

The earliest Dr. Ruth; the fairy tales were absolutely teeming with sexual instruction. They were told to prepare children for life, to teach children about growing up, about their sexuality, romance and marriage, and all the things that children in a peasant environment would have needed to know about their own psychological life. Psychologically, they're incredibly complex and deep.

So you found them useful?

I found that one useful ["The Frog Prince"], considering what I wanted to deal with in that book: romantic love and objecthood. I wanted to write about inanimate objects in a way they had never been written about before. There have been some good books in which inanimate objects played a large role, but invariably as a symbol. They were dealt with symbolically, like the pistol in James Jones' great little novella [*The Pistol*], or the overcoat in Gogol.

But I wanted to write about an object in a non-symbolic way, where the secret life of the object itself, the energy of the inanimate object itself, was as real as a character in the book, as a human being.

In a fairy tale, are all the objects charged with a certain supernatural energy?

They have meaning, largely symbolic. I chose a fairy tale

where an object was a symbol, but I also chose another object, a Camel pack. The golden ball remained a symbol. It symbolizes unity.

When we were children, people would say, "Look at that kid. He's a ball of energy." And while they might think that they were using a mere figure of speech, when we're young our energy is very contained, we *are* like balls. The older we get, the more dispersed it becomes; we lose that union with the universe.

That's what the golden ball represented. When the little girl lost her golden ball, that was her loss of innocence, her loss of universal unity. Of course, she wanted it back, but it was very difficult to get back.

I dealt with it on that level, but the Camel pack I chose to deal with non-symbolically, as a real object standing only for itself. Even though it was rich in association and meaning, and engendered games and riddles and puns, it nevertheless had a life of its own.

Why did you choose the pack of Camel cigarettes?

I wanted to use something human-made. I didn't want a seashell or a pine cone, something from nature. I wanted it to be something that had been shaped by a human hand, I wanted it to be something that was in common usage, that you'd be likely to see anywhere, in anyone's home or car. So I thought, "Something from the supermarket would be just right."

I'm really attracted to package design, cans and labels. It occurred to me that the Camel pack had the most potential because of all the lore that accompanies it, all the games and riddles and things that had been invented by sailors and convicts, men who are alone with objects. The design, of course, is quite appealing; maybe the most successful package design of all time, plus it had all these other psychological and aesthetic associations. The Camel pack was a very rich subject. I collected a lot of stories about it and only used a few of them, one-tenth of what was available.

Did you try to see the whole universe in that one object?

Yeah, Blake's idea of seeing the universe in a grain of sand, the macrocosm in the microcosm. I actually shut myself up in a room for three days with nothing but a pack of Camels.

Just like Princess Leigh-Cheri in the book?

Yes, although I only did it for three days. But I got the essence of it. I just meditated on it for three days.

That must have been a strange experience.

Strange experiences can be the best experiences.

A pack of cigarettes is normally something we take for granted. Were you trying to reanimate the object?

Quite the contrary. I wanted to explore and to celebrate the inanimate. My goal was the opposite of anthropomorphism. There may be a million stories in the Naked City, but there are a trillion dramas unfolding every fraction of a second on the subatomic level. Even on the molecular level, there are amazing bonding romances going on. Who knows what secrets an object really holds? I guess I was trying to say that we should *not* take them for granted. In the socialist countries that I've visited, there was a severe shortage of interesting objects, and I keenly felt their absence. Bare shelves signify more than one kind of deprivation. They must emaciate the imagination.

There's a method of looking at the world, maybe we could call it "poetic awareness." That sounds pretentious, but it's just a way of training yourself to be constantly aware of the vitality and connectedness of the things around you. You automatically begin to register the vectors or association between unlikely objects and images and events. You spot a can of Red Devil lye in the supermarket, for example, and you're instantly reminded of thirteenth-century Christianity. Then and there, you could compose an essay on the relationship. Cross-reference to the max. It's an interesting exercise in mental aliveness. The world becomes one big poem. Or one big parlor game.

You seem to do that a lot in your writing.

Well, it's my way of defining reality. Or *not* defining reality.

How about cartooning? Do your books owe something to cartooning?

Hardly a thing. That's a fake notion that's been perpetuated by the press. Cartoons, more specifically comic strips, are an integral part of American popular culture. Now popular culture possesses a tremendous energy, vitality and humor that can be tapped by the serious artist and put to higher purposes. I certainly do that, and I'm amazed that so few serious writers have harnessed the power of pop culture to illuminate their fiction. Maybe they're afraid of being considered lightweight or frivolous by the academic dullards. In any case, pop culture, comic strips included, has great potential as literary fuel. You have to keep in mind, though, that it's only the fuel, not the vehicle, itself. I learned a lot about structure from George Herriman, creator of "Krazy Kat," as did Philip Guston, the late painter. But Herriman was a structural genius and most cartoonists are not.

In fiction, the bottom line is language, and my language owes no more to cartoons than does the language of Henry James. True enough, I don't paint deep, detailed psychological portraits. But that doesn't mean my characters are cartoons. What it means is that I find that sort of writing boring, boring to do and, increasingly for me, boring to read, although there are writers who've done it exceedingly well. I employ a different dynamic, one that in the interest of freshness and swing—"It don't mean a thing if it ain't got that swing"—requires the reader to fill in some of the blanks, some of the notes. It is more accurate to compare it with jazz than cartooning.

The surface of your prose is like a package design—bright, shiny and alive—but there always seems to be something going on underneath.

Well, I hope that's true. That's part of my approach. I've described my books in the past as being cakes with files baked in them. That's kind of an obsolete image, but years ago in movies and in comic strips, prisoners would receive a cake from a friend and there would be a file hidden in the middle and they would file their way out of jail. I try to create something that's beautiful to look at and delicious to the taste, and yet in the middle there's this hard, sharp instrument that you can use to saw through the bars and liberate yourself, if you so desire. It's not imperative. You can just eat the cake and throw the file away if you want, but the file is there; it is always there in anything I write.

Is it important for you to have an audience, or would you write the books anyway?

I certainly wouldn't write as much.

When you're writing are you aware, like a circus performer, that an audience is there?

No, and I don't think Karl Wallenda would have thought about the audience very much when he was up on the wire. You're too busy trying to stay on the wire. I think about the wire and how I'm going to get from this side of Niagara Falls to the other without falling off. You don't think of the people down below until you're safe and sound on the other side.

Nowadays, I write under contract. I thought that might be a problem, knowing that I had a deadline and all that, but I don't think about that, either. When I go in to write, I forget everything else. I don't feel any pressure from the publishers, not that they put any on me. And I feel no pressure of trying to please an audience. It's just between me and the page. I'm lucky that way.

Do you feel that your reputation is always on the line when you do a book?

I don't give a rat hair about my reputation.

But you were talking about writing being a high wire act?

I was probably just being fanciful. I'm a long-time admirer of aerial acts, and I'm capable of fancy. No, the problem with reputation is that it's bound up with egoism. And the ego is the source of most of humanity's unhappiness. Hell is a solidified ego, heaven is a dissolved ego. Simple as that. The reason so many writers are depressed and dismal is that they tend to have large, stiff egos. Look at Saul Bellow. Now, he has a great reputation. He's rich and famous, he's won a Nobel prize, critics everywhere wash his feet with their slobber. But Saul Bellow is one miserable old hound dog. And he's merely one example. If you think a grand reputation will bring you joy, think again.

To return to the original analogy, the real joys and thrills and fulfillment in writing don't come from audience or critical response, they come from working high up on the wire, alone, without a net. But I really should apologize to Karl Wallenda's ghost for that presumptuous analogy.

Does it scare you to work up on that wire?

Always. That's good, because if it isn't scaring you, you have to figure that you're becoming a formula writer. If you're not scared, then you're too comfortable, too smug. There's something missing when you're not scared. Terror is very inspiring.

Scared of what?

Of falling off the wire, writing a stilted paragragh or a stupid book, or at least one that doesn't work for me. The ones that work for me, other people might consider stupid, so that's neither here nor there. You can write bad books and still have a good reputation. If I do something that *I'm* not proud of, then that's what I have to deal with, that's the fall that'll break my bones. I'm making it sound more dramatic than it really is.

Do you try to write back to the people who write to you about your books?

I get an awful lot of truly wonderful fan mail, and I don't think it's because my audience is so huge, it's because we have a special relationship, my readers and I. Thus, they write. Someone who likes my books is more apt to write me a letter than, say, someone who likes John Updike is apt to write him. I answer as many as I can, but too often people expect me to be their pen pal.

Do you like the solitude of being a writer?

A writer has got to like solitude. It's a solitary and lonely business. A lot of talented people have failed as writers because they couldn't stand being alone.

Do you work every day?

Five days a week.

Early morning?

It's not healthy to get up too early. [Laughs] I work from ten to three, approximately. That's the time I'm at my desk with implement in hand. Actually, I'm working almost all the time. When I'm in bed at night waiting to go to sleep, I'm working. When I'm walking the fields I'm working, when I'm playing volleyball or honky-tonking, I'm working; it's always on my mind.

So every part of your being goes into a book?

Dream and imagination, wit and sexuality, insight and intuition, *weltschmerz* and wang-dang-doodle. You stir in every spice on your shelf, although, ideally, in amounts and combinations that won't spoil the stew. But you've got to hold some stuff back for yourself and your loved ones. I, for one, refuse to use up my life in literature.

Is it fun to sit down at the writing desk? Do you feel you're discovering things?

Well, it's definitely a journey, an odyssey. It's fun and it's edifying and it's laboriously hard work and it's terrifying and it's very, very mysterious.

The truth is, I don't know how to talk about writing. Authors such as William Gass and Stanley Elkin speak so beautifully about the act of writing, in all of its various ramifications. But you ask me to describe the writing process, all I can think to say is that it's like a cross between flying to the moon and taking a shower in a motel.

Are there a lot more books you want to do?

To paraphrase every football coach in the country, I just take 'em one book at a time.

Murray Morgan

THOUGH *Murray Morgan has written about subjects as diverse as the World Health Organization and the* C.S.S. Shenandoah, *he is particularly renowned for his vivid and colorful histories of the Pacific Northwest. His history of Seattle,* Skid Road *(1951), found an enthusiastic audience early and it remains the most popular history on the subject to date. In this and other works, Morgan uses novelistic techniques such as dramatic scenes and careful individual characterizations to bring historical events to life. By describing events from the point of view of the principal participants, he makes history interesting and meaningful to modern readers.*

Currently Morgan is working on a history of the sea otter trade in the North Pacific, a project he's been pursuing for over forty years. He has written some fifteen books of non-fiction, including The Last Wilderness *(1955),* The Dam: Grand Coulee and the Pacific Northwest *(1954) and* Puget's Sound: A Narrative of Early Tacoma and the Southern Sound *(1979). He is the author of two works of fiction,* Day of the Dead *(1946) and* The Viewless Winds *(1949), and numerous articles, essays and stories.*

Morgan was born February 16, 1916 in Tacoma, Washington.

He was educated in the Tacoma public schools where he acquired an early interest in history and in writing. He began his journalistic career at the University of Washington, where he edited the University of Washington Daily. *Morgan received a master's degree in journalism from Columbia University in 1942. He has worked for* Time *magazine, the* New York Herald Tribune, CBS World News *and other news organizations. He has taught Northwest history and journalism at colleges and universities in the Puget Sound area.*

Morgan and his wife, Rosa, live in a house on Trout Lake, near Auburn, Washington. The interview took place there in January of 1985, where, over several cups of tea, Morgan talked about Northwest history and his methods of bringing it to life.

What are the boundaries of the Northwest region?

The part of the Northwest that I react to as homeland really ends at the crest of the Cascades. I'm visiting when I'm over on the other side in Yakima. It's the Indian separation really, between the plateau Indians and the coastal Indians. My empathy is with the area near the salt water. As a matter of fact, I'd go on down the California border. I think of San Francisco as part of the Northwest.

People commonly consider Idaho and Montana part of the Northwest. Do you agree?

The area of the Northwest I feel personally involved in is much smaller, but I have no quarrel with Idaho, eastern Oregon, and parts of Montana being lumped in the Northwest. But when I'm in Bend, Oregon, I feel as far from Northwest concerns as when I'm in Mexico.

What makes the Northwest region unique?

It's simply geographic. When you're talking about regions, you have to divide them up somehow. The natural division in this area lies along the mountains, but the political divisions are what made it a region. The most absurd of course is the forty-ninth parallel, the area where our rivers rise, which has the same forest covering, had the same indigenous population, and which has drawn pretty much the same white population.

To what extent has the human history of the region made it distinct?

It's made it fresher. We haven't had quite as much chance to get solidified in our errors as the East Coast. Because our history is quite recent, it gives us a somewhat colonial status and attitude. Major decisions are made for us back East or in corporate headquarters elsewhere. We don't have as much control as we might wish of our economic destiny.

The blessings of nature have been left all around us, and in spite of our record of exploitation, they have given us a wider feeling for environmental issues than you find back East.

Is a concern for the environment something new to the area?

As an organized movement, it certainly is new, but there were voices raised right from the start. A hundred years ago, one of the Tacoma newspapers, which failed quite quickly, was writing editorials against the destruction of the forests. So there were always people around who were concerned. If you live around trees and see the trees disappearing, you're going to start valuing trees a lot more than if you never had trees, or if you didn't have trees in your time.

Do you see a continuity in the history of the Northwest?

Yes, but it's a disguised continuity often: the same problem comes up in a somewhat different form. There's always been the problem here with distance from major markets and the seat of government. We've always had an exploitative economy, one which has taken what was here without replacing it. That includes the major grain-growing areas east of the mountains. We're washing away much of the soil with the current agricultural methods.

We've been shaped by our position on the Pacific Coast, with the dream of this being the gateway to the trade of the Orient. There was a time when the idea was that we would ship sophisticated materials to the Orient and bring back raw materials like silk. Then it turned around so that now Japan is shipping us the sophisticated materials and taking our logs. But our history is determined by proximity to the ocean and ocean transport.

When did your family move to the Northwest?

At the turn of the century. My father was a minister. He was born in Canada, and came first to Portland, and then to Tacoma.

Why did he move to Tacoma?

He thought that Tacoma was a place that was growing, but he had a somewhat mocking attitude toward visions of Tacoma's economic growth; he wrote some mocking poems about business club meetings. But he was very much in love with the area, and responded to it, as my mother did.

Where was your mother from?

Nebraska. Dad met her on a lecture tour. She was a widow with two sons and he had a son and daughter by a former marriage. I was the only child of their marriage. Mother was part Indian. I always felt that her response to the land around here was the Indian response.

Why did you start writing?

Both my mother and father wrote. Someone was always writing around the house. Dad published poetry, and a little religious magazine. Some of my first memories are of folding his magazines. We used to fold them by hand and stuff them in envelopes. The magazine had a worldwide circulation but it was small. Mother wrote children's plays.

I always was going to write; it was just a matter of what I was going to write. I knew I was going to be a journalist early. I was on the junior high school paper, the high school paper, the college paper.

How did growing up in the Northwest shape you as a writer?

It was decisive in what interested me. I like to write histories in terms of personalities which represent a period. Since I was here most of the time, this was where the research was easy. It was never a conscious plan of mine to wind up writing Northwest histories, but it just grew out of my doing journalism in a bit more depth than most daily stories covered. The first history I wrote was up in the Aleutians when I was a private in the signal corps during the war. I wrote to my wife, "Send me a history of the Aleutians." She wrote back that none had been published. "Why don't you write one?" she said. And I responded that there was no way to do the research. We didn't have libraries. Rosa wrote, "I'll do the research down here, send you the material, and you write it." Rosa did the research in Seattle, sent it up to me and I wrote it. When it was published, I thought, "Why not another?"

Have you been able to make a living writing local histories?

Well, I'm not rich, but I don't envy other people their lives. Mine's the way I like it. We've traveled a lot. I've been all over North and South America, spent a lot of time in Europe, kayaked with Eskimos in the Arctic, caught fish in a fishing boat on the Bering Sea, canoed the Danube, gone up the Amazon on a medical boat, been in Upper Volta when it gained its independence, lived in Geneva. I don't know what else we could have done if we had had a lot more money.

We have seldom been in the position of living entirely off the receipts of the books, and I've tried not to be, because I want to write the books my way, and not have to write them to a publisher's demand. So I've done journalism, I've taught. But I've usually made about the same amount of money off the books as off the other sources.

Who are the writers you emulated?

When I was just starting to write, my major heros were Steinbeck and Hemingway; Steinbeck for some of his lyric qualities, especially in descriptions of landscapes, and Hemingway for the wonderful conciseness, especially in reporting action. When I started writing historical pieces I was most interested in Lewis Allen, who wrote *Only Yesterday* and *Since Yesterday*. I remember reading *Only Yesterday* as a sort of revelation of what in-depth journalism could be. Also, Malcolm Cowley recommended *The Outlaw Years*, by Robert Coates, as a model. I read it, reread it, and tried to see how he did things.

How did you meet Malcolm Cowley?

He came up to give the Walker Ames lectures at the University of Washington. It was a very controversial appointment at that time. It was just before McCarthy, during a lot of the red-baiting. Malcolm had very briefly been a Communist Party member, and he was picketed by the American Legion and so on. The Northwest writers went out of their way to make Malcolm and his wife Muriel happy.

Malcolm was very interested in the environment. He was the first intellectual environmentalist I'd really encountered. The guy wasn't essentially a camper or a fisherman or a logger.

He suggested that I write a book on Seattle. I said that Dutton, my publisher, didn't think that Seattle could stand another book—Archie Binn's *Northwest Gateway* was still on sale. Malcolm was one of the editors at Viking, and he said if I could get a release from Dutton, he was sure Viking would publish it. He was my editor for two books, *Skid Road* and *The Last Wilderness*, and seeing what he did to my copy was by far the most shaping experience as a writer that I had. I tended to write in a newspaper short sentence style. He said, "That's fine in places, but you have to learn to be more flexible if you want somebody to read 200 to 300 pages." I worked on it. One of my great triumphs was getting him to tell me that I had written a sentence that was too long [laughs].

How do you choose the subjects for your books?

What interests me. I've written three commissioned books, but the rest of the books I just became interested in.

How do you organize your books?

I look for a significant personality, and then try to get enough background to show him in action against events contemporary with him. When Cowley worked on *Skid Road*, we incorporated a 2,000- to 3,000-word essay into each of the narrative sections on a personality. These essays dealt with that person's importance to the topic, but they were concealed as essays. It was a real trick of writing. Between these narrative chapters that illustrated development, we had a series of short vignettes of important events like the Seattle fire or the general strike. There's really a rather mechanical format to that book, but it has enough variety that people tend to read it more like a novel.

How do you research your books?

I just try to learn as much as I can. It's very much like reporting; just hit as many different sources as you can. I started off using journalist's sources. In *Skid Road*, for instance, I was mainly at the city hall looking through old court records, that kind of thing. Across the years I've learned the professional historian's sources, the more formal archives.

Why do you focus on individuals in writing histories?

It's where my interest lies. I like to read biographies. I like narrative history much better than the kind of history you get in textbooks. It's an outgrowth of writing feature stories and magazine profiles of people. If you write a magazine piece about a guy, you're explaining him against his background.

Do you think that individual lives are illustrative of a larger period?

Sure. The danger of course in writing it that way is that it can't be a comprehensive picture. It gives the picture of the period by implication. The rest of history is distorted by being seen through this particular prism. But it's distorted in some way no matter what you do; everyone sees it a little differently. For me, the advantages are overwhelmingly on the side of doing it this way. When I'm able to do it this way, I have no trouble with people finding the book uninteresting.

In Skid Road, *you use a lot of dramatic scenes. How do you get the dialogue right in these scenes?*

The only time I ever have put into quotation marks things that I didn't have an absolute source for was in *Dixie Raider*, a book on the cruise of the *Shenandoah* during the Civil War. Wherever I wrote "Catch that ship!", the captain would have said someplace, "I gave orders to capture the ship." But I've hesitated to do that since then. I try to keep it in third person or use a quote that either the person himself said, or the person listening to him put down.

When you wrote the scene in Skid Road *where John Considine was outside the People's Theater, you described him as "watching thoughtfully" the spectacle before him. How did you know what he looked like at that particular moment?*

It would have been some letter of his or something he was quoted as telling somebody in grand jury testimony or in the newspaper.

Are there some ways in which your writing is fictional?

I hope it reads like a fictional narrative, but it certainly is not fictional in the sense of having been fabricated. The events happened and this is as close as I can get to them. But I try to build scenes with suspense, and have characters develop. They start one place and they're somebody else by the time you're through. Either they have changed or the reader's perception of them has changed because of the events he's seen them go through.

Did you consciously choose a style of writing that would make history come alive?

Sure. I came into history from writing. I never took a course in Northwest history.

Do you consider yourself an expert on Northwest history?

Yes, at least for the Puget Sound area.

And what is your specialty?

Seattle and Tacoma history and the sea otter trade. I use the history of the sea otter trade as a means of emphasizing the themes that we talked about earlier—the importance of the Pacific, the continuity of the exploitation of natural resources. The sea otter was our first natural resource that was exploited. It was the first thing that we exported and it was almost wiped out. Its history emphasizes an ecological concern.

Does knowing the history of the area enrich your living here?

Sure. I remember nutty things that happened almost anyplace I look in Tacoma and Seattle. I enjoy thinking about what used to be here, what the land must have been like, and how it has been remade. A sense of place and of the continuity of the place is as important for me as any other part of living.

What were some of the major events that shaped the Northwest?

The first was Americans finding a way through the mountains by wheels. The British were getting out here by the canoe route across Canada and by ship. They were establishing a very firm hold on it until the covered wagon migrations began.

The next big thing was the Gold Rush, which drew people to California. Its effect up here was creating a market for Northwest lumber. Before that, the lumber availability meant almost nothing to the Northwest because if you had to haul it all the way around Cape Horn you couldn't compete in the Eastern market.

The third thing was the trouble with Indians, which slowed the population growth for a while.

Then the next was the coming of the railroads, which allowed the population to pour in. Once people could get here cheaply, we were much more at the mercy of national and international events. It wasn't an isolated economy, then. The lumber, agricultural and mining industries suffered terrible blows during the '90s. We broke out of that with the Gold Rush and the American eruption of trade with the Spanish-American War, and the acquisition of the Philippines which helped underwrite the Pacific timber trade. The Northwest was shipping lumber to our occupying force there, trying to keep the Philippines from being independent.

Was it the railroad that introduced the Northwest to the national scene?

Yes, it tied it in tightly. Once the rail system was here, the population poured in. The transcontinental railroad was completed in '83. In 1880, Seattle's population was 4,000, Tacoma's was 1,000; in 1890, Seattle's population was 43,000 and Tacoma's was 36,000. The population wouldn't have exploded without the railroad.

Do you think that relations between the Indians and the whites in the Northwest could have been handled differently?

They were handled miserably by Governor Stevens. He was a brilliant man, but he was in such a hurry and he had such confidence that the Indians were a disappearing race. With his attitude it's hard to think a conflict could have been avoided. I've never made up my mind whether he was deliberately trying to confuse the Indians by having the Medicine Creek treaty translated into Chinook instead of the Salish languages, or whether he just didn't understand what he was up to. But clearly the Indians weren't aware of what they were doing when they signed the treaty.

East of the mountains it was different. The Indians there were pretty sure of what they were doing, but then they got double-crossed. Since eventually the whites were going to have more power than the Indians in the area, there was very little chance that the Indians would have ended up holding onto the land.

One of the things you have to remember, though, was that the Indians were really in a position to drive the whites out if they had been organized. We keep forgetting that they outnumbered the whites here by a great amount and that there were fewer than 1,000 soldiers west of the Rocky Mountains in 1854. There were 20,000 Indians. If they had been united, there would have been a lot of whites killed.

*Did the nature of the Indians' culture prevent them from put-
ting up an organized opposition?*

Yes. And furthermore, the Indians west of the mountains, in
this area, had been ravaged by disease, unlike the great horse
tribes in the interior that had much less contact with whites. Here,
the coastal Indians had been in contact with whites since the late
1700s and they'd picked up malaria, smallpox, whooping cough,
and alcohol.

*Has Northwest Indian culture totally died out, or do remnants
of it remain?*

Some remnants remain, but the concept of living in an un-
changing land is gone. They've become acculturated toward the
exploitation of resources.

Where do you see the Northwest heading in the future?

It will be profoundly influenced by trade across the Pacific,
but that depends so much on events in China and Japan. It
depends on whether the really unique relationship we have with
Japan will continue: Japan not having to support an arms industry
and therefore in a fine position to outcompete us, and the strange
maneuverings we have to go through to keep the Japanese from
pumping too many cars into this country. With China, it depends
on whether Deng's policies can be maintained against the old-time
Maoists. Our future lies in trade with the Orient. For the rest of
the world we're a long way off.

The timber base is shifting its importance. The problems that
lie ahead are going to come from economic changes; the timber
base will be a smaller part of our overall production.

Where does your work fit within the field of historical writing?

I think of it as reporting, really. Though I've taught, I'm not
an academic historian. I simply don't have the degrees. I was a
one-course historian. I taught a good course on Northwest history,
but if they had asked me to teach a course on the history of the
American Revolution, I wouldn't have been qualified. I'm a writer. I am appreciative of the fact that I'm now accepted by the formal historians as having done my homework and not making up
the stuff. I guess I'm pleased at the review I got on *Puget's Sound*
in the *Pacific Northwest Quarterly*, but I'm not really one of the

tribe. I write for people who are just interested in the area. I would rather have the book read by 50,000 people than have it read and admired by 300 or 400, which academic history tends to be. I don't argue that my way is the more valuable way, it's just that journalism is what I do, and journalism is supposed to be interesting.

Ivan Doig

*I*VAN *Doig grew up in northern Montana along the Rocky Mountain Front where his novels* Dancing at the Rascal Fair *(1987) and* English Creek *(1984) take place. He has worked as a ranch hand, newspaperman, magazine editor and writer.*

His memoir, This House of Sky *(1978), was nominated for the National Book Award in contemporary thought. "The language begins in western territory and experience but in the hands of an artist it touches all landscape and all life," wrote Robert Kirsch in the* Los Angeles Times. *"Doig is such an artist."*

Winter Brothers (1980), a nonfiction book on the past and present of the Pacific Northwest, received the Pacific Northwest Booksellers Award, as did The Sea Runners *(1982), Doig's first novel.*

Throughout his work, Doig has found new ways to conjure up the people and country of the Northwest. He says, "My theme will remain what it has been —the American people and the westering expanse of this continent they happened to come to."

Born June 27, 1939 in White Sulphur Springs, Montana, Doig received a B.S. in journalism from Northwestern University in

1961, an M.S. in journalism from Northwestern in 1962 and a Ph.D. in history from the University of Washington in 1969. He won a National Endowment for the Arts Fiction Fellowship in 1985. He lives with his wife, Carol, in north Seattle. The interview took place at their home in the winter of 1984.

The author has red hair, blue eyes, and the air of a philosopher about him. He is fond of hats, and turns his phrases with the care of a craftsman.

How did you get started writing?

I suppose I was going to be a writer of some kind from about my junior year in high school. My notion was to go away to college to break out of what seemed to me not a very promising ranch future in Montana. So I went to Northwestern, specifically to the school of journalism. I thought at the time I was going to be a newsman. That idea held through college and through the first couple of jobs. I began to shift when Carol and I were living in the Midwest, where we were both working on magazines. I wanted to have more time to think about things. That's when I thought I would like to become a journalism teacher. So we came out here with the notion that I would get a Ph.D. in history and would know more background to bring to journalism teaching.

Graduate school taught me that I didn't want to be on a university faculty. I was continuing to free-lance magazine pieces even during graduate school and I began, to my surprise, writing poetry—which I'd never done before.

Have you ever published it?

Eight or nine published poems—mostly during the graduate school years or just afterwards. But I don't have any great facility in it, that I can see. Once I began *This House of Sky*, I began working on what Norman Maclean has called the poetry under the prose—a somewhat poetic kind of language. That fulfilled whatever urge I had toward poetry.

So you could do in fiction writing what you were doing in poetry?

Yes, as I savvy it. I've read and learned a great deal from

Richard Hugo's book *The Triggering Town*. Looking at the individual vowels and consonants, the interiors of words, for instance. I imagine my use of rhythms in some of my prose has a kind of poetic urge behind it, too.

Did you know Richard Hugo?

Yes, Carol and I knew Dick and his wife, Ripley, to a point where we were friends but not close friends. We were around them six or eight times. We never lived in the same community. He was someone of considerable stature by the time I got to know him. I was just glad he was around, writing as he was about Montana, living that sometimes outrageous life he did. I knew him during his great spate of creativity when, Christ, every time we saw Hugo he had a new book of poetry coming out. I got to know him well enough to kid him about that a little bit, and he'd say "Aw, I wrote these *years* ago. They just happened to come out *now.*" You'd look up next and he'd have a mystery novel out.

Was it both his lifestyle and poetry that impressed you?

I think it was his commitment to language—his burning himself and his life up for the sake of his language. This was a guy doing the job to his fullest. I like writers who pour themselves into their work.

Did you have an affinity for Hugo's subject matter?

It was more his verve. You got that not only in his poetry, but being around him and hearing stories about him. There were more stories about him than any other writer out here. There was a dimension to Hugo; there was a lot of him [laughs] in every way. I don't know that we could have stood each other as roommates for more than twenty-four hours. But he was someone very bracing and he was very generous to me in his estimation of my work, in his comments.

As a full-time writer, what keeps you going? What about writing is continually demanding?

It may be because I look on it as a craft that it's perpetually interesting to me. I've done it as various phases of craft. At the newspaper phase I wrote editorials, did a bit of reporting, book reviews, editing. I mentioned the poetry, and free-lance magazine pieces are entirely a craft in and unto themselves. Then, trying to stretch the craft toward the areas where it mysteriously starts to be something more than craft—art, literature or whatever you want to call it. Above all, I'm interested in the language. Language is the alpha and omega. I'm working now on this trilogy [*English Creek* is the first book of the trilogy] where I'm trying to use the Montana slang and get at the flow of life, the deep aspects of life, as well.

And to get at the deeper aspects of this life, you have to use the idiom of Montana?

That's what I'm interested in doing, currently. Having a first-person narrator, as each of these three books will, provides me a distancing device—the way Marlow is in some of Conrad's material. A person is there speaking in ways which I want him to, but he is not me, and therefore he can say more, in some ways, than I can. Because I'm inventing him he's going to have aspects which I don't particularly have myself. There's a richness to be got at by having a Montanan narrator speak Montanese.

Did journalism help your later writing?

Yes, it did help. Much of the course work I had at Northwestern was in what was called radio/television editing. I was taught by excellent journalistic craftsmen. Among other things, they taught me to write for the ear—because that's mostly what radio news is about. They taught me to write bright leads because you have to attract the listener. No one is being paid to listen to you or to read your stuff.

I see mine as similar to the way writers used to get their training. Hemingway and O'Hara worked on newspapers. Until the rise of writing courses at colleges and universities, that's the way you did it. Both journalism school and the almost ten years I put in as a magazine free-lancer were part of that training. Not always the most pleasant training, particularly in free-lancing, because of the financial impossibility involved. But it does teach you to do certain things with words.

Does there come a point where journalism will hurt your writing?

If you don't keep pushing the form of whatever you're in, you simply curl up and die away. I don't think it's the genre or form itself that is necessarily constricting, if you try to reinvent it.

Why did you move to Seattle?

We came out here largely pushed by the flatness, the lack of distinction of the Midwest. Both Carol and I were hungry for mountains and water.

What makes the Northwest distinctive?

In a lot of ways, the geography is its attraction. But I think out here—in the Mountain West as well as the Coastal West—you're around people choosing to live here for the sake of geographic place, rather than profession or family or social class. There's a force field attractiveness to that.

What are people's reactions to your books, say, This House of Sky, *for instance?*

There's much enthusiasm for *This House of Sky,* which is taught in courses in Montana starting with high school English, and then the Montana and Western literature courses at colleges and universities. It ranges from that to phone calls and letters I've had from ranch foremen, forest rangers, saying, "Godammit, I don't read that many books, but that was sure a good one."

That must be very gratifying.

Yes, it is. Again, when you work at this as a craft, to have it recognized by the people who know the country, who know what you're writing about—that is gratifying.

I try to run as much of my writing as I can in manuscript past people of this sort. The payoff on that is, when it finally gets into print, it's been tinkered with, corrected if necessary, to the point where people are not sending letters all the time saying, "God, you got that assbackwards."

What's the value of that strict authenticity?

Well, intrinsic [laughs]. It takes on a rightness in itself. I can't defend it financially. A lot of writers would not bother to defend it in terms of the time and energy it takes. But by God, you ought to do it right, it seems to me, even if it does take more time and energy. Nobody ever said this was going to be an easy business to be in. Some of this goes back to people I grew up around. There simply was a right way to build a haystack or fix a fence, in these people's minds—my dad among them.

What is distinctive about the writing that comes out of the Northwest?

In terms of living out here, some of the writers I'm aware of as fellow professionals and craftspeople are Ursula Le Guin, Frank Herbert, Tom Robbins, Ernest Gann, and certainly Ken Kesey. Of those, what I have in common with Robbins and Herbert is our journalism background, which is not much recognized because now our writing and the topics we work on go in three very diverse directions. But all three of us paid our dues. All three of us are fairly productive writers, fairly regular writers. And Ursula Le Guin probably produces more than any of us. So, there are a number of us out here who have the right work habits. We hole up and do our work.

Do you feel your writing grows out of a certain tradition?

Not literarily. Socially and culturally, I'm aware of being part of a lineage, a family tree of Western writers, because I have read and know of Wallace Stegner and Mari Sandoz and Hamlin Garland. They are people whose growing up was somewhat along the lines of mine—on ranches, farms, homesteads. People who came out of rural places to be writers. A.B. Guthrie is also in that family tree. He was around as an example, when I was a kid, that a Montanan could, indeed, grow up to write famous books.

The Western tree continues in my own generation—Jim Welch, Bill Kittredge, and Mary Clearman Blew, up in Havre, Montana. Norman Maclean is kind of an honorary member of our generation, even though he's thirty-five years older, because he began publishing about the same time we did.

I'm aware of being a part of these people, because some of them are friends and people I admire for how they've made their way in life. But professionally, I don't compare my work to other regional writers. Or anybody, for that matter.

Where does your writing fit within the scheme of Western writing?

What seems to me most distinctive about what I'm trying to do is an interest in working people in the American West. Currently, in this trilogy, my interest is in using working language of the area, trying to find a style within it for these three Montana novels.

Because this hasn't been done before?

Well, I don't know and I don't much care if it's been done by other people. Again, I feel it's worth doing in its own right. You don't use up a literary topic by writing about it once. Who's going to write better about the sea than Joseph Conrad? And yet there are other sea stories to write. There have been endless coming-of-age stories—none of which bothered me one bit in writing 340 pages about a fourteen-year-old, Jick, in *English Creek*. His coming of age was unique to me. I don't think you have to forever be searching for the topics that haven't been done. If the story is coming out through you, then it hasn't been done. I don't think there need to be new literary fashions and topics constantly. When they are done, that's fine, but they shouldn't be done just for their own sake. If you're going to do them, do them right, as Garcia Marquez has or Vargas Llosa or Russell Hoban in *Riddley Walker*.

When you first started publishing books, why did you choose to write a memoir about your growing up, rather than a novel?

I'm quite literal minded, and a memoir seemed to be the best way to tell the story, and so I didn't see why it shouldn't be done that way.

Do you think your writing is moving away from personal experience and history? Are you moving toward writing solely fiction?

Well, the project of the '80s is this fiction trilogy. That's as far as I can say. When I'm done with that—the third book is to appear in 1989—I don't know whether I'll be tired of writing fiction for a while or whether I'll have new stories, new angles and roads I'll want to take. Fiction in these past two books has been a liberating and exhilarating phase for me. You're no longer bound to the fact of the people you're writing about. You're free to make up the book's population. I still feel bound by the authenticity within which they live, but the people themselves are a liberation.

Are there things that you can accomplish in fiction that you can't in non-fiction?

There are things that I wouldn't know how to get at in nonfiction. The circumstances would have to present themselves in nonfiction for me to equal it, and that's not too likely to happen. In writing fiction about the Depression generation in *English Creek*, or now the homestead generation as I'm starting the next book—there are scenes I feel I can get at that I couldn't otherwise, simply because the people are no longer alive, or I can't see the actualities. So I create the actualities. I've been working on the opening scene of my two young Scotchmen on a dock on the River Clyde, getting ready to come to America. I can't see them, back there a hundred years ago. I've seen the dock, I've seen the River Clyde, I've seen the town these guys come from—I've seen a lot but I have not and cannot see these two actual guys. So the way to see them, therefore, is fiction.

So fiction fills in what you can't discover otherwise?

Yeah, and as it fills in it takes its own forms. It pushes the bounds of actuality. It's a hot, molten mass. It moves the form of the writing around to new patterns. You find your fictional people getting into predicaments, having troubles, having good times, which maybe people do and maybe they don't in actuality.

But the fiction must still be authentic, it still could have happened?

Yes, so far, my writing "could have happened." I don't believe you have to be goosing the reader with outlandish surprises all the time, the notion that fiction has to be hyped up—Ho! Here comes an axe murderer! Huh! Here's a Russian submarine! Jesus! Here's the killer comet from outer space! Life is vivid enough in itself. Look what happens to people as they go through their years. Everybody's got a story, everybody's got drama, good times and bad. There's a lot of intrinsic drama, and I think it cheapens fiction by having artificial sweetener in the plot all the time.

Why did you base The Sea Runners *on an actual event, rather than making it up out of thin air?*

It didn't occur to me. I had lived out here at that time twelve to fourteen years, I've been along the coast as a hiker and had thought at various times of trying to write something about it, but it never dawned on me that anybody could have, would have, made that particular voyage by canoe.

I turned to fiction in *The Sea Runners* because I didn't see any way to do it as non-fiction. So it looked like the best way to do that particular story was to take the historical kernel—the fact that it happened—and base fiction on it. My imagination works off facts, by and large.

Is that your newspaper training?

Well, could be. Could be 700 years of Scotchmen in my background. It's simply there and it's what propels me through life, and I try to work with it. Once I do have a fact, I'm perfectly game to do something imaginative from it if I'm working on fiction. But apparently I need that seed of fact.

In Winter Brothers, *you quoted extensively from the diaries of* James Swan. *Does your own writing build on writers like Swan?*

In that they are the eyes and ears into a time we can't reach ourselves, yes, they're utterly invaluable. Swan would prove in his diaries to be so good, so deft a writer, that I would find a kinship and admiration and a reminder to myself, "Okay, he is doing something I would like to do in his situation." Sometimes it might come just out of the words, whatever their topic might be. But I—maybe it's the direction my writing has taken in fiction—I tend to look on people like Faulkner as the real liberators.

Liberators in what sense?

Through their particular obsessions in language, obsessions in their work, they have shown us what is possible and make our own obsessions a bit easier. Faulkner has shown us that you can live in backwater Mississippi and be great. Maybe your neighbors didn't even know it and maybe if they did know it they were against it. That didn't matter. You could still be great.

To see greatness in writing come out of a guy like Faulkner, that's exciting to somebody trying to work with words. You don't have to be striving to be great—I don't mean anything that extreme—but just to see how proficient a guy like that could be in his circumstances. That's a wonderful example for a writer.

In writing This House of Sky, *did you need several years to get an emotional distance from the story?*

It took me quite a while to accumulate the emotional ingredients of *The House of Sky*, to get the material brought out of memory and taken back to Montana and expanded or verified by talking to other people and seeing the places where things actually took place. The work on the prose, of trying to make each sentence carry its weight, took two and a half years at the typewriter.

Did the book flow out of you or was it painful to write?

It did not flow, but none of my writing flows [laughs]. It comes out a word at a time and a sentence at a time. Because of the way I work, carving away at this craft of mine, that's simply the way things happen. I don't feel I was emotionally blocked, no. It was simply a matter of needing the time to work on the language, and find the stuff and think about it. The old-fangled philosophy of taking some time to think produced a lot of that book.

What about the Montana landscape inspires you to write so movingly about it?

You can't be around that landscape without it being on your mind. The weather governed our lives on the ranch, often determined whether the entire year was a success or not. Our lives turned on the weather, in combination with the landscape. This carries over into my writing.

So in a way you're still working the landscape like your dad was?

An even smaller patch of it than he was. I work on these small sheets of paper, still trying to make a living out of the landscape.

One of the reviewers of English Creek *criticized the book as slow-moving while another reviewer contradicted this and said the pace was entirely appropriate for the period and the characters. Did you design the pace so that it would reflect the way life was during that time?*

It never dawned on me that the actualities of life and how working people lived and went about their labors could be considered plodding; that you had to have green-eyed invaders from outer space before anything was happening. I thought, and still think, a lot of things do happen in *English Creek*.

Along with its seasonal life had to go, I believed, description of the country—sense of the country, sense of the past, as people tell stories and listen to stories. This does not bother me at all as a reader and so it doesn't as a writer. But, Christ, you can edit Faulkner and Conrad and Shakespeare and everybody else down to a third their length and pretty much preserve what ostensibly happens. What you'd lose is the richness in life, and the richness in life is what I'm trying to get at. If a reader or reviewer is bothered by that, he's got the greatest fast-forward ever invented—the human eye. Just flip ahead in the pages.

So, yes, the pace was meant to be natural. I'm trying to write each book on its own terms. The pace of *The Sea Runners*, which is much swifter, is meant to match the tension in that book. In

English Creek, you're meant to take in the seasonal change as it comes month by month through the summer, and meant to be catapulted into what's coming next in history.

Do you have any other books planned after you finish the trilogy?

I always have other books in mind, but it remains to be seen which of them will hold up as intentions over the next five years, and which will look most appealing then. I have ideas all the time of things I'd like to do. We say around this house, "Life is choices. Decide what seems most worth doing and work on that."

Gary
Snyder

SINCE *his early years growing up on the edge of an old clearcut in
north Seattle, Gary Snyder has felt a close kinship with the natural
world. His sense of himself as part of organic evolution, literally
kin to all other life, has given focus and power to all that he has
written, whether poetry or prose.*

*As a youngster, Snyder made numerous trips into the back
country of the Cascade and Olympic mountain ranges. On the
great snowpeaks of the Northwest—Adams, Rainier, St. Helens,
Hood—his calling in life became clear to him: he would become a
poet and make known human responsibilities to the earth.*

*He has been true to that calling. A deep and abiding sense of
the landscape pervades all of his poetry; the need to protect and
live well within the natural world is one of the principal themes of
his prose. All of his works are rich with the texture and poetry of
place. These include:*

Myths & Texts (1960), Riprap and Cold Mountain Poems
(1965), Six Sections from Mountains and Rivers Without End
(1965), A Range of Poems (1966), The Back Country (1967), Earth
House Hold (1969), Regarding Wave (1969), Turtle Island (1974),

The Old Ways: Six Essays (1977), He Who Hunted Birds in His Father's Village: The Dimensions of a Haida Myth (1979), The Real Work: Interviews and Talks 1964-1979 (1979), Axe Handles (1984).

Snyder was born in San Francisco on May 8, 1930. His family moved to Seattle before he was two and stayed until 1943, when they left for Portland, Oregon. In 1951, he received a B.A. in anthropology and literature from Reed College. He won the Pulitzer Prize for poetry in 1975 for Turtle Island, *the Levinson Prize in 1968, a Guggenheim Fellowship in 1968, and numerous other awards.*

Snyder now lives with his family in the foothills of the Sierra Nevadas, northeast of San Francisco. He often travels during the spring and fall. During a trip to Seattle in September, 1986, he took some time out for an interview in his room at the Camlin Hotel. Snyder wore his sandy-brown hair and beard cut short, and two turquoise pierced earrings in his left ear. When answering questions, he often would stroke his beard contemplatively before responding in a rich, resonant voice, a voice reminiscent of forests and woodsmoke, of campfires and Douglas fir trees.

Where did you grow up?

I grew up in Lake City. There were very few neighbors. The neighbors to the north of us, the Scandinavians, were dairy and goat farmers. The neighbors across the street were Japanese who were trying to farm. Most of the rest was second growth woods. Within the woods were very tall stumps with springboard notches cut in them, western red cedar and Douglas fir stumps with wild blackberry growing around them in profusion, a lot of madrona, and a strong sappy growth of cascara widely spread through the woods. There were a very small number of trees of mid-range age. I remember them: Douglas fir, and then one western red cedar in particular. It essentially was the aftermath of a giant clearcut. All of the fields and hills in that area up north of Seattle were totally denuded of trees in the early years of this century.

By the time I was a little boy, in 1936, a brushy second growth was underway. We cleared some of that for cow pasture and kept some cows, planted an orchard and kept a garden. My father was out of work for eight or nine years and we lived in a house that was covered with tarpaper.

My father was the youngest of five brothers who grew up in Kitsap County and Seattle. My grandfather was a homesteader in Kitsap County who settled and homesteaded some land directly after it had been logged in the first phase of logging, in the days when they felled trees directly into the water and then towed them off in logbooms.

Did growing up near the woods make a big impression on you?
It *was* me.

Please explain that.
It's the difference between being made an impression on and being something.

So you didn't see a clear separation between yourself and the woods.
No, it made me what I am. It didn't just make an impression on me. I was part of the woods. I grew up normally, in other words. I grew up in terms of planetary normal, which is to say growing up in close contact with the fabric of nature, rather than removed from it. I had a normal childhood. As Fran Shephard points out, in two books, *Thinking Animals* and *Nature and Madness*, human beings probably get a little crazy if they don't grow up close enough to the fabric of nature.

As in Manhattan?
Or in Seattle. People who have not experienced the fabric of nature in childhood are slightly impoverished, morally and imaginatively. Growing up in that fabric gave me a powerful moral perspective of respect and regard for all sentient beings and gave me a powerful sense of membership in a real world. I imagine that maybe the ghosts of the great trees that had gone down in the clearcut of 1905 were still hovering over the landscape, instructing me somehow.

If you felt so at home in the Puget Sound region, why did you feel the need to leave?
The territory is vast. Douglas fir goes all the way down to the Big Sur River and as far north as the Skeena River. It's a natural ex-

tension of the space you can walk in. It's a natural part of one's exploration of the planet. When you start out walking in the world from the position of having been somewhere, then you always know where you came from, and you are always informed by that. I can recollect with almost photographic accuracy everything that was on our farm and the way it smelled. So if somebody asks me, "Where are you from?" I never have the least difficulty in answering them. Where are you from?

You mean specifically? As far as my neighborhood?
See, I'm asking you how do you answer that?

I would say Seattle.
So you don't entirely know where you are from.

Well, we moved around a little bit, but. . . .
You don't have a precise answer. It's a vague answer.

I suppose it's made up of several different places.
So you hesitate. You hesitate as to how to answer that. The only reason I bring this up is to demonstrate the difference and to demonstrate that I mean what I said a moment ago, "I never have any difficulty in answering where I am from." Most people have difficulty answering that. I would not say Seattle, I wouldn't say Lake City, I would say, "I'm from some cutover slopes lying between Puget Sound and northern Lake Washington in a little valley with an unnamed creek running through it. This is the second drainage west of the lake. The creek heads south. We were about a mile below the headwaters. That's where I'm from."

So you'd be that specific?
That's because I know it. If you don't know it, you can't be specific. The answer I've just given you would be the common answer of anyone from China or Japan, or the common answer of a native American. They would give you the village and the location of the village, up what river, what branch of that river, what valley.

Why wouldn't you say that you were from a city or town?
It's because I belong to America the continent, not to the America of cities and towns. I'm a member of the continent, not a member of any particular political entity. Seattle's only 125 years old. That's not much of an entity to be from.

Did you have a desire to find out more about the place where you grew up?

The question is not, "Did I have an interest?" but "How did I do it? By what steps?"

How did you do it?

By bicycling out to Lake Washington. By bicycling to the head of Lake Washington. By canoeing up the length of Lake Washington. By bicycling to Puget Sound. By gathering clams and fishing in Puget Sound. By fishing in Lake Washington. By gathering cascara bark for sale and selling it. By trapping *aplodontia* [ground squirrels]. By picking wild blackberries and selling them at the roadside. By gathering discarded stubby and jumbo brown glass beer-bottles, for which you could get three cents on the stubbies and five cents on the jumbos, causing you to explore the edges of all the roads and creekbeds to get all of them you could, because that was how you got some spending money. That was the first step.

The second step was coming in on Saturday afternoons to the University District branch of the public library and checking books out and reading a lot.

What I first perceived was contradiction. What first sharpened my wits was contradiction. I saw the contradiction of living in a place that was real to me and seeing it populated by hordes of ghosts for whom the place was not real. That's what I saw when I came to downtown Seattle. So that politicized me. And then I also became a mountain climber, and I started going into the Cascades and Olympics. And finally I got down to Portland to go to Reed [College].

Why was that a necessary step?

Well, anybody who has been politicized by the awareness of contradiction is good material for college. Right?

That's probably true.

And Reed has always been a good secular humanist college, with an intention of doing searching criticism of history and society. So that was just the right place for me to go. That's where I was introduced to the Marxist critique and other critical methods, all of which have been very valuable to me since.

When did you begin to write poetry?

When I was about fifteen.

Did writing poetry have anything to do with a sense of your-self as part of the wilderness?

I started writing poetry because I couldn't find any other way to express what I was feeling about mountaineering on the great snowpeaks of the Northwest. I climbed St. Helens when I was fifteen, Hood when I was sixteen, Mount Adams when I was sixteen, and then Mount Baker and Mount Rainier when I was seventeen. That was a powerful teaching for me. It was an initiation by all of the great gods of the land here. And so I began to write poems.

Why did mountaineering affect you in this way?

Young men in our culture have a hard time getting initiated. They usually end up initiating themselves in some messy and possibly dangerous way, or being initiated in a messy or dangerous way by their peers. By some great chance of luck and fortune I was initiated by the mountains of the Northwest.

What did your parents think of your literary ambitions?

My mother had always wanted to be a writer. She was very supportive. My father, too. Both of my parents were grassroots radicals; they belonged to the native Northwest socialist tradition. My grandfather was an IWW [Industrial Workers of the World].

Did you think of poetry as a vocation?

At some point along the line, when I was twenty-eight or twenty-nine, I realized that poetry was one of the things I did best, and that I was more cut out to do that than I was to be an academic. But at the same time I realized that you can't make a career out of being a poet, so I never expected to be able to live off it, and I kept myself handy in other ways so that I could always make a living. As it turned out, much to my surprise, I ended up being one of the few poets in the United States who does make a living writing poetry.

What did the Beats see in your poetry? Why were they at-tracted to you as a poet?

In Jack's [Kerouac] case, Jack was interested in everything, and was open to the America of that time. I was something new to him, an authentic West Coast mountain person with a working the woods, climb the mountains, work on the trail crews, go out on the look-outs kind of background. And at the same time, I practiced meditation and was studying Chinese.

Partly it was just new information for him, new territory to get to know things in. From his somewhat jaded East Coast background, he, and Allen [Ginsberg] too, enjoyed our fresh West Coast naiveté and energy, plus our physicality. The Eastern intelligentsia, especially in those days, did not get out and climb glaciers or run rivers or sleep out in the rain or anything like that, whereas a lot of us did it as a matter of course.

Were you, Kerouac and Ginsberg rebelling against the dominant American culture?

It would be a little vainglorious to call it rebelling, I would say critiquing.

Was poetry then your way of responding to issues of the day?

Not necessarily. Sometimes yes, but also I wrote prose, and also I wrote letters to senators; that's another kind of literature. [Laughs] I wrote prose essays. I took part in protests and demonstrations.

Why did you leave the States for Japan?

To study Zen Buddhism.

Why did this study appeal to you?

Travel to the Far East appealed to me and took particular focus around Zen Buddhism for two reasons, an intellectual reason and a personal reason. The intellectual reason was an ongoing interest and concern for the possibilities of a civilized society operating in harmony with nature. My reading of Taoist texts, Chinese and Japanese poetry, and my experience of Chinese landscape paintings, led me to think that the Far East had been a high civilization that had somehow done this. I was aware of how primitive cultures were very intimate with nature, but I also wanted to find out what the chances were of a civilization, a more complex social system with a larger population, being able to do something like that.

This intellectual and aesthetic interest in the Far East came to me initially in a visit to the Seattle Art Museum when I was nine years old. I can vividly remember walking through various rooms. I noticed that the English and European landscape painters were not very interesting. But in the Chinese room, the hanging Chinese scrolls looked like mountains that I knew.

The Cascades?

Yes. I said, "Those guys know how to paint." And that was the beginning of a deep respect for Chinese culture; and that was carried along by literary exposure to Chinese poetry and Japanese poetry and so forth. So those were intellectual reasons.

On a personal level, I found that the Ch'an tradition's course of study on how to empty the self really attracted me. It seemed like a continuation of mountaineering on another plane. Not that I ever quit mountaineering on a physical plane.

How did studying Zen change your poetry?

The practice of meditation, where you become intimately acquainted with your own breath, your own pulse, your own belly, and the twists and turns of your imagination and finally with your own emptiness, totally frees you from the notion that poems are written with words, and opens up all the different angles and sides of things. It's a tremendous freedom.

I came back to writing poetry granted permission to do exactly what I wanted, able to call up imagery, information, from all sides freely, and able to do it occasionally from a perspective of intimately knowing the oneness of everything, from inside—to write about a pine tree as a pine tree would want to be written about, from inside.

Were the forms of Oriental poetry appropriate to what you wanted to say as a poet?

No, of course not, but certain things that had been done in Oriental poetry were instructive: secular mysticism, for instance, that's a Chinese invention. All the mysticism of the West is theological and religious. No one ever thought of secular mysticism until the Chinese came along, the mixture of the personal and the political, the involvement of the personal and historical, and the deep sense of nature and landscape that was in Chinese poetry. The fact of no reliance on complex symbolism or mythologies or theologies, but presentation of the thing itself, in the most direct language, was always a characteristic of Chinese poetry.

And then Japanese poetry, the haiku in particular, was an

extraordinary tradition of refinement of the image and of imagistic imagination, a great leap beyond the rational and the theoretical into direct perception.

Did you find it difficult to transfer what you'd learned from Oriental poetry into English?

No, I didn't, because I just did it. I never set about doing it as a deliberate project, I just went ahead and wrote my own poetry. Whatever I learned came into my poetry. That's all I was doing.

Why did you come back to the United States?

Everything has its period. My roshi, Oda Sesso Roshi, died. Shortly after he died, I met my wife-to-be. We got married and had our first child. The Vietnam War was beginning to wind down and I could sense the ecology movement beginning to rise. I felt it was time to come back to the United States. And my wife wanted to go to the United States. I felt I'd been in Japan long enough and I had learned what I went to Japan to learn.

Do you consider yourself a Buddhist?

Oh, yes. In fact, I would say I'm a peasant Buddhist; that means I'm a Buddhist who believes in all of the local spirits and gods as well.

Is Buddhism ideal for you because it allows you to incorporate a lot of different traditions?

Buddhism is ideal for me, and it's ideal for anybody who wants to be both planetary and local at the same time, to have roots in a place and still have a sense of planetary cosmopolitanism.

Did your time away allow you to get a perspective on the Northwest?

Oh, yes. When I first went to Japan, I thought it was going to be like the Pacific Northwest. I was amazed how different it was. It's 180 degrees opposite in a way.

So you saw this place a lot more distinctly when you came back?

Yes. It really focused what the West Coast was like. I could see its planetary uniqueness. I came to realize, for example, that old growth stands of deciduous hardwood and coniferous trees disappeared from the Chinese lowlands about 1,500 B.C. Similar old growth stands disappeared from Japan, pretty much, by about 700 or 800 A.D. Stands like that disappeared from northern Europe by around 800. What we have on the West Coast in tiny amounts are the only temperate zone old growth stands left in the world. When we look into some of these forests we are standing where China was in 2,000 B.C.—makes it all the more poignant when you realize that there's not much of that anywhere in the world.

And then that North Pacific coast from Puget Sound to Bristol Bay is one of the little windows into the Pleistocene, one of the few remaining samples of the biological richness of our planet, the way it's supposed to be. The diversity and the richness are still there —the salmon, bald eagles, orcas, deer and bear—but there aren't many places you can see it any more.

Being in Japan and China, realizing how totally cut over they are and how wasted their wildlife has become, made me appreciate all the more the wealth and treasure that we have on this coast. People that live here have no idea.

Does being close to these things affect the people who live here?

A lot of the people who live here don't really live here. Their bodies are here but their minds are elsewhere; they haven't seen anything. That's a big problem with Americans in general; most Americans' minds are elsewhere. And so it has no effect on them.

When you came back to the United States, why did you settle on San Juan Ridge?

By the time I came back to the United States, my sense of membership in place had expanded so much that there was a much huger territory in which I could feel at home. By that time I had worked in the woods east of the Cascades and gotten to know ponderosa pine trees, and I had hiked and traveled and worked in southern Oregon, northern California, as well as Japan, Okinawa, Vietnam, India and so forth. So it didn't matter to me so specifically; there was a much bigger territory I felt at home in.

By chance, a piece of land became available up in the Sierra Nevada. When I went up and looked at it—there was some Douglas fir, black oak, ponderosa pine, madrona, manzanita—it just felt fine.

Was it difficult to stay in one spot after traveling so much?

No. I still had to go out and travel three months out of the year anyway because that's where a lot of my income comes from. So I settled right in there and it's been a very good place to live ever since.

Did the commitment to one place change you in any way?

It had been in the back of my mind that sooner or later I would do that. It gave me the opportunity to see what happens in time in a given spot, to really become aware of the minor seasonal differences from year to year. Yes, it's a great experience, and as I said earlier, it's perfectly normal. I live in Shasta, that's the natural nation. This is the natural nation of Cascadia, within which you are in the province of Ish.

Is this Indian terminology?

Samish, Salish, Snohomish, Stillaguamish, Squamish, Duwamish, Skykomish. Now what does Ish mean?

River?

Yes. Salish means "People of the River." The Ish nation is the drainage of all of Puget Sound and the Straits of Georgia about halfway up Vancouver Island.

Recently there was a Pacific Northwest bioregional congress near Bellingham. They blocked out the language of Ish nation. The delegates came from north and south of the Canadian border to declare that we live in the same nation.

So you don't agree with the political boundaries of the Pacific Northwest?

Why should I? They don't represent anything real to me.

But hasn't the history of the place been influenced by these boundaries?

For the worst, for the worst. It's not an interesting history; it's a history of exploitation and ignorance.

So you think it makes more sense to divide up areas by regions?

It's a starter in learning where you are. For example, it's a great help in realizing where you are to know that the border between Canada and the United States is illusory; there's nothing to stop you from going over there and feeling as at home as you feel here, and vice versa. It comes down to the nitty-gritty when you get into water quality control, air pollution control questions, or salmon runs. The salmon don't give a fuck which border it is, nor does the air pollution or the water pollution. So we're talking about administering things for human affairs in consonance with their natural regions so that human affairs may be non-harming to natural affairs. That's called social ecology.

Do you think that at some point things may be administered that way?

Some people are saying it's an idea whose time is about to come. At least it's very instructive, very educational, for people to have to bend their heads in a new way. I started that with *Turtle Island. Turtle Island* is the first literary surfacing of the bioregional concept. It's all right there in the introductory paragraph explaining why the name Turtle Island. That's the declaration of independence from Europe and also from the American flag.

Do you try to conform your life to the rhythms of the natural world?

Yes. You can't avoid it, but I don't live that differently from anybody else either. I do cut my own firewood, and we burn wood for cooking and wood for heating. We have some fruit trees and some gardens and chickens. I do a lot of my own work on machinery. Naturally we're close to the weather and we're close to the seasons.

Why is physical labor important?

First of all, it's normal. It's important to any normal human being. It empowers you. It makes you aware of your own capacity to take care of yourself and your family, to do what has to be done. You're not someone who has to look for somebody in the Yellow Pages every time something breaks. It's disalienating, but also it's meditative; it's close to the things that are real, or have a stronger appearance of reality, anyway. And physical work gives you time to think; it frees the mind.

So it's something like yoga?

It could be for someone who wanted to use it that way.

Are there things that you can get through physical labor that you can't get by sitting?

Well, you might be able to get them by sitting, but then you wouldn't have hoed any corn either.

How does writing fit in with the rest of your life?

Writing is my metier. After all the things I've told you, it will sound somewhat paradoxical for me to say I'm an intellectual, but I am. I'm a rural intellectual, I'm a shamanist Buddhist intellectual, but I'm still an intellectual. Ideas and language are the sharpest tools in my tool kit. So I use my tool kit to the best of its advantage.

Could you do without writing?

If I was to do without writing I'd tell stories and sing to make up for it.

Do you do that too?

Sure.

How do you choose the subjects for your poems?

They choose me.

Is there a lot of rewriting involved?

A moderate amount. It depends. Some pieces require more than others. You never can tell.

Do you read them aloud?

Always.

Do you write them to be read aloud?

Poetry, yes. I consider poetry an oral art form.

Are your poems mostly autobiographical?

Oh, heavens no. A great many of them are celebratory—celebratory of different nodes and intersections in the world and have nothing to do with me at all.

Is your voice consistently speaking throughout them?

I don't know about you, but I have very many different voices, because I am not just one self. Who is this *you* you're talking about? I have half a dozen selves that I can speak from, if I want to, although there is a consistently clearer one, which is the one that's most detached.

To what extent do you speak for Gary Snyder and to what extent do you speak for the larger human community?

I would have a hard time figuring that out. It would be

presumptuous to declare I speak for the larger human community, in a way, but it also would be presumptuous for any of us to declare that we were individual and unique, since we are really constructed out of bits and patches, starting with the language. I didn't invent the English language, it was handed to me. But if I were going to speak for something larger, I wouldn't call it the human race, I would call it the biosphere. I would hate to limit myself to the human concern. In fact, part of my life project has been proposing the possibility of speaking from the nonhuman to the human, because the human does not hear enough from the nonhuman. That could be described as what I've been doing, being a spokesman for the nonhuman.

How do you do that as a writer?

By doing Zen, and meditating. By opening your mind to the point that it's empty enough that other things can walk into it, so that a rabbit can walk into your mind, so that trees or rocks can become part of your mind. By giving up on your strict boundaries of self-definition, letting go, letting go of the question, "Who am I?" It's a useless question. It's breaking out of narrow self-concern and narrow self-identity, and into big imagination, big mind, big belly, that allows a person to become a spokesperson for the nonhuman, which is the nonhuman in us if anything.

Do you think that poetry should be the outgrowth of a particular place, like a coho salmon or a rhododendron bush?

Let's put it this way: every person should be the product of a specific place, like a coho salmon or a rhododendron bush, and then something in their work will reflect that. We are both specific creatures and, in a certain way, universal creatures. Whether we give the universal side of things the main weight or the specific side of things the main weight is in response to the needs of the times. The needs of the times right now are that we become aware of the specifics. It's my faith that appreciating specifics is also a road to appreciating the universal.

There are too many people who have either a political or a spiritual rhetoric of oneness, who can talk about oneness, or who must talk about oneness because they don't know anything specific. And so it remains just rhetoric. What kind of oneness would be a one-world globalism where you travel from Hyatt

Hotel to Hyatt Hotel in different capitals of the world, eating the same food and wearing the same clothes? That's one kind of oneness. Who wants it? The only oneness that's interesting is the oneness of a mosaic of diversities, which is the nature of the ecosystem as well.

We live in a time when people need to be taught to pay attention to the specific before their insistence on oneness can have meaning. People who want to talk about spiritual oneness should learn to tie their shoes and roll their sleeping bags and sweep their floors.

And there's something similar in politics, too. It's great that people want to save the world from nuclear confrontation between superpowers. They should go to school-board meetings, too. They should be concerned about what's going on in their block.

So that's what we're doing. It might be that in another century we'll have to stress it some different way. But the basic materials will be the same: the human mind, the mind of all things and our irreducible embeddedness, localness, specificness.

We get all this television, media and books, and we imagine ourselves as being gigantic universal beings, but we stand on only one square yard of ground and move within certain limits. It's exciting to learn what those moves are and what those limits are. To know your localness is as important as to know your universalness.

To what extent do poetry in particular, and art in general, help in establishing a regional identity?

Well, let's take Northwest Coast art. What is Northwest Coast art? It's cedar, the most beautiful wood that grows naturally everywhere around here, carved. And what is carved? Ravens, salmon, beavers, sculpins—all the beings who live in Ish country. And what are the masks? The masks are the animals and some of the creatures from dreams. And so the songs and the masks and the dances and the carvings made out of the prime material of the region are all a perfect expression of what the region is. Now that's what art does, when it's doing its job right. There's truly a spiritual exchange then between the physical ecology and the mental ecology of the people. It's extraordinarily profound.

What is the relationship between the wilderness and the unconscious mind?

That's a complicated question. We would have to say first of all that it's just a metaphor, but a metaphor is not just a metaphor; metaphors are pretty important. I would say that the similarity between the wilderness and the unconscious mind is that they are both wild, and wild means self-maintaining, self-creating, self-transmitting, unpredictable, full of surprises, running according to its own system, with the system not evident for your analysis, mysterious, creative and subject to exploration if you follow the right etiquette and apply yourself to it.

By applying the term "wild" to the two, you can see that the same criteria begin to apply. So that's our analogy. Now how would the analogy be literally true? It would be literally true if that mind were inherent in the physical universe from the beginning. If there's such a thing as a wild ecosystem and it moves according to some remarkable rules and connections that we can rarely fathom, then it's no surprise that there's also a wild mind.

Now Christians and Platonists would have it that we are another order of being, and that our intelligence puts us on a radically and qualitatively different plane from the natural world. This is a very dangerous idea—self-justifying and self-excusing.

Organic philosophy, East or West, would assert that intelligence of the highest order is implicit and inherent from the beginning in all things. And so it would be no surprise to find a "mind" as something which reflects the qualities of wild ecosystems.

So one of the reasons wilderness must not be destroyed is that it will keep us in touch with the wild part of ourselves?

That's true, but the most important reason is that it's the right thing to do. You don't torment the cat. You don't do silly vandalism. You don't do vandalism on nature either. It doesn't need any more justification than that. You could come up with more sophisticated arguments later. But it should be taken right from the beginning: it's the right thing to do and we'll feel better if we do it, *just like your mother said.*

If not available at your
local bookstore, this book may
be ordered by sending the cover price
plus one dollar for postage and handling
to the address below.

Madrona Publishers
Department X, P.O. Box 22667
Seattle, WA 98122

Prepaid orders only, please.
Add one dollar for postage and handling
for the first book,
fifty cents for each additional book.

Mastercharge and Visa cardholders
may order by calling (206) 325-3973.